Mule Deer

Carol
France
©

Mule Deer

A Handbook for
Utah Hunters and Landowners

Dennis D. Austin

Utah State University Press
Logan, Utah

Utah State University Press
Logan, Utah 84322-7800
USUPress.org

Manufactured in the United States of America
Printed on acid-free, recycled paper

ISBN: 978-0-87421-741-4 (paper)
ISBN: 978-0-87421-742-1 (e-book)

Library of Congress Cataloging-in-Publication Data

Austin, Dennis D.
  Mule deer : a handbook for Utah hunters and landowners / Dennis D. Austin.
       p. cm.
  Includes bibliographical references and index.
  ISBN 978-0-87421-741-4 (pbk. : alk. paper) -- ISBN 978-0-87421-742-1 (e-book)
  1. Mule deer hunting--Utah. 2. Mule deer--Utah. 3. Wildlife management--Utah. I.
Title.
  SK301.A97 2010
  799.2'7653--dc22
                                    2009048012

Contents

Determining Management Decisions

Preface

In writing this book, I attempted to cover the entire scope of mule deer management in Utah. Although most of the information in this text may be found scattered in numerous technical publications, occasionally in popular articles, and in chapters of specialized books, I believe the entire range of information about mule deer is presented here for the first time. I intended each chapter's topics as an independent reading. Consequently, sequential reading of the book is unnecessary.

The purpose of the book is to give hunters, landowners, and others interested in deer management and wildlife in general an overview of mule deer biology and management. In order to present a synopsis of the enormous mass of technical information available, I employed a narrow filter of relevance and avoided unnecessary details. Although many biologists may find much of the information useful as general reference material, this volume was not directly written for the professional biologist. In most cases I have avoided using long lists of supporting citations, but have included critical references to support the material presented. I used references primarily from Utah-based studies, and secondarily from studies within the Western states. Professionals and other interested parties may obtain more detailed information via the literature cited within the text and from the complete listing of the references at the end of the handbook.

In many cases, the information presented was based on my own unpublished observations and experiences. For clarification, in these instances I have added phrases such as *in my opinion/experience*, or *I recommend/determined*. Intermittently throughout the book, I have given personal examples or remarks to illustrate or emphasize points. These comments simply begin with the word *Note*. Frequently I have used the initials DWR in the text to refer to the Utah Division of Wildlife Resources.

Chapter 1 describes the history of mule deer and the development of deer management in Utah. Chapters 2-8 deal with the biology of mule deer. Hunter preferences, ethics and hunting success are covered in Chapters 9-11. How, when, and where to hunt, guns, strategy, equipment, and the like are not detailed in this book because that information can be obtained from numerous magazines and hunting guides. Data on Utah harvests of mule deer are covered in Chapter 12. Chapters 13-17 explore various aspects of managing mule deer.

The descriptions, analysis, and recommendations in this handbook are solely the conclusions of the author. This handbook does not represent the views of any agency, organization or other individuals. All errors in this handbook are solely the responsibility of the author.

Acknowledgments

The author is grateful to numerous individuals for their assistance in reviewing, supporting, encouraging, and suggesting this work. In particular, the superb reviews by Chris Peterson, Gary Austin, Rick Danvir, and the anonymous reviewers from Utah State University were extremely noteworthy. The author wishes to thank his former mentors at Utah State University, Arthur D. Smith, Phillip J. Urness, and Charles H. Jensen, for many years of good times, and detailed training in research and environmental awareness.

Thanks to Carol France for contributing her deer drawings; Alan Gardner and *The Herald Journal* for his cartoon; Becky Blankenship for her photos, especially the front cover; Dick Spencer for his photos, especially the back cover; and Micah Austin, Patricia Cramer, Mark Elzey, Mitch Mascaro and *The Herald Journal*, Larry McCormick, Dan Miller, and Philip Urness for their photo contributions. John Alley and his USU Press team are recognized for their publication expertise and dedication.

The author is extremely grateful for the Utah Division of Wildlife Resources for providing opportunities for a fulfilling career. The author's five children, Daniel, Alicia, Jared, Micah, and Mary-Marie, and sweetheart and wife, Annie, are deeply thanked for a lifetime of support and joy.

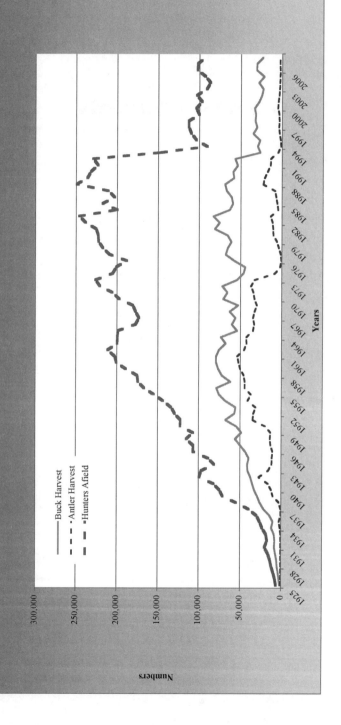

Utah Deer Harvest and Hunters Afield 1925-2008

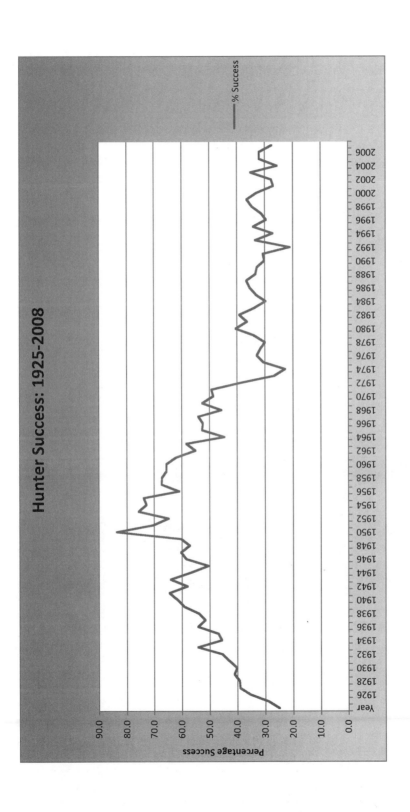

Hunter Success: 1925-2008

The adult, four-point, mule deer buck has become an icon of
the American West

Historical Overview

During early winter, large, mature bucks may be found on
every Utah deer unit.

Chapter 1

A Brief History of Mule Deer Management in Utah

Prehistory Period: Before 1776

Indirect sources provide the only records of the diversity and abundance of wildlife prior to the Domínguez-Escalante historic exploration of Utah in 1776. For an estimated 10,000 to 14,000 years prior to written records, Native Americans evolved culturally and flora and fauna evolved biologically in Utah and throughout North America. Evolution in western North America, where water resources were limited, led to dry climate adaptations and decreased land productivity to support flora and fauna. Because of the dryer climate, the abundance of flora and fauna resources necessary for human survival probably fluctuated over time and space, and Native Americans developed community mobility to relocate readily to take advantage of food resources. However, it is also clear that some locations having reliable year-around or at least seasonally abundant food resources served as permanent quarters for at least a portion of the year. At least some of those quarters were probably located in the vicinity of big game and mule deer winter ranges. It is likely populations of Native Americans over these thousands of years increased and decreased with the availability of food resources. It is also likely that as human populations increased, their vulnerability to population collapse also increased because of rapid seasonal or annual changes in climate. Surely populations of mule deer followed similar cycles controlled primarily by climate, especially extremes in climate. Thus, frigid and extended winters or severe droughts over several years resulted in fluctuating food resources and limited populations of mule deer and many other species, including humans, in western North America.

The primary indirect sources of reliable information on wildlife prior to 1776 are from Utah's abundant rock art and the findings of archaeologists (Jennings 1978). Occasionally petroglyphs provide hints of the prehistory of wildlife in an area. In Cache Valley, Utah, for example, rock art is rare. However, at the only known rock art location in the Blacksmith Fork drainage, one of the few remaining petroglyphs shows two human figures, one small and standing, and the second larger, kneeling and pointing at a clearly defined mule deer with distinctively branching antlers.

> *Note:* My interpretation of this rock art comes simply from a father teaching a son the skills (and joys) of hunting. The lesson is equally simple, that is, teaching in the field by example and by a parent is the most precious and lasting of all educational experiences. If children are to obtain the same joys from the fields and woods as experienced by their parents, the parents must take the time to provide those lasting experiences. In today's fast driving, high tech, multi-communications world, it remains a parent's privilege, opportunity, and responsibility to show and teach their children in the out-of-doors.

Based on petroglyphs, pictographs, and excavation sites, archaeologists judge that compared to human populations in the early 21st century, only small and scattered populations of Native Americans lived in Utah prior to 1776. Those peoples apparently relied heavily upon fish and wildlife for survival, especially during those seasons when plant foods were scarce.

The mule deer was probably moderately important in the diet. In one comprehensive study, of 193 rock art locations inventoried in Utah, mule deer were identified at 59 sites (31 percent) (Castleton 1979, 1984). For comparison, bighorn sheep were identified at 134 sites (69 percent), bison at 19 sites (10 percent), elk at 7 sites (4 percent), and pronghorn at 6 sites (3 percent). Moose, mountain goats, and white-tailed deer were not identified.

Results from many archeological studies indicate wildlife were probably never very abundant, except perhaps locally, in Utah, the Great Basin, or more broadly, in the Intermountain West. Numbers of big game and mule deer fluctuated primarily due to climatic cycles, and the animals were decimated by the occasional severe winter. Predators—primarily wolves, coyotes, black bears, bobcat, and cougar—limited population growth, but the key long-term factor was climate, which controlled population size and geographical range.

Probable Origins of the Mule Deer

Archeological records suggest the mule deer evolved from a combination of specialized hybridizations from the white-tailed deer (Geist 1990). The white-tailed deer has been found on the North American continent for about 4 to 4.5 million years. Most other members of the deer family are relatively new inhabitants since about the last 13,000 to 14,000 years. At one time in the distant past, estimated at 700,000 to 1,000,000 years ago, white-tailed deer were found across the continent from the Pacific to the Atlantic oceans. However, climate changed separating and isolating the west coast deer from those on the rest of the continent. Over many thousands of years of isolation, speciation occurred, and the west coast white-tailed deer gradually developed into a new species or subspecies, named the black-tailed deer. Climate changed again for a geologically short period of time near the end of the Ice Age, allowing the white-tailed deer to again advance toward the west coast and the black-tailed deer toward the east. The ranges of the black-tailed and white-tailed deer temporarily overlapped. On these areas of sympatric ranges in the Intermountain West, 11,000 to 13,000 years ago, interbreeding and hybridization occurred; the progeny were the beginning of the mule deer. The hybridization probably occured one way, that is, from white-tailed deer females and black-tailed deer males.

Climate changed once more and mule deer of the Intermountain West were again separated and isolated from the white-tailed and black-tailed deer. White-tailed and mule deer were separated on the east by the barrier of the Great Plains with the great herds of bison and other, now mostly extinct, ungulates. The deer species could not successfully compete with the grazers on the Great Plains. On the west, the Sierra Nevada Mountains separated the black-tailed and mule deer.

During about the last 13,000 years, the deer species within the Intermountain West slowly evolved into today's mule deer. With mid-twentieth century expansion of agriculture from coast to coast, white-tailed deer expanded westward and now are once again found in all continental states. The first Utah white-tailed deer in recent times was verified in North Logan in Cache County in 1996 (McClure et al. 1997), and populations have since slowly expanded throughout many counties of Utah. White-tailed deer were not found in Utah before 1996 (Durrant 1952, McClure et al. 1997).

Also occurring about 13,000 years ago, near the end of the Ice Age, but before the draining of Lake Bonneville, was the migration of humans into the Western Hemisphere. At that time, the oceans were about 500 feet lower in elevation than today, due to the colder temperatures and the immense build-up of polar ice. A land bridge formed between the continents, and humans migrated from Siberia to Alaska across the Bering Strait. Along with humans, numerous mammals, including elk, moose, caribou, grizzly bear, and gray wolf, migrated from Siberia, adapted, and became established. These new species gradually evolved away from the species found on the European continent and added to the established fauna of North America.

Based on archeology an estimated 70 percent of the large mammal species native to North America became extinct between 10,000 and 13,000 years ago. This massive extinction was previously considered as caused primarily by changing climate, but newer findings have indicated disease and hunting by humans as significant, perhaps controlling factors. Species evolving on the North American continent had no previous contact with the human predator, and many species may not have been able to adapt to humans' increased intelligence, which led to hunting effectiveness. In addition to climate change, disease, and hunting, a fourth theory on North American extinctions is evidenced by numer ous geologic reports indicating that an extraterrestrial comet, meteor, asteroid or inter-stellar object exploded over North America between 11,500 and 12,900 years ago, with the impacts having global effects, but particularly over North America (Allan and Delair 1997, Firestone et al. 2007). The much smaller and diminished but perhaps similar Tunguska Event occurred over Siberia in 1908. In my opinion, all four factors probably contributed to the extinctions to varying degrees depending upon the adaptability, mobility, population dynamics, geographic range, and ecology of each species. Further, it appears plausible that following this period of major shifts in populations North American mammals began a new era of adapting to climate and environment.

Nevertheless, several established species of North American mammals did survive and adapt to human presence. The most prominent of those mammals included the black-tailed deer, pronghorn, black bear, llama, the only large native mammal from North or South America domesticated for human use, the highly adaptable white-tailed deer, and the extremely adaptable coyote. Since the massive extinctions near the end of the Ice Age, it is noteworthy that the mule deer has become the only known mammalian species to have evolved into a separate species in North America.

1776–1846: The Period of Explorers and Trappers

Early Utah explorers and trappers recorded variable abundance of wild-life, but only rarely mentioned mule deer (Rawley 1985). Although horses were occasionally sacrificed for food, as with the Domínguez-Escalante expedition, most trappers and explorers lived primarily off the land. Fish were found in the streams and lakes, and waterfowl were abundant around the Great Salt Lake and other marshes. Bighorn sheep, bison, and pronghorn were mentioned frequently in journals, with elk and mule deer noted occasionally. Some examples (Rawley 1985) include the following:

In 1825, William Ashley recorded several species of big game in the Uinta Basin, but did not include mule deer.

During 1825–1830, Peter Skene Ogden on several trips in Box Elder and Cache Counties of northern Utah recorded numerous kills of pronghorn and an occasional bison, but no deer.

In 1840, Osborne Russell recorded eating abundant bighorn sheep, elk and deer in Cache Valley.

In 1846, Edwin Bryant described good fishing on the Weber River. "Every angler was more or less successful. . . numerous water-fowl in the Farmington Bay area . . . and some abundance of big game . . . and [Indians]brought deer and elk skins, which they wished to trade."

In 1846, John C. Fremont wrote about an area in Beaver County as "containing more deer and mountain sheep than we had seen in any previous part of our voyage."

From these early journals, one may surmise mule deer were seen infrequently along the explorers' routes. Since most of the trapping was for beaver and river otter at lower elevations during fall and winter, it is not surprising that only 'few' deer were seen in those habitats. It seems probable that mule deer existed in only very low numbers, and mostly in the higher mountains. Interestingly, there were never any reports of moose.

Russell's 1840 report of abundant big game, including mule deer, seems somewhat inconsistent with other observations. However, it is very possible that concentrations of big game occurred in very well defined pockets of winter range where slope, aspect and vegetation combined to create a more favorable microclimate and allowed big game to flourish in limited, distinct areas.

1847–1906: The Period of Settlement and Pioneers

When the Mormon pioneers arrived in Utah in 1847, wildlife in the Salt Lake Valley and adjacent valleys was very scarce. Indeed, during the first years of pioneer settlement, the settlers struggled with finding enough sustenance. Generally, mule deer were not easily found by settlers, although they were relished and hunted whenever possible. In some valleys, such as Cache Valley before 1880, even finding a mule deer track during winter was a rare occurrence. However the abundance of mule deer was undoubtedly variable throughout the state with several small areas containing good populations during at least some years.

For examples, in Cache Valley two "warmer" winter ranges are apparent. These lie between Logan and Green canyons, and between Millville and Blacksmith Fork canyons. During deep snow conditions in winter, an observer looking east from the Mendon bench across Cache Valley can note that these two areas are the first in the Bear River Range to show bare ground; therefore, they are traditional winter ranges for big game. The Utah Division of Wildlife Resources recognized the value of these two ranges and purchased most of the Millville-Blacksmith Fork range and part of the Green-Logan range in the 1930s. Although wildfire has destroyed parts of both ranges, and most of the Green-Logan Canyon range has been sold to Logan City, these rangelands continue to support significant numbers of mule deer and elk in winter. Similar warmer winter ranges are located throughout northern Utah, such as in Rich County along the east side of Bear Lake and the south facing slopes of Otter Creek near Randolph. Another example of an area with a good population was recorded in 1884, when John Brown reported seeing "plenty of deer . . . and getting three or four of them" north of Paragonah, Utah.

Commonly, settlers recorded taking big game species other than mule deer. For example, in 1863, Charles C. Rich recorded in his journal killing two elk and one bear on a trip from Cache to Bear Lake valleys.

This trip most likely was taken between Preston and Liberty, Idaho, over Strawberry Canyon, now Idaho State Road 36, but could have been taken up Blacksmith Fork Canyon and down Cottonwood Canyon into Round Valley. Elk were later extirpated from northern Utah and were reintroduced into Cache Valley from the Yellowstone herd in 1917.

Primary Reasons for Low Deer Numbers before 1906

The most significant factor in consistently low numbers of mule deer across varied geographic areas was the extreme winter weather conditions. Journal entries during the 1800s as well as natural evidence, such as tree rings, strongly suggest that occasionally winters were extremely severe prior to and during the nineteenth century. Evidence suggests these severe winters usually occurred at intervals of between seven and twenty years. A period of seven to twenty years would not usually be of sufficient length for a population to fully recover to the carrying capacity of the range, especially if the population was almost annihilated at regular intervals and if population recruitment was greatly curtailed by uncontrolled predator populations.

The second factor likely limiting mule deer population was competition for prey species among Native American and mammalian predators. The presence of mammalian predators was a chief concern of the early settlers. Journal entries often noted the presence of predators, the difficulties of protecting livestock from predation, and pioneer efforts to not just control but eradicate predators. During the winter of 1847–1848, which in many locations was considered a severe winter, pioneer hunting parties in the Salt Lake and nearby valleys recorded killing 2 bear (likely black bear), 2 wolverines (likely now almost extirpated from Utah), 2 wildcats (probably bobcat but possibly cougar), 783 coyotes, 400 foxes (possibly gray, kit, and red), 31 mink, 9 eagles (probably both golden and bald), 530 magpies, hawks, and owls (probably mostly great horned), and 1,629 ravens (possibly included American crows) (Rawley 1985). Unquestionably, these predatory animals helped stock the settlers' meager food supply.

Hunting by Native Americans certainly contributed to the scarcity of prey species. Game species were harvested over the entire year whenever opportunities occurred. The comparative effectiveness of Native Americans and mammalian predators is unknown. However, it is likely the Native Americans were at least as effective in harvesting prey species as the entire group of mammalian predators, especially in the vicinities of the Indians' winter quarters.

The third major factor that limited big game and particularly mule deer was the vegetation on winter ranges. In the 1850s during the period of settlement, the foothills of the valleys had far different vegetative cover from that observed a century later in the 1950s. Utah juniper (*Juniperus osteosperma*) and big sagebrush (*Artemisia tridentata*), now the vegetative symbols of the western valley and foothill big game winter ranges, grew in low density on most ranges. Instead of the shrubs and trees found at the turn of the twenty-first century on productive winter ranges, the foothill winter ranges contained luxuriant growth of perennial grasses (Christensen and Johnson 1964; Hull and Hull 1974). Because mule deer require browse for food in winter, especially when snow depth exceeds about 8 inches, and because dry grass has little, if any, nutritional value for deer, few deer would be expected to survive (Austin and Urness 1983). Of interest, elk, bison and probably moose and bighorn sheep, but not pronghorn, are much more capable of digesting dry grass for forage during winter, and consequently, would have been more likely to have persisted under those early pristine vegetative conditions.

> *Note:* Wildfire was certainly a factor in maintaining grasslands on winter ranges under pre-settlement conditions. The common winter range perennial bunch grasses, including the widespread bluebunch wheatgrass (*Agropyron spicatum*), as well as the native perennial forbs such as Utah's state flower the sego lily (*Calochortus nutallii*), easily recovered and maintained populations after periodic fires. Big sagebrush and other shrubs invading the grassland community were mostly killed by fire, whereas the roots of grasses and bulbs of forbs were protected by the soil; the grasses and forbs would sprout vigorously in the spring following fire. Following a foothill fire, soil nutrients contained in the shrub's leaves and stems were, in part, returned to the soil, adding to the quick recovery of the native grasses and forbs.

Livestock Grazing—The Necessary Factor for Maintaining Browse on Winter Ranges

When the Mormon settlers arrived, they brought with them considerable numbers of livestock. With open rangelands and high forage availability, livestock numbers rapidly increased. Intensive grazing, particularly in the spring and fall, of the foothills, now mule deer winter ranges, occurred. Since livestock mostly graze grasses and forbs in spring and summer, domestic grazing shifted the growing advantage to shrubs and trees less palatable to grazing livestock. Heavy livestock grazing in the spring not only reduces understory growth and reserves soil nutrients for shrubs, but also leads to longer retention of soil moisture for continued growth of shrubs later, into the summer. As a direct consequence of heavy livestock grazing, shrubs became an increasingly dominant vegetative type on winter ranges.

The shift in vegetation from grasslands to ranges dominated by shrubs steadfastly continued throughout the West until about the 1930s. Although vegetative changes were evident throughout the Intermountain Region, changes were particularly obvious along the Wasatch Front, where the Mormon settlers and their livestock operations were first concentrated.

However, in the 1930s, mud rock slides and massive soil erosion—caused by decades of heavy overgrazing on protective plant cover and the subsequent slow destruction of grass root systems, followed by more recent years of drought—forced state and federal agencies to begin to reduce and eventually in some cases to eliminate grazing from sensitive watersheds. With the reduction of livestock grazing, many of these ranges have slowly returned to domination by grasses with associated native grassland species (Austin et al. 1986).

First Estimates of Big Game Numbers in Utah

It is likely that throughout most of the nineteenth century big game animals and particularly mule deer were generally scarce in Utah. Orange Olsen, the first regional forester in charge of wildlife management, worked for the agency which was to become the United States Forest Service; he estimated in 1900 that the total Utah population of mule deer was only 10,000! In addition, he estimated the population for Utah of other big game species as 500 pronghorn, 200 bighorn sheep, and only 25 elk. It is interesting to note that Rocky Mountain goats, moose, whitetailed deer, and bison were not included in his estimates.

The first law protecting big game in the territory of Utah was written in 1876 under "Laws for the Preservation of Game and Fish." This law simply established that the taking of big game, defined as mule deer, pronghorn, bighorn sheep, and elk, could only occur during the period July 1 through December 31, a six-month season. No bag limits were established and hunting from January 1 through June 30 was only a misdemeanor (Rawley 1985). It is again interesting to note that Rocky Mountain goat, moose, and bison were not included on the big game list. It is likely that populations of two of these species, moose and bison, were very low or nonexistent, in part due to their high vulnerability to hunting. Rocky Mountain goats were not present in Utah at that time.

> *Note:* The Rocky Mountain goat is generally not considered a native species to Utah, even though sufficient habitat is available in the Wasatch and Uinta Mountains. Through transplanting efforts the Utah Division of Wildlife Resources has established numerous small populations in northern Utah Mountains. The USFS is monitoring sensitive alpine vegetation for any negative effects grazing by Rocky Mountain goats may have on this habitat type. It is my opinion that it is very unlikely any Rocky Mountain goat lived in Utah during historical times, since about 1800. However, over the last 13,000 years, in consideration of the great cycles in climate, the probability that Rocky Mountain goats migrated into Utah and temporarily became established seems reasonable. Nonetheless, even if this scenario is correct, migrating populations were unable to withstand mortality factors such as climate and predators and a permanent population was apparently never established under presettlement conditions. The ability of populations to become temporarily established on fringe or marginal habitats is a common occurrence with most species of wildlife including mule deer. That is, under favorable reproductive and survival periods, populations expand into marginal habitats and regress slowly back to primary habitats under unfavorable conditions.

By 1894, the need to manage Utah's wildlife resources was clearly recognized, as demonstrated by organization of a new branch of the territorial government, currently named the Division of Wildlife Resources, and the appointment of a fish and game commissioner. However, little control over hunting occurred during the next 12 years, and the six-month season continued.

Table 1-1 summarizes, in chronological order, the major events defining mule deer management in Utah from 1876 through 2008. Emphasis in this table was placed on the research and development of Utah's critical winter ranges.

1907–1913: The Period of Complete Protection

Utah received statehood in 1896, but it was not until 1907 that the first license fee of $1.00 was required to hunt big game. In 1907, only a few hunters participated in the hunting of big game, primarily because the number of big game animals available in Utah was very small, and probably less than the numbers that were estimated by Orange Olsen in 1900. Big game populations had been decimated by years of hunting seasons lasting six months, high predator populations, intermittent but extremely harsh winters, and still a preponderance of grass on many winter ranges, although shrubs were increasing. Unfortunately, no data on licenses sold or harvest are available for 1907. It is likely no data were recorded for the 1907 hunt, particularly because prior to that year the only hunting restriction had been the six-month season. Since hunting had previously been free, it is quite likely that only a few hunters bothered to purchase a license and most hunters continued to hunt without the newly required license.

By 1907, Utah's wildlife commissioner as well as hunters clearly recognized the absence of big game in the State and the need to protect remaining animals from all hunting. As a consequence, all big game hunting was closed for the next six years between 1908 and 1913.

> *Note:* During this period of closure, unquestionably poaching occurred, especially in the remote rural communities. However, it should be noted that poaching before the latter half of the twentieth century was much different from the last 50 or 60 years. That is, most of the current poachers are dedicated to killing trophy animals, often leaving the carcass and only taking the head or antlers, whereas almost all of yesterday's poachers were simply trying to put a supply of meat on the family table.

1914–1950: The Period of Buck-Only Hunting

The 'buck-only' law was passed by the Utah State Legislature in 1913, ending the moratorium period of no hunting. The new law became effective at the beginning of the hunting season in 1914. In that first year an estimated 600 buck mule deer were harvested in Utah. No record is available on the number of hunters.

Under buck-only hunting regulations, numbers of mule deer gradually increased. In 1925, the Board of Elk Control, renamed the Board of Big Game Control in 1935, was established to determine elk regulations. In 1927, the duties of this board were expanded to cover all big game regulations. Between 1914 and 1933 only buck deer were hunted in Utah. By 1934, deer populations in the State had increased to the degree that depredation problems were causing significant crop losses in some agricultural areas. The board responded and established the first antlerless-control deer hunts in 1934.

Research into deer problems, data collections on deer herds throughout the state, and management expertise improved rapidly, leading toward more scientific management during the 1930s and 1940s. Before about 1946, Utah regulations were very simple and applied over the entire state. Differences in population sizes, productivity, hunter impacts, and numerous other factors were generally not considered.

After the end of World War II returning veterans showed renewed interest in hunting and the deer resource. In response, important changes in the management of Utah's mule deer resource were adopted abruptly in 1946. In that year, 53 individual deer units were identified based on geography and migration patterns, Utah State University established a big game–livestock relationships and research problem-solving project, and with interagency cooperation and contributions, detailed research into mule deer ecology was begun on the Oak Creek deer unit. In 1948, the three-person Interagency Committee was formed to determine big game regulations. This committee was composed of a representative from the Division of Wildlife Resources, the Bureau of Land Management, and the U.S. Forest Service. Also in 1948, the first description of overall range conditions for the State was published. In 1949, the first attempt at identifying the summer and winter ranges of mule deer was completed. In 1957, The Great Basin Research Center, which continues the essential work of range revegetation, was established in Ephraim. In 1958 the big game range trend surveys were begun.

By the late 1940s, deer numbers had expanded to extremely dense populations throughout Utah. Deer populations had gradually increased in response to increased browse availability on winter ranges, increased predator control, and buck-only hunting in most areas. The limited number of antlerless-control permits issued before 1950 accomplished little in curbing the growth of most mule deer populations. At this time the high deer density was observed to be out-of-balance with the forage available on the winter range. On most ranges it is estimated the appropriate balance between deer numbers and available forage on winter ranges occurred between 1940 and 1945. By 1946, the number of deer on winter ranges greatly exceeded the carrying capacity of most ranges. Consequently, because of the extreme overwinter utilization of shrubs, winter range conditions rapidly deteriorated and grasses replaced winter browse forage. Even more importantly, overutilization of the browse resource was leading to shrub decadence and mortality, reduced browse productivity, and decreased future carrying capacity. Annually during the late 1940s, overwinter mortality losses caused by starvation and harsh winters were staggering, particularly during the especially severe winter of 1948–1949.

1951–1972: The Period of Either-Sex, Hunter-Choice Hunting

Finally in 1951, after at least five years of significantly overpopulated herds of mule deer throughout most of Utah, the Utah legislature repealed the 1914 'buck only' law and hunters were allowed to harvest 'either-sex' on their deer hunting permit. Tangential to the initiation of either-sex or hunter choice hunting, the Department of Fish and Game began an aggressive harvest program designed specifically to decrease herd sizes, including the establishment of two deer permits, pre-season hunts, post-season hunts, extended hunts, conditional hunts, and others. Deer were plentiful everywhere, so to attract hunters, areas distant from human population centers had fewer restrictions and more opportunities than areas along the Wasatch Front where hunter pressure was higher. For a few years around 1960, a hunter could have legally harvested up to 11 deer during a single season in Utah. Either-sex hunting opportunity continued on most units through 1972. In addition to either-sex hunting, the number of antlerless-control permits reached the peak in 1961 at about 40,000 statewide and slowly declined during the 1960s and into the 1970s.

During the 1950s, permanently marked pellet group plot transects, browse utilization transects, pre-season classification counts, post-season classification counts, and checking station data collection points became standard tools for wildlife biologists to assess populations. In 1953, the Utah Legislature established by statute the Saturday nearest October 20 as the beginning date of the general deer hunt, due to established tradition, optimum physical condition of deer in the fall, and average weather conditions. In 2008 the Utah Legislature gave the Wildlife Board the authority to change the date, and thus, the date for opening day may be changed in the future.

1973–1974: The Period of Rapid Population Decline

The numbers of mule deer significantly and drastically declined in the early 1970s (Workman and Low 1976). After a decade of generally average climatic conditions with high reproductive and recruitment rates, which had led to very successful hunting during the 1960s, the early 1970s marked the beginning of a long decline in mule deer numbers. Several factors contributed to this decline of mule deer (Utah DWR 1951-2008, Hancock 1981, Utah DWR 2003). The harsh winter of 1972–73 showed a significant loss of deer due to starvation, and as a consequence, most of the 1972 fawn crop was lost. Antlerless harvest had remained high during the first four years of the new decade: 1970, 1971, 1972, and 1973. Poor fawn crops were produced during those same years. Cold and delayed spring seasons continued into May and weakened does in the later stages of gestation. Summer drought in several parts of the state dried up many traditional watering places. The effects of predators increased with declining deer populations. Finally, a statewide jump in hunter license sales from about 180,000 in 1969 to 200,000 in 1970 caused a noticeable increase in hunter pressure, particularly on does, and an observed decline in deer numbers.

In response to these conditions the Division of Wildlife Resources established hunting regulations that were much more restrictive and the period of either-sex hunting came to an abrupt close. Few antlerless deer permits were issued in 1973 and 1974. By 1975 buck-only hunting regulations, which had not been in place for 25 years, replaced either-sex hunting. In that year a statewide total of only about 6,000 hunter choice permits were issued.

1975–1984: The Period of Conservative Antlerless Harvest

The solution to the decline in deer numbers adopted by the Division of Wildlife Resources was to revert back to buck-only hunts with antlerless-control permits. Under conservative doe harvest regulations, deer populations increased quickly. In many areas deer numbers again soon exceeded range carrying capacity. In just two years, by 1977, statewide buck harvest had recovered to harvest levels achieved before 1973. However, the hunters' and general public's desire to maintain high deer numbers on public lands often resulted in harvest considerably below the biological goals of maintaining populations within carrying capacity. The difficulties of harvesting adequate numbers of antlerless deer on privately owned ranges, where landowners controlled hunter access and the effectiveness of antlerless-control permits, also contributed to harvests considerably below biological goals.

The extremely harsh winter of 1983–1984 was a grim reminder of the consequences of excessive populations. For most of Utah's deer units, the severe winter weather caused total herd losses usually in the range of 50% mortality, and on some units as high as 70%.

1985–1992: The Period of Experimental Seasons

Hunters and wildlife biologists desiring a higher quality hunt and a higher proportion of mature bucks in the harvest, as were often available during the 1950s and 1960s, caused the establishment of special hunts: limited entry and high country (hunter restriction), and three point and better (antler restriction). The advantages and disadvantages of these hunt types were intensively debated. The continuance of special hunts in the twenty-first century will probably depend less on biological inputs and harvest and more on hunter preferences. Indeed, the need to evaluate the quality of the hunting experience was poignantly recognized during these years. The two major issues of hunting quality—too many hunters and too few mature bucks—led to the major changes in regulations and hunter choices in the 1993 fall hunts.

1993–2009: The Period of Reduced Public Hunting Opportunity but Increased Opportunities for Higher Quality Hunts

In 1993, hunters were required to choose and hunt only one season: archery, rifle or muzzleloader. This was a very significant and primary change from the wildlife management policy adopted and practiced for 80 years, since 1914. Prior to 1993, hunters obtaining a deer tag could hunt any legal season. This new policy, which has continued through the 2009 season, was adopted to reduce hunter crowding during the rifle hunt and increase the percentage of surviving bucks. To meet that goal, a secondary regulation restricting hunters with an antlerless tag from also hunting bucks was adopted, but that regulation was repealed the following year.

Hunting opportunity was again significantly restricted in 1994 when deer permit sales for the general season buck hunts were capped at 97,000. That was an even more significant and primary change from the 1914 wildlife management policy. Prior to 1993, deer license sales were not limited. However, because of the difficulty of monitoring sales throughout Utah, sales exceeded the cap by several thousand through at least 1998. In 1999 and thereafter, the monitoring of license sales was greatly improved and the 97,000 buck deer hunter permit cap became firmly established and enforced. With considerable discussion, the deer permit sales cap has been widely accepted by hunters and has continued with only minor changes.

In the mid to late 1990s, the economic value of hunting on private lands finally became evident. Ranchers wanted to make a profit from hunting, even though the state owned and controlled all game animals. The Wildlife Board, which had replaced the long established Interagency Committee, adopted the concept of Cooperative Wildlife Management Units (CWMUs) to allow private landowners to share in the profit of hunting. Ranchers who maintained big game on their lands during the fall hunting seasons, and owned a minimum of 5,000 contiguous acres, were given monetary incentive and the opportunity to privatize big game hunting in Utah. This was the third departure from long-term wildlife management policy established in 1914. Ranchers who maintained big game on their lands only during the winter had little or no advantage, and continued to struggle with depredation problems and crop losses. In some cases their depredation problems in winter were augmented and exasperated by the management of adjacent CWMUs. The Cooperative Wildlife Management Unit opportunity has continued to be a successful economic venture for many large acreage landowners, and over the state has decreased depredation problems.

Also in the late 1990s, the Wildlife Board approved the dedicated hunter program. This special interest program allowed hunters who were willing to donate labor for various habitat improvements or other approved wildlife projects to hunt all three seasons: archery, muzzleloader, and rifle. However, they were only allowed to harvest a maximum of two bucks every three years. The potential hunter success rate was 67%, or about double the actual success rate for the general public hunter. The dedicated hunter program has also continued through at least 2009 with enthusiastic response from many hunters.

Prior to 1994 hunters could hunt almost anywhere open in the state of Utah using the same permit and tag. Beginning in 1994, as a result of low deer numbers, hunter crowding, the influence of special interests groups, and for improved management, the state was divided into five regions. Hunters were forced to select and hunt in a single region. Many families with brothers, uncles, and other relatives living in diverse parts of the state encountered tough decisions on which region to hunt. For example, some hunters had to choose to hunt close to home for the entire season or far away, usually with family, for only the opening weekend. Many family hunting groups, some comprised of many generations, were divided. The regional requirement has also continued through at least 2009.

Following closely behind the designation of region-restricted hunting was the development and establishment of the Regional Advisory Councils (RACs). These councils are comprised of government-appointed sportsmen, biologists, and individuals from numerous outdoor interests. The RACs hold public meetings for the purpose of obtaining managerial opinions from the general public, various sportsmen groups, and other interested organizations. Meeting discussions center on current DWR management regulations and issues. The RACs take the public input, determine solutions, and present management recommendations to the Wildlife Board, which makes final policy decisions. The RACs have become a strong voice for Utah's sportsmen, and the work of these councils will continue through at least 2009 and probably indefinitely.

Note: Considerable discussion has occurred on changing state regulations to strictly limited-entry deer hunting on all units. Statewide limited-entry hunting would have the advantage of improved harvest control, but the disadvantages of fewer hunting opportunities and limiting hunters to smaller geographical locations.

Several other less significant changes were also made during this period. Most of these changes favored special interest groups and were designed to increase hunter interest. These changes included lowering the age required to obtain a hunting license from 16 to 14 years with recommendations in 2006 to lower the age to 12 years; allowing young hunters under the age of 18 years to hunt all three seasons; shortening the rifle hunt from 11 to 9 or fewer days; bonus points and preference points for hunts having limited permits and high demand; increased complexity of the proclamations; separating into two proclamations the antlerless and bucks/bulls regulations; and sales of limited special buck tags available to the highest auction bidder. Receipts from these sales are mostly earmarked for habitat projects. Other changes included maintaining a minimum ratio of 15 bucks (of which 5 must be mature) to 100 does during post-season classification counts on every unit. This management goal was mostly achieved by regulations limiting hunter pressure.

Although deer numbers unquestionably declined during the period, alternative solutions to decreasing hunter numbers, decreasing geographic range available to hunters, and attempting to satisfy the desires of several special interest groups were and continue to be available to the state for deer management. The first and obvious solution was not to change policy or add any new restrictions, thereby allowing decreased hunter success and hunter discouragement to be the controlling factor in license sales, and also allowing buck-to-doe post-season ratios to be controlled by hunter efforts. This solution is biologically sound as long as buck-to-doe ratios do not become so wide as to affect reproductive and recruitment success. A second solution was to restrict license sales to only a single big game species per hunter per year. A third solution of restricting hunters to a single hunt for each species per year has been adopted, but was probably weakened by allowing the dedicated hunter program.

A fourth potential solution was to apply adaptive management strategies to each unit. Adaptive management is based solely on the resources within each unit. Under this solution, the strategy for each unit would be different and determined by many factors including population dynamics, habitats available, land ownership, acreage of summer and winter ranges, location with respect to human population centers, hunter access, etc. Selected criteria and population dynamics' data collected by DWR would directly define the hunt restrictions for the following year based on the adaptive management plan for individual units. For example, units having poor population dynamics and low deer populations would have more restrictions, such as road closures, shorter seasons, weapon restrictions, or muzzleloader hunters moved to the rifle (any weapons) hunt, whereas units having very good population dynamics and high deer populations would have no restrictions and probably increased opportunity, such as longer seasons or an increase in the number of antlerless permits. In my opinion, adaptive management strategies provide the highest population oversight and control, and will likely be adopted at some future time.

Before 1993, the direction of the DWR was clearly to provide, within resource boundaries, the maximum hunting opportunity, equally available to anyone, and with family-friendly regulations. Indeed, the fourth or fifth most important Utah "holiday" during the school year was the opening weekend of the general deer hunt. Guys went hunting and gals went shopping. However, the restrictions imposed during this period, and especially during the 1990s, were clearly in response to the decrease in the number of deer. Unquestionably, the Division of Wildlife Resources had to make difficult choices.

Hunting opportunity and deer numbers are clearly not dependent, and management decisions may be altered according to numerous factors and interests related to the uses of the deer resource. Nonetheless, a management philosophy focused on providing the optimum hunting opportunities for Utah hunters, but including input from other interest groups, will continue to be a primary consideration for the state of Utah.

Table 1-1. Chronology of the major events defining the management of Utah's mule deer and winter range resources.

1876   First law protecting big game in the Utah territory titled, "Laws for the Preservation of Game and Fish."
1894   Utah Fish and Game Department organized.
        First fishing and hunting regulations adopted.

1908   State legislature closes mule deer hunting in Utah for six years.
With the previous six month hunting season (1894-1907), mule deer had become extremely scarce, and extirpation was possible in many Utah counties.

1913   "BUCK-ONLY" law was passed by the state legislature.
Antlerless mule deer were completely protected.

1916   U.S. Biological Services began control of large predators to protect livestock.
This action increased protection for mule deer from predators.

1930   Excessive utilization of winter ranges by mule deer was first recorded.
At least some of Utah's deer herds were approaching or exceeding carrying capacity of winter ranges.

1933   Board of Big Game Control was established.
The Board was given the authority and responsibility to regulate the number of mule deer in Utah.

1934   First antlerless deer hunt was approved and conducted.
First efforts were made to balance mule deer numbers with available winter habitat and forage.

1937   Purchase of the Mule Deer Research Management Area near Utah State University.
This site became the focus area for most of the research on mule deer and habitat requirements. *Note:* Most of the Management Area and associated winter range was sold to Logan City in 2001 for a cemetery, development, and other uses.

1944   Publication of the initial Doman and Rasmussen manuscript on supplemental feeding and nutritional experiments on the Mule Deer Research Wildlife Management Area.

1946   Definition and establishment of 53 mule deer units.
First efforts were made to manage mule deer populations within individual units.

1946   Establishment of the big game-livestock relationships project at Utah State University.
Research begins on winter range relationships. *Note:* This project was terminated in 1994 when the Division of Wildlife Resources was financially compelled to an action of 'Reduction in Force.'

1948   Establishment of the Interagency Committee.
Cooperation improved between state and federal agencies.

1948   Description of overall range conditions.
Conditions of the range were defined with respect to big game and livestock grazing.

1949   Recognition and identification of summer and winter ranges.
The critical value of winter ranges was clearly defined.

1950   Publication of USFS Research Paper Number 24.
A thorough review of Utah's' big game, livestock and range relationships problems was completed. Research needs associated with mule deer were defined. The herd unit management concept was developed.

1951   Annual report of mule deer harvest in Utah was initiated.
Data collection and reporting were greatly improved. This effort has continued through to the present.

1955   Publication of the textbook *Range Management* by Stoddart and Smith.
This was the first textbook dealing with range management.

1957   Establishment of the Great Basin Research Center in Ephraim.
Extensive research on rangelands revegetation was begun. This project has continued through 2009 and hopefully will continue indefinitely.

1957   Systematic collection of range trend data and analysis was initiated.
Selected winter range sites were first characterized by vegetative data. This project with incremental improvements has continued through 2009 and hopefully will also continue indefinitely. First publication in 1958.

1968   Publication of Smith and Doell's manuscript on livestock grazing benefits for mule deer.
Initial guidelines for grazing cattle on mule deer winter ranges were established.

1968   Publication of the booklet *Restoring Big-game Range in Utah* by Plummer et al.
Initial methods for revegetation of winter ranges were established.

1976   Publication of the symposium *Mule Deer Decline in the West*.
Public recognition of the decline of mule deer populations throughout their entire range, and recognition of the significance and decline of deer winter ranges was stated.

1976   Division of Wildlife Resources publication on limiting range factors.

Defined each unit as limiting deer populations by available summer range, winter range, or units were both summer range and winter ranges were equally limiting.

1977   Publication of the *Oak Creek Mule Deer Herd in Utah* by Robinette et al.

A major source of information on mule deer biology and population dynamics was made available.

1981   Publication of Hancock's manuscript on mule deer management in Utah.

Management synopsis for the past and framework for future management.

1984   Massive, statewide winter (1983–1984) kill of mule deer.

Hunters, environmentalists, conservationists, and citizen groups as well as wildlife biologist realized the folly of carrying excessive numbers of mule deer on winter ranges. This resulted in the initial increase of public involvement with wildlife management.

1993   Substantial, statewide winter (1992–1993) kill of mule deer.

Substantial reduction in harvest and deer numbers due to a combination of factors.

It was realized that decades of periodic overutilization of ranges by deer and livestock have resulted in long-term loss of habitat. Due to changes in winter habitat, deer populations statewide were now unable to recover to pre-1993 levels.

1993   Hunters restricted to one hunt - rifle, muzzleloader, or archery.

1994   Total number of general season buck deer hunting permits capped at 97,000. Hunters required to choose hunting Region.

1997   Publication of Division of Wildlife Resources document on "Deer Herd Units."

Prioritization system for land acquisition of winter range was developed.

1997   Wildlife management units and boundaries redefined.

Thirty, more clearly defined and larger management units in Utah, were established.

Data collection needs and biological efforts were reduced to a more manageable number of units.

1998   Establishment of permanent annual range utilization transects on the Cache unit.

1998 Beginning of several years of statewide drought especially in southern Utah. Drought continued in parts of Utah through 2005.

1999 Range trend data analysis altered to use only permanently marked end points.
Greatly improved data accuracy and precision of range trend data.

2000 Publication of Austin's manuscript on mule deer-livestock relationships.
Summarized 50 years of research and updated recommendations for livestock grazing on mule deer winter ranges.

2002 Division of Wildlife adopts aggressive programs on habitat revegetation.
Reestablishment of vegetation on depleted winter ranges becomes a major priority.

2003 Comprehensive statewide management plan for mule deer was developed and published.

2005 Total number of general season buck deer hunting permits reduced to 95,000.

2006 Declining statewide range conditions recognized. Primary factors defined as drought, invasive plant species, wildfire, frequent overgrazing by livestock, and over population by mule deer on summer and winter ranges. Predators, hunter and human harassment, and highway mortality listed as limiting and decreasing deer numbers. The long-term goal of maintaining 426,000 deer in Utah was temporarily reduced to 412,000. Number of general season Utah buck deer hunting permits remains capped at only 95,000, with less than 1,000 limited-entry buck permits, and with fewer than 1,100 antlerless permits. Statewide buck deer harvest determined at a little over 30,000.

2007 Wildfires blacken over 600,000 Utah acres mostly on big game winter ranges.
Statewide buck harvest determined for a second consecutive year at a little over 30,000.

2008 Following a moderately harsh winter, buck harvest significantly declines to less than 23,000.

Photo by Becky Blankenship

The behavior of buck deer during the rut is always
fascinating to observe.

Mule Deer Biology

Photo by Becky Blankenship

In Utah a buck deer is defined as, "a deer with antlers that are longer than five inches." This small yearling barely qualifies.

Chapter 2

Life Cycle and Behavior

Utah mule deer fawns are mostly born in late spring within one or two weeks of June 20, the approximate mean birth date (Robinette et al. 1977). The short fawning period has natural survival values for the fawn crop. Foremost, the effects of predators in reducing deer numbers is lessened because of the short time interval when fawns are especially vulnerable. Because almost all does have been determined to be carrying fawns in spring, long fawning periods would generally produce about the same number of fawns as shorter fawning periods; however, fawns would be vulnerable to predation over a longer period of time.

Physiologically, fawns are born after the does have had sufficient time to recover from the stresses of winter (Wallmo 1981). Does may lose as much as 30 percent of their body weight during winter. Does regain vitality and physical condition rapidly in spring from the early and highly nutritious growth of grasses and forbs. Usually when fawns are born, vegetation is abundant and at its nutritional best. Forbs are lush and plentiful, and young fawns, although nursing several times each day, adapt rapidly to the succulent vegetation.

About a week before fawns are born, and during the first few weeks after parturition, does become very secretive and stay mostly alone (Reynolds 1960). The small family groups, including the previous year's fawns, with which deer often associate during the winter, temporarily disband during this time period. Does usually select secluded areas of brushy rangeland for fawn birthing areas. After birth the fawns are licked clean and nursed by the does. Fawns can usually stand within a few minutes. During the next few days the fawns mostly stay hidden with little movement, while the does return at intervals to nurse and care for them.

Rapid summer growth and storage of body fat by fawns is necessary to help them survive the rigors of winter. By the October deer hunt, male fawns weigh about 70 pounds and females about 65 pounds (Austin and Urness 1976). Bucks and does also replenish their body fat stores during the summer months and by fall have accumulated thick deposits of body fat. The thickness of the fat deposit in fall is a good indicator of summer range vegetative condition. Thick subcutaneous deposits on the rump and at the xiphoid process at the base of the sternum usually indicate lush summer range conditions, while thin deposits often show up during droughts or on areas of marginal summer range (Austin 1984). Occasionally deer that foraged on alfalfa hay or other agricultural crops throughout the summer are harvested with fat thickness exceeding one inch.

Antlers mature and begin to harden in late August and September, and bucks begin the ritual of horning. Horning is the scraping of the antler velvet, which is mostly removed by the first week of October, when the antlers are fully hardened. Subsequent rubbing, often resulting in scraping and debarking of trees and shrubs, continues until antlers are dropped four or five months later. Horning is used by deer as an auditory signal for dominance, similar to the well-known bugling in elk.

During September, sparring between bucks, usually initiated by the more dominant buck, is common. Sparring is comparable to a sporting contest, as opposed to fighting during the breeding season between equally ranked and sized bucks. Sparring usually occurs between bucks of different dominance ranks, and is usually terminated by the subordinate buck.

Breeding begins about the first of November with the midpoint about November 20, soon after the end of the rifle season hunt in Utah, and is mostly completed by mid December. The gestation period is usually near 205 days. With very few does being incapable of bearing young, pregnancy rates for most herds in Utah exceed 95% for mature does aged one and a half years and older after the period of conception. Unlike white-tailed deer, conception in mule deer fawns, aged about half a year, is very rare (Hall 1984).

Breeding behavior in mule deer can often be observed on winter ranges following the hunting season when the breeding interests of bucks lessen their fear of man. Mature dominant bucks may court and breed 20 to 30 females or more during a single season. It is of genetic advantage for fawns to have been sired by the most dominant bucks, which generally pass on their large size and vitality. Consequently, does attract many bucks, which compete and occasionally fight to determine dominance. Also, from natural selection advantage, each male works to breed as many females as possible with dominant bucks accomplishing the clear majority of the breeding.

During the breeding season bucks roam constantly, searching for does in estrus (Geist 1980). Bucks determine if does are in heat by first stimulating the female to urinate and then, by the "lip curling behavior," test the urine. Through this method bucks can detect not only if a doe is in heat, but also if estrus is imminent. In the latter case, bucks will tend the doe, chase off other bucks, and wait for estrus. Usually after a doe begins estrus, she is courted and bred by the dominant buck in the area. After an average of five pre-copulatory mounts, the doe is bred. Usually after the initial breeding, the buck will continue to court the doe and after three to several hours may again copulate. It is estimated that a doe will be bred four to six times during the day and a half estrus period. Toward the end of the rutting season bucks become decreasingly aggressive and less active, and are often exhausted. Conversely, does which have not been bred become more aggressive and initiate breeding.

Following the breeding season, deer often gather in large groups with the dominant and often oldest doe becoming the leader. When snow depth increases to over 18 inches, groups often trail onto lower elevation ranges in single file to minimize loss of energy. These larger groups often remain intact until mid spring when vegetation becomes abundant and deer begin to physically recover from winter.

In January or occasionally in late December, bucks begin to shed antlers, with older and healthier bucks shedding first. By the first of April, antlers from all healthy bucks are shed, and growth on next years' rack has begun.

When overwinter losses occur, fawns are found much more frequently than bucks or does. Most deer killed over the winter from starvation and weather die in a curled fetal position with the carcass intact, whereas accident and predator mortalities show the carcasses in various positions and often with disconnected and scattered body parts. Overwinter mortalities of bucks, yearling does, and does older than eight years are found less frequently. Mature does, aged two to eight, are uncommonly found and have the highest overwinter survival rate. Overwinter losses of mature does normally occur only during severe winters, and thus, the critical reproductive segment of the herd has the highest potential sustainability. During average winters, about 15% of the deer entering the winter are lost from the combination of all mortality factors, with about 5% being adults and 10% being fawns.

Chapter 3

Forages, Nutrition, and Water Requirements

Sometimes to survive, deer must take what they need from what they can get.

Forages

Deer are highly adaptable to available forages within most Utah habitats and readily consume various plants, from succulent forbs found in alpine meadows to brittle shrubs on the desert floor. In any particular location deer will generally select the more palatable, lush, and usually nutritious forages available during any season. The tapered snout and sticky tongue of the mule deer enables it to carefully choose selected forages. For example, at the big game research facility near Utah State University, rolled barley (equivalent to ice cream for deer) and alfalfa hay deer pellets (bread or potatoes) were mixed and fed daily to tractable deer during winter. After each feeding some of the pellets remained, but rarely did a single grain of barley stay hidden.

A second fascinating example occurred during summer feeding trials of diet and nutrition determination in the Uinta Mountains. I observed that, toward the end of each feeding trial period when the desire for food was mostly satisfied and the rumen was filled, deer became very selective in forage choices. When the wild strawberries, about the size of a green pea, began to ripen, deer would search diligently for many minutes before finding and picking an occasional sweet, red berry without consuming any of the strawberry's palatable green leafy forage. The same selectivity was observed for mushrooms in late summer.

Because deer are more commonly observed during winter, they are usually considered browsers, which eat primarily shrubs, as opposed to grazers, which eat primarily grasses and forbs. However, deer are actually opportunistic feeders, that is, selecting the most palatable forage class available during any season. It is true that in winter when snow cover limits availability of other forages except shrubs, deer are browsers. However, given a choice, deer usually select other forages.

When winter snows melt from south-facing hillsides in spring, the first green shoots of grasses are highly nutritious and palatable forages. In early spring deer are grazers, and particularly on ranges with healthy stands of grasses, browsing decreases to minor dietary significance, usually less than five percent of the total diet. Where available, the non-native crested wheatgrass, which has been seeded on many ranges throughout the western United States for increased forage and livestock production, is an important source of nutrients and energy following winter. As much as 90 percent of the diet may be comprised of various species of grasses in early spring before bulbous forb forages begin to be available (Austin and Urness 1983).

> *Note:* Grasses and forbs begin to grow in the spring as a direct response to increasing soil temperatures. Grasses are usually first to "green-up" in the spring because their root systems begin just under the soil surface and new growth is triggered with the initial warming of the soil temperatures. Bulbs are often six to twelve inches or deeper under the soil surface, and usually several days are required for increased soil temperature flux to penetrate to those depths and stimulate new growth on forbs. New growth on forbs must also push through several inches of soil before reaching the surface, whereas grasses are initially at or near the soil surface.

Usually one or two weeks after spring growth in grasses begins, the first of the forbs in Nature's high variety garden becomes available. As forbs become increasingly available, the deer diet switches over to a variety of forbs. By May, forbs usually comprise the majority of the diet, up to 85 percent (Austin and Urness 1985). Some of the important spring forbs include wild onion, milkvetch, water leaf, phlox, violets, spring beauty, spring parsley, steers head, yarrow, and the common dandelion. Wherever available, alfalfa hay is always an important source of forage.

As summer progresses, the early spring forbs begin to mature and dry and are replaced by forbs growing in late spring and summer. At middle elevations usually within the mountain browse zone, important forbs during June and July include penstemon, geranium, vetch and mules ear. At the high elevations within the conifer and quaking aspen zones, forbs dominate the diet throughout the summer with some important species being heartleaf arnica, goldenrod, bluebells, and cinquefoil. Forbs remain the major component of the diet for as long into the summer as they are available. At middle elevations around the middle of July, later at upper elevations, succulent forbs dry out with summer's heat and slowly biodegrade. Only a few forbs such as pale bastard toadflax and some species of aster remain at lower elevations throughout August. At high elevations during favorable growing years, the highly palatable and very nutritious mushrooms are sought after and eaten with relish (Launchbaugh and Urness 1992).

By September the deer diet gradually switches over to browse. Acorns from Gambel oak and nutritious berries from chokecherry, snowberry, twinberry, serviceberry, elderberry, currants, Oregon grape and others add to the rapidly building fat stores essential for winter survival.

When hunters head for the field during the Utah general October deer hunt, deer are at or near their annual peak of physical condition. Fat stores and deer weights slowly decline beginning from about the first of November and continue until new vegetative growth becomes available in the spring.

In October, November, and December deer migrate to traditional winter ranges where few nutritious plants are available. Only a few forbs such as thistle and bushy bird beak provide more than one or two percent of the diet, with the large majority comprised of browse species. However, during years where snow depth is not excessive and fall rains and warm temperatures have stimulated plant growth, fall regrowth of grasses becomes available and is highly nutritious. Regrowth grass forage may constitute more that 50 percent of the late fall diet (Austin and Urness 1983). Regrowth often occurs on rangelands where some of the winter range was left ungrazed by livestock during the spring and summer. The black-body effect of sunlight—radiant energy absorbed by exposed plant biomass under snow depths of about 6" to 18"—causes snow around the base of shrubs and grass clumps to melt, resulting in warmer micro-enviromental temperatures and grass regrowth (Austin et al. 1983).

When snow cover and depth eliminate access to grasses and forbs, deer are forced to become browsers. Snow depth exceeding about 12 inches causes the deer diet to approach 90% browse. At snow depth exceeding 20 inches browse constitutes 99%+ of the diet. Palatable shrubs, such as antelope bitterbrush, serviceberry, and Douglas rabbit brush are rapidly consumed. Several species, such as Douglas rabbit brush, require a heavy frost and freezing temperatures that cause chemical changes in the plant for the shrubs to become palatable.

Big sagebrush and Utah juniper are the bread and potatoes of the winter diet. Without these two species on winter ranges, deer numbers would be drastically lower, especially in northern and central Utah. Based on other browse species available on winter ranges, I estimated deer numbers may be reduced by as much as 50 to 80 percent depending on the composition of the total forage base.

In later winter as bare ground and snow cover alternate between snow storms, the diet of deer rapidly shifts between winter and new spring forage, but quickly the new growth of palatable and nutritious species becomes the primary forages.

For mule deer, the best spring ranges contain a good groundcover and mixture of grasses and forbs within the sagebrush-grass community. From spring through early summer deer move to the mountain browse zone, with Gambel oak and Rocky Mountain maple being preferred habitats, particularly for birthing fawns. During mid to late summer the quaking aspen community provides the best array of forages for deer, especially if the zone is not heavily grazed by livestock. By early fall, the moist zones, which often produce highly palatable berries, on north slopes and in the bottom of draws become prime habitats. However, the critical habitat for most of Utah's deer herds is winter range. The best winter ranges contain a variety of deciduous shrubs and Utah juniper, and always include healthy stands of big sagebrush mixed with multiple species of perennial grasses and forbs.

I compiled Table 3-1, which is based on numerous dietary studies of mule deer forages and lists the major plants consumed by mule deer in Utah (Kufeld et al. 1973; Deschamp et al. 1979; Wallmo and Regelin 1981; Austin and Urness 1983, 1985; and others). Nomenclature is from Beetle 1970, Welsh and Moore 1973, Welsh et al. 1993, and Anderson and Holmgren 1996. Numerous—hundreds and probably thousands—other species are consumed in minor amounts. Although additional major plant species would be added for specific ranges, particularly outside of Utah, this list generally applies over the entire range of the mule deer. The forages are listed by the habitats where they are commonly found. The forages are also listed by the most likely season(s) of use. However, depending upon availability, individual forages may be consumed during other seasons and in habitats not designated.

Nutrition

Similar to all mammals, mule deer have specific minimum requirements for energy, minerals and vitamins (Hall 1984). Unfortunately, few quantitative requirements have been defined. The two factors which are referred to most often in assessing deer nutrition are percent crude protein and percent dry matter digestibility. Generally, winter deer diets containing a minimum of seven percent crude protein and being 40 percent digestible will sustain mule deer (Wallmo and Regelin 1981). Overwinter losses are often high when nutritional values fall below these minimums. However, much higher nutritional levels are required for reproduction and growth. Optimum nutritional levels are reached at about 16 percent crude protein and 65 percent digestibility. Early growth spring grasses, succulent forbs in spring, various autumn fall berries, mushrooms, fresh wildflowers, riparian zone forbs, and field-growing alfalfa hay are forages which provide optimum nutrition.

For example, on a typical good deer winter range near Henefer, Utah, overwinter diets ranged in percent crude protein from 7.4 to 11.5 percent, with digestibility between 37 and 47 percent. On that same winter range in spring, percent crude protein exceeded 25 percent and digestibility ranged from 57 to 75 percent (Urness et al. 1983). Crude protein and digestibility generally remain above 10 percent and 50 percent, respectively, on good summer ranges. Values exceeding 20 percent protein and 70 percent digestibility are obtained on the highest quality mountain ranges (Collins and Urness 1983).

Since mule deer are small ruminants and have limited capacity to digest low quality forages, such as dry grass and twigs, a variety of quality foods is important. Unlike most mammals, foods eaten by mule deer are first processed or fermented in the ruminant stomach. Through regurgitation foods are often rechewed or cud-chewed to aid in later digestion. Most of the volume of the forage at any one time in the total gastrointestinal tract of mule deer is found in the rumen. The rumen is a special adaptation in mule deer and some other herbivores that is necessary to reduce cellulose, a major constituent of range vegetation. Through acids, enzymes, and bacteria, dietary foods are broken down into usable materials. After foods pass through the rumen, they are digested similarly to most other large mammals.

Whether alfalfa hay is eaten by deer while growing in fields during the spring through fall season or from dried baled hay in winter, alfalfa hay is always beneficial to the diet. The idea that deer cannot eat alfalfa hay in winter is simply not true. In the 1930s and 1940s experimental feeding of alfalfa hay to deer on the foothills of Cache Valley showed supplemental feeding was very successful, although expensive (Doman and Rasmussen 1944, Urness 1980). The bulk of the year-round diet fed to tame mule deer, as well as elk, bison and pronghorn, for 40 years at the Utah State University research facility was alfalfa hay. Also, when wild deer are fed in winter, the best feed is often alfalfa hay. Second or third crop alfalfa hay is preferable to first crop because of the higher protein content and higher digestibility. Furthermore, commercially prepared pellet feeds for deer or domestic livestock usually have alfalfa hay as the primary ingredient.

Water Requirements

The mule deer's need for surface water varies by season, vegetative succulence within the home range, and weather. Generally water is not a limiting factor controlling deer population in most areas because several water sources are usually within the home range of deer. In winter deer do well with only snow, and during spring and early summer, consumption of forages high in moisture content reduces the need for surface water to almost zero. Nonetheless, water becomes critical in desert habitats in late summer and early fall from about July through September.

Adequate water distribution is critical to mule deer in desert environments. The western third of Utah and many of Utah's southern units maintain many desert environments. Based on home range sizes of deer in desert areas, water locations need to be available within at least two miles of summer deer habitat. However, as the distance from water further increases, the likelihood of deer using the range forage resources or the water rapidly decreases. For adequate range utilization and deer density, I recommend water sources should be spaced such that all deer summer habitat is within 1.5 miles of water. Consequently, water sources spaced at three mile or closer intervals will adequately serve mule deer in desert environments. As may be expected, when water sources are developed on previously dry desert rangelands, such as the west deserts of Utah, deer densities and populations have been observed to increase (Wood et al. 1978).

Where natural springs are sparse or cannot be developed in desert habitats for wildlife, artificial water sources should be constructed. Guzzlers, which are constructed for deer as well as upland game, non-game birds, and mammals, consist of a precipitation catchment surface, storage tank, and small watering basin. The catchment surface is usually made of corrugated aluminum roofing placed over a wood frame and built several inches above the ground surface. Catchment surfaces usually measure 10 by 20 feet or larger, and the catchment area is often fenced to prevent damage to the structure. A concrete catchment surface also works well and has lower maintenance, but is more costly. Rain and snow falling on the catchment surface is drained into an underground 1,000 gallons or larger storage tank. By use of a pipe connected to the bottom of the tank and float valves that open when water is being used, about two inches of water depth is maintained in a small drinking basin usually measuring less than two by two feet. If juniper trees are unavailable, structures are often built to shade the water. Hundreds of desert guzzlers have been constructed and maintained by the Division of Wildlife Resources.

Generally even under very dry and hot weather conditions, deer only visit water sources once daily, usually at night. However, daily consumption of surface water in desert environments has been determined to be almost one gallon per deer. For examples, on Utah's desert Sheeprock Mountains, I measured that deer averaged 0.95 and 0.84 gallons per day during August 1982 and 1983, respectively, and at Promontory, Utah, in September 1990, the average was 0.81 gallons. In an Arizona study by Hazan and Krauman (1988), does drank 0.92 gallons per day, and bucks consumed 0.78 gallons per day.

Table 3-1. Major forages of mule deer by habitat types and season of use.

Plant Class	Common Name	Habitat Types*	Winter	Spring	Summer	Fall
	Serviceberry	3, 4	x	x	x	x
Shrubs	Big Sagebrush	1, 2, 3, 4, 5	x			
and	Saltbrush	1	x			
Trees	Oregon Grape	3, 4	x	x		x
	Buckbrush	5, 6	x		x	x
	Mahogany	3, 4, 6	x		x	x
	Rabbitbrush	2, 3, 4	x			x
	Utah Juniper	2, 3, 4	x			
	Western Red Cedar	4, 5, 6	x			
	Myrtle Mtn. Lover	4, 5, 6	x		x	x
	Pine Trees	3, 4, 5, 6, 7	x	x		
	Quaking Aspen	5, 6	x		x	x
	Chokecherry	2, 3, 4, 5, 8	x		x	x
	Antelope Bitterbrush	2, 3, 4	x		x	x
	Gambel Oak	3, 4	x		x	x
	Squaw Bush	2, 3, 4	x		x	x
	Current	4, 5, 6, 7, 8	x		x	x
	Wild Rose	2, 3, 4, 5, 6, 8	x		x	x
	Willow	7, 8	x		x	x
	Elderberry	3, 4, 5	x		x	x
	Snowberry	3, 4, 5	x		x	x
	Blueberry	6			x	x
	Wild Onion	2, 3, 4, 5		x		
Forbs	Pussytoes	3, 4		x	x	
	Heartleaf Arnica	6, 7, 8			x	
	Fringed Sagewort	2, 3	x			

Plant Class	Common Name	Habitat Types*	Seasons of Use			
			Winter	Spring	Summer	Fall
	Aster	2, 3, 4, 5, 7			x	
	Milkvetch	1, 2, 3 , 4, 7		x	x	
	Balsamroot	2, 3, 4		x	x	
	Indian Paintbrush	2, 3, 4		x	x	
	Thistle	2, 3, 4	x		x	x
	Bastard Toadflax	2, 3, 4			x	x
	Bushy Birdbeak	2			x	x
	Hawksbeard	2, 3, 4		x	x	x
	Larkspur	2, 3, 4, 5		x		
	Willowherb	2, 3, 4, 7		x	x	
	Fleabane	2, 3, 4, 7		x	x	
	Wild Buckwheat	2, 3, 4		x	x	
	Wild Strawberry	4, 7, 8			x	
	Wild Geranium	4, 5, 6, 7			x	
	Sunflower	2, 3		x		
	Wire Lettuce	2, 3		x		
	Lupine	2, 3, 4, 5, 7		x		x
	Alfalfa	1, 2, 3, 4	x	x	x	x
	Sweet Clover	2, 3, 4		x	x	
	Bluebells	5, 7, 8		x		
	Prickly Pear Cactus	1, 2, 3, 4	x		x	
	Penstemon	2, 3, 4, 5, 6, 7, 8		x	x	
	Phlox	2, 3, 4		x	x	
	Cinquefoil	2, 3, 4, 5, 7, 8		x	x	
	Goldenrod	3, 4, 5		x	x	
	Common Dandelion	2, 3, 4, 5, 6, 7, 8		x	x	
	Yellow Salsify	2, 3, 4, 5	x	x		
	Clover	4, 5, 7, 8	x	x		
	Vetch	2, 3, 4, 5, 6		x		

Plant Class	Common Name	Habitat Types*	Seasons of Use			
			Winter	Spring	Summer	Fall
	Mulesear	2, 3, 4, 5, 7			x	x
	Wheat Grasses	2, 3, 4		x		x
Grasses	Cheatgrass	1, 2, 3, 4	x	x		x
and	Sedges	4, 5, 6, 7, 8		x	x	x
Sedges	Blue Grasses	2, 3, 4, 5, 6, 7, 8		x		x
	Rushes	7, 8		x	x	
	Wild Rye Grasses	2		x		
	Brome Grasses	5, 6			x	
Other Plants	Mushrooms	5, 6, 7, 8		x	x	x

*Habitat Types:
1 Salt Desert Shrub   2 Sagebrush-Grass   3 Pinyon-Juniper
4 Mountain Browse   5 Aspen   6 Conifer
7 Upland Meadow   8 Riparian

Chapter 4

Antlers, Carcass Measurements, and Venison Quality

Harvest Age and Carcass Weight Relationships

The size of harvested mule deer is important to hunters for antler, meat, hide, and self-satisfaction values. In reporting deer weights, three different measurements are used: (1) live or total weight, (2) field dressed weight, which equals total weight including heart and liver but minus the blood and viscera, and (3) hog-dressed or eviscerated carcass weight, which is field dressed weight without the heart and liver. In all three measurements the hide, legs, and head are intact. Hog-dressed weight is the most commonly used measurement and hog-dressed weights are often collected at Utah's deer checking stations.

The average and normal range of hog-dressed weights for hunter-harvested mule deer in Utah are shown in Table 4-1. These data from a study by Austin and Urness (1976) represent deer harvested from good-quality ranges, such as along the Wasatch Front. Deer harvested from lower-quality ranges, such as the Oak Creek and Vernon deer units, are slightly smaller.

Table 4-1. Hog-dressed weights (lbs) of hunter-harvested
Utah mule deer in October.

Age (years)	⅓	1⅓	2⅓	3⅓+
Bucks	Fawn	Yearling	Twoling	Prime
Mean weight	50	98	122	166
Normal range	40-60	70-120	100-165	120-220

Age (years)	⅓	1⅓	2⅓	3⅓+
Does	Fawn	Yearling	Twoling	Prime
Mean weight	44	86	94	96
Normal range	35-60	60-105	75-115	80-130

The average yearling buck weighs about the same as a prime doe, or slightly under 100 pounds hog-dressed weight. Female deer are smaller than bucks at all age classes, including birth (Robinette et al. 1977). Does gain very little additional weight following their fourth summer. Buck deer, however, continue to make significant weight gains for ages up to seven to nine years if they manage to survive hunters, accidents, predators, disease and harsh winters. Under buck-only hunting, during the 1980s where less than one percent of the harvested bucks exceeded five years of age, very few bucks, less than one in a hundred, weighed over 200 pounds. Before 1976 about three to four percent of the harvested bucks in Utah exceeded 200 pounds hog-dressed weight.

The hog-dressed weight of 200 pounds is a fine benchmark and represents a mature, physically healthy, and genetically rich buck mule deer. Units where 50 percent or more of the bucks aged six years and older exceed 200 pounds in hog-dressed weight should be considered excellent in year-round forage quality and having a proper balance of deer numbers with available rangeland. Although highly dependent on management strategies and goals, I estimate that to maintain near optimum health of Utah deer herds, where summer and winter ranges are in at least fair condition, a physical index to successful management is to maintain two to eight percent of hunter-harvested bucks exceeding 200 pounds hog-dressed weight.

Venison Quality

The table quality of venison depends primarily on field care up to the time of butchering and freezing, and secondarily upon cooking and physical condition of the animal when harvested (Cook et al. 1949, Mendenhall 1967). When venison is properly cared for, it is superior to beef in most respects. Studies at Utah State University compared carefully handled venison with similarly handled beef in paired sample tests. In one test the panel of nine judges rated the unknown meats for tenderness, texture, juiciness, and taste appeal. Venison excelled beef in all categories except juiciness (Smith and Smith 1959). A later study by Bardwell and others (1964) using the same rating scale and 119 harvested deer reported similar results. It is noteworthy that they also reported no differences in taste between bucks versus does, or older deer versus younger deer.

Not only does venison compare favorably with lean beef in taste appeal, but venison is generally more nutritious, as shown in Table 4-2. When compared to lamb, beef, and veal, venison is similar in protein, fat, niacin and food energy, slightly lower in calcium, but higher in phosphorus, thiamin and riboflavin (Chatfield 1940; Cook et al. 1949; Watt and Merrill 1963; Adams 1975).

*Table 4-2. Nutritional comparison of lean, raw venison of mule deer, lamb, beef, and veal per 1,000 grams of meat weight.**

Meat	Protein	Fat	Calcium	Phosphorus	Thiamin	Riboflavin	Niacin	Energy
Venison	205	45	103	2490	2.4	5.0	63	1285
Lamb	199	47	119	1848	1.8	2.5	57.5	1269
Beef	216	54	130	2009	0.9	1.9	51.8	1410
Veal	199	59	119	2057	1.4	2.6	66.7	1390

*Protein and fat in grams, calcium phosphorus, thiamin, riboflavin, and niacin in milligrams, and energy in calories.

Venison Yields

The amount of venison a deer carcass yields is dependent upon the size of the deer, the method of butchering, the amount of meat wasted from bullet damage, and the care taken to remove all the meat. From an unpublished study I conducted from deer checked at the Daniels Canyon checking station near Heber City, Utah, where butchering was compared between the hunter, a friend/relative or meat cutter, only small differences in the average amount of venison were found. The results are presented in Table 4-3.

Boned butchering means the venison was removed from all bones. Most hunters use boned butchering. Unboned butchering means some portion of the bone was cut and left attached to the meat. Unboned venison yields are about 25 percent higher than boned venison yields due to the addition of the bone.

A good rule of thumb is to expect that 50 percent of the hog-dressed carcass weight is available in boned venison. For examples, the average yearling buck or mature doe weighing about 100 pounds in hog-dressed weight will yield about 50 pounds of boned venison. Similarly, a 200 pound hog-dressed buck will yield over 100 pounds of boned venison. The percentage of venison compared to hog-dressed weight increases slightly as the size of the carcass increases. For the hunter who bones all possible meat from the carcass including rib meat, lower leg, and neck, the percentage may be increased to 60% or slightly above. For the hunter who only bones off the major cuts, the percentage may drop to 40% or lower. The relationship between hog-dressed weight and mean venison yield is shown in Table 4-4.

Table 4-3. Venison yield by butchering method as a percentage of hog-dressed weight from hunter-harvested and processed mule deer.

Method of Butchering		Number of Deer Processed	% Venison
Boned			
	Self	56	46
	Friend/Relative	10	50
	Meat Cutter	18	48
Unboned			
	Self	30	62
	Friend/Relative	5	63
	Meat Cutter	23	63

Table 4-4. Relationship between hog-dressed weight (lbs) and mean venison yield (lbs) for hunter-harvested and processed mule deer in Utah.

Hog-dressed Weight	Boned Venison Weight	Unboned Venison Weight
40	18	25
50	24	31
60	29	38
70	35	44
80	40	51
90	45	57
100	51	63
110	56	70
120	62	76
130	67	83
140	73	89
150	78	95
160	84	102
170	89	108
180	94	115
190	100	121
200	105	128
210	111	134
220	116	140

Physical Condition Indices

Good physical condition of mule deer in fall is critical to winter survival and optimum reproduction. Fat storage reflects the annual nutritional cycle, reaches a maximum in the fall, and is a measure of summer habitat quality. However, even during normal winters and with deer entering the winter with heavy fat stores, subcutaneous, internal and marrow fat deposits are mostly depleted by spring. Of the various fat deposits subcutaneous fat is deposited last and is used first, and is not found on deer in emaciated or very poor condition (Kistner et al. 1980, Anderson 1981). Hunters and biologists can easily determine the condition of fall-harvested deer by measuring the fat depth at the base of the sternum (Austin 1984). With a sharp knife, simply cut the underside of the carcass below the ribs to the base of the sternum and through the xiphoid process. Measure the fat depth in millimeters adjacent and perpendicular to the xiphoid process between the hide and the next layer of muscle tissue. Physical condition of the deer is estimated in Table 4-5.

Table 4-5. Relationship of fat depth and physical condition.

Fat Depth	Physical condition
0-2 mm	Poor
3-4 mm	Fair
5-6 mm	Good
7-8 mm	Very Good
9+ mm	Excellent

Annual Antler Cycle

Small antler pedicels are first observed on male fawns at about three months of age (Robinette et al. 1977). The small pedicels, usually less than two inches in length, are retained by the fawns throughout their first winter. By late March or early April the small pedicels on last summer's fawns as well as the pedicels on all older bucks begin growth. Antlers, not horns, are grown in only a few months during the spring and summer at an amazing growth rate, which may exceed two inches per week during peak growth. Growth rates gradually increase as summer progresses with most growth occurring in July. However, by the first of August growth quickly declines and is mostly finished by mid-August, when archery hunting season often begins. The soft furry covering called velvet, which supplies blood to the growing antlers during spring and summer, begins to dry in late summer with increasing levels of blood serum testosterone. By mid-September, the velvet, which has no additional value for the buck and covers the bone-hardened antlers, is purposefully rubbed off by the buck. Buck rubs on trees and shrubs are common signs of fall buck activity. By the October deer hunt only about one in 500 bucks still retain any velvet. Bucks retaining a significant covering of velvet during the October deer hunt have usually suffered a major injury or illness during the previous one to four months.

Bucks retain antlers throughout the fall breeding season. Generally, mature bucks will shed earlier than young bucks, and healthy bucks will shed before bucks in poorer condition.

Factors Affecting Antler and Body Size

Antler development and size in mule deer are highly sensitive to yearly changes in environmental conditions. On the original Vernon deer unit in Utah's west desert areas, for example, my data showed that during a three-year period, 1980 to 1982, deer antler size responded to changing summer range conditions, particularly precipitation levels. That is, in 1980, following a very dry summer, 60 percent of the yearling bucks harvested were spikes; in 1981, a wet summer, the percentage of yearlings harvested as spikes was 35 percent; and in 1982, an average to slightly dry summer, 51 percent were spikes.

Antler development can also be affected over many years by slowly changing environmental and biological conditions. For example, on the Oak Creek deer unit between 1951 and 1959, only 33 percent of harvested yearling bucks were spikes, according to a study by Robinette and others (1977), whereas during the drought years of 1990 and 1991, my data indicated an alarming 48 percent were spikes. It is interesting to note that no spike bucks, aged two and a half years or older, have been harvested or documented in Utah, although one such animal was reportedly taken in Nevada.

Biological Considerations of Hunting Mule Deer during the Month of August

Hunters must act quickly to avoid meat spoilage in August. The timing of Utah's early deer hunt dates corresponds to warm but decreasing temperatures, and improving physical condition of deer.

Air Temperatures and Meat Spoilage Rates

Except at cold temperatures below the threshold for bacterial growth, increases in rates of bacterial growth are directly and positively related to air temperature. Bacterial growth rates increase geometrically with increases in temperature. The most commonly used measure of bacterial growth is the time and temperature relationship needed to double the bacterial growth count. A food safety representative for Millers Packing of Hyrum, Utah, provided the following data and analyses of the bacterial growth time and temperature relationship in big game.

(1) Initial bacterial counts of big game harvested in the field would be expected to be about 1,000 (designated as log 3, or 10 raised to the third power) per square inch. However, initial bacterial counts could be as high as log 4 or 10,000 per square inch.

(2) Spoilage occurs between log 7 and log 10.

(3) Bacteria doubling rate is a function of temperature in degrees Fahrenheit (F) as:
   (a) 40 degrees F equals 6 hours
   (b) 50 degrees F equals 3.7 hours (This is the standard processing temperature for the packing industry.)
   (c) 60 degrees F equals 2 hours
   (d) 70 degrees F equals 1 hour
   (e) 90 degrees F equals one-half hour

(4) Example: With a beginning count of log 3 and constant temperature of 60 degrees, spoilage would begin during the twenty-seventh hour. At 70 degrees spoilage would begin during the fourteenth hour. At 50 degrees spoilage would not begin until after four days. Furthermore, with a beginning count of log 4 and using the same parameters, spoilage would begin during the fortieth hour at 50 degrees, the twentieth hour at 60 degrees, and during the tenth hour at 70 degrees.

(5) It is extremely important to quickly cool a harvested animal to 50 degrees or lower. It is also evident that a few hours in warm temperatures during the day will quickly spoil meat, even though nighttime temperatures may be quite cool.

A climatologist at Utah State University provided the information in Table 4-6, which shows the average change in temperature every five days from August 15 to September 15. Climatic temperature records were used from the stations at Utah State University, Salt Lake City, Brigham Young University, Levan, Vernal, Calleo and Monticello. Temperatures represent the combined daily means of years of records available.

Table 4-6. Change in temperature (F) August 15 to September 15.

Degrees Fahrenheit (F)

	Maximum	Daily Mean	Minimum
August 15:	87	72	56
August 20:	87	71	56
August 25:	85	69	52
September 01:	84	68	54
September 05:	83	67	51
September 10:	81	65	49
September 15:	78	62	46

A difference of about three degrees F usually occurs between August 20th and September 1, with the earlier dates and higher temperatures leading to more rapid meat spoilage of the carcass. The difference of a mean temperature of 70 degrees F versus 67 degrees F, using graphic interpolation, is about 0.25 hours per time interval needed to double the bacterial count. Therefore, with meat bacterial count at log 3 and temperature at 70 degrees, spoilage would begin to occur during the fourteenth hour, whereas at 67 degrees spoilage would begin during the eighteenth hour or about four hours later. Adding 2,000 feet to the mean elevation of 5,100 feet and incorporating the revised adiabatic lapse rate of five degrees F per 1,000-foot increase in elevation, at the 7,100-foot elevation, where many archers hunt, the mean temperature would be about 60 degrees. Using the same analysis, the difference of three degrees between August and September would delay spoilage by about 13 hours. Using the same analysis at 9,000 feet at 50 degrees, the difference of three degrees would delay spoilage by more than 30 hours.

The simple conclusion is that a three-degree difference in temperature between mid-August and early September may be a significant factor in the potential spoilage of hunter-harvested deer.

As a general rule to avoid meat spoilage, I suggest that deer carcasses harvested during August should be removed from the field and butchered or brought to a meat cooler on the same day the animal was harvested, or by noon of the day after the deer was harvested if the deer was taken during the cool hours of the later afternoon or evening.

Physical Condition

The timing of the hunting period from the standpoint of meat palatability and physical condition of the mule deer was a question explored several decades ago in numerous studies.

A study of Idaho deer clearly showed physical condition reached a peak after September 1. This study reported that from May through August less than 10 percent of deer were found in good condition, whereas during September through December the percentage of deer in good condition more than doubled. The authors of the study wrote, "During this period [May through August] the physical condition of the deer ceases to deteriorate and the animal regains health and vigor. The fat reserve buildup period occurs from September through December. At this time, fat is deposited in the bone marrow, mesenteries, and on the rump and kidneys" (Trout and Theissen 1973).

In a study from Nevada, Papaz (1976) reported the peak physical condition and fat stores were determined to occur near the first of September.

A 1964 study conducted at Utah State University showed the palatability of venison to be best during the late August to early September period, and declined slowly after mid-September (Bardwell et al. 1964).

One of the earliest yet very comprehensive studies was conducted in Utah in the late 1940s. This study showed that physical condition and weight of mule deer rapidly increased during the month of August. Few differences were noted in palatability scores between August and October. This study also showed nutritional value of venison was high during the late summer through fall period (Cook et al. 1949). Numerous subsequent studies have shown similar and consistent high nutritional values for venison.

Although physical condition and venison palatability are clearly acceptable in mid-to-late August, fat content and weight reach a peak in early to mid-September and palatability remains constant through about December 1. After about December 1, the quality of venison apparently declines in response to forage availability, nutritional stresses, and the severity of weather. Numerous studies dealing with the physical condition of other ungulate species through time indicate similar results.

Effects of Hunter Disturbance

Specific studies on the effects of hunter disturbance as related to survival of fawns are scant. However, certainly the effects of disturbance become more significant as the age of the fawn decreases and the level of disturbance increases.

Studies on mule and white-tailed deer as reported in books published by the Wildlife Management Institute suggest fawns are weaned after about 10 weeks. Since parturition occurs in mid-June, fawn dependence upon the doe for nutritional supplement continues until about September 1. The period for behavioral and survival dependence is unknown, but would most likely be considerably longer. Some declining degree of fawn dependence on the doe certainly continues at least through the first winter of the fawn's life to about spring green-up. However, by early June as the fawn approaches one year of age and the doe approaches parturition, fawn dependence is essentially ended, sometimes abruptly by the doe chasing off the yearling fawn.

Clearly, the effects of temporary fawn displacement from the doe during the period of nutritional supplementation until about September 1 would most likely result in increased mortality rates for fawns. For permanent separation from the doe during this period, I estimate the mortality rate approaches 95 percent.

The potential mortality effects of temporary fawn displacement from the doe or from the normal home range, caused by the activity patterns of hunters or other human disturbances, between September 1 through about December 1 have not been quantified. Even though fawn weight in fall appears to be positively correlated with overwinter survival, and some loss of fat reserves due to disturbance is inevitable, neither the degree of disturbance nor the consequential effects have been sufficiently studied. Equally important, the effects of doe mortality or wounding from hunting after September 1 on subsequent fawn mortality have not been quantified. Nonetheless, fawn survival rates certainly increase as the length of time of the fawn-doe relationship increases.

Historical Perspective

The beginning date of the archery hunt has varied in Utah from about mid-August to early September. Generally, the beginning of the archery hunt has gradually been set at earlier dates than the other hunts since its inception in the 1940s. In 1956, the archery season was September 8 through 23. During 1957 to 1966, the season began between August 28 and 31 and continued for 16 days. Similar dates were observed between 1969 and 1971, with earlier starting dates during 1967 and 1968. Since 1972 through 2009, beginning dates have varied from August 15 to August 23. Season length was increased from about 16 to 21 days beginning in 1982.

The period of 1956–1971 was a very stable period in deer management and the archery season reflected that stability. It is reasonable to assume the research conducted on the Utah Oak Creek deer unit and other western locations contributed to the decision to begin the archery hunt near the first of September. The beginning of buck-only hunting in 1973 coincided with the setting of the earlier date for the beginning of the archery hunt. This change was probably made due to the restrictions of archers harvesting only bucks, and therefore the archery hunt was assumed to have no effect on does, fawns, or deer populations.

Conclusion

Additional research into the question of when to begin the archery hunt, and significantly, depredation hunts, seems appropriate. With the lower deer recruitment rates and lower numbers of mule deer available on most units than during the previous half century, it may be prudent to err on the side of conservative hunting. Thus, an archery date beginning in late August or nearer the first of September, and continuing for about 16 days, may result in higher fawn survival, especially on units where antlerless deer may be harvested.

Chapter 5

Winter Range, Habitat Types, Migration, and Home Range

To most people: In a developing urban community, open space lands become increasingly valuable until they become invaluable. To most species of wildlife: Progressing human developments lead to population declines and finally extirpation.

Defining and Understanding Utah's Mule Deer Winter Ranges

Winter range is simply defined as the area used by the majority of the mule deer population during the wintry months. The time period during which deer utilize their winter range is about November 15 through April 15, although two to three week variations are common at the beginning or end of winter. Most winter ranges occur at lower elevations. The Utah Fish and Game Department recognized winter range as the limiting factor in controlling sustainable populations of mule deer at least as early as 1930, when excessive utilization of some winter ranges was first recorded.

The first action to study the relationship between mule deer and winter range occurred in 1937 with the purchase of the Mule Deer Research Wildlife Management Area near the campus of Utah State University. This key area became the focus for applied research pertaining to numerous aspects of mule deer management in Utah and the West. The land was initially acquired because "it formed a natural congregating place for mule deer and [it] was purchased to provide range for deer and minimize damage to private property" (Smith 1948). Areas of investigation included deer-livestock relationships; dietary and nutritional habits; behavior; alfalfa, cereal grain, and orchard depredation;

54

and changes in winter range vegetation. Big game species studied on this project were usually both tame and wild and included mule deer, elk, pronghorn, and bison. Domestic animals studied included cattle, sheep, goats, and horses.

Although some research and investigations on winter ranges had already been implemented, such as the Doman and Rasmussen manuscript on deer feeding and nutrition in 1944, the key year for the beginning of intensive deer management in Utah was 1946. The big game–livestock relationship project, which included the Mule Deer Research Wildlife Management Area, was established that year in cooperation with the Range Science Department at the Utah State Agriculture College, later Utah State University. The original Research Committee on mule deer in Utah was also organized in 1946.

This Research Committee, composed of D. M. Gaufin, O. Julander, W. L. Robinette, J. G. Smith, and A. D. Smith, published the benchmark paper in 1950 entitled, "A review of Utah's big game, livestock and range relationship problems." This key manuscript reviewed the range problems and defined the mule deer research needs. The committee members spent most of their careers researching those defined problems, exploring management options, preparing data and maps defining summer and winter mule deer ranges, and refining and defining the concept of herd unit management.

By their definition, a herd unit is "an area comprising both summer and winter ranges, and enclosing a distinct deer herd on a year-round basis." This definition remains as a corner post for big game management. This landmark publication established the direction of research and management on mule deer in Utah until about 1973, when housing and business developments, highways cutting corridors, increased numbers of people, and especially politics began to alter and dictate new research directions and management decisions.

However, from the Research Committee's recommendations, annual systematic data collection by mule deer herd unit began in 1951 and was established statewide by 1956. Also the first maps of summer and winter ranges for mule deer were prepared. These maps have been updated and redone several times as new technologies have become available. The more recently prepared maps, since about 2002, show considerable detail of winter ranges for each deer unit. Defining of winter range is a continuous activity as landscapes are altered by urban developments, highways, changes in agricultural lands, reservoirs, and other man-made changes.

The massive winter kill of mule deer during late winter 1984 led to management changes re-emphasizing the need to balance deer numbers with available winter range forage. Parallel to this escalated management emphasis, the era of increasing public involvement with deer management began through expanded participation in public meetings and establishment of hunter organizations. Public comments into management eventually led to the establishment of the Regional Advisory Committees.

Since the late 1980s numerous fires have caused massive reductions of deer winter ranges throughout the state. Not only have fires eliminated the current forage base, but with the introductions of numerous exotic weedy species, it has become clear that the reestablishment of native browse species on burned areas proceeds much more slowly than previously predicted and in some cases not at all. Maintenance and re-vegetative management efforts on winter ranges have increased greatly in priority.

Although the majority of mule deer data collected in Utah concern population dynamics, the importance of the winter range and the associated data is evidenced in both the compiled reasons for the decline of mule deer populations, and the data necessary to effectively manage a deer herd. I have identified six prioritized factors that have been recognized as contributing to the decline of mule deer since 1970. These six factors include: (1) decreased carrying capacity on winter ranges, (2) increased human populations, (3) changes in livestock grazing on winter ranges, (4) increased effects of predators, (5) increased competition with elk, and (6) changing public values. Of these six factors, three (1, 3, and 5) directly concern winter range. These factors are discussed in chapter 15.

In addition to the six factors considered as contributing to the decline of mule deer, I have identified seven sets of data that are generally considered essential to be collected on each unit. These non-prioritized sets of data include: (1) buck and antlerless harvest, (2) age determination of harvested buck and antlerless deer, (3) reproduction rates obtained from fawn-to-doe ratios and buck-to-doe sex ratios in the post-season classification, (4) recruitment ratios obtained from fawn-to-adult ratios in the spring classification, (5) annual browse utilization and winter range assessment, including deer density and mortality estimates, (6) winter range condition and trend assessment evaluated about every 5 years on each unit, and (7) periodic randomized hunter or citizen opinion surveys. Of these seven

Photo by Becky Blankenship

A buck deer surveys its winter range. Winter range is the critical
habitat on most of Utah's deer units.

sets of data, essential to understanding the dynamics and management of any deer herd, two (5 and 6) are directly concerned with habitat changes on winter ranges. These factors are discussed in chapter 17.

Habitat Types

In terms of potential deer herd population size, of Utah's original 53 deer units 36 were considered to be limited by the extent of winter range, 9 were limited by summer range, and 8 were considered to be limited by both summer and winter range equally (Utah DWR 1976). Of the current 30 deer management units, about 20 are considered limited by winter range, 5 by summer range, and 5 by both summer and winter range equally.

Twenty range types are usually identified in Utah, from salt-desert shrub to alpine tundra (Johnson 1989). Each range type is the result of precipitation regimes, elevation, soils and topography. Although deer are found on all range types occasionally and seasonally during the year, I consider four types—big sagebrush, pinyon-juniper, mountain browse, and aspen—as the most important and essential to maintaining deer herds with sustainable hunter-harvest in Utah.

The two most important range types for wintering mule deer are big sagebrush and pinyon-juniper. These types are usually found in the foothills above Utah's valley floors and extend up to about 8,000 feet in elevation. The big sagebrush type is usually found in elevations below the pinyon-juniper type, and on many winter ranges, the big sagebrush type gradually interfaces into the pinyon-juniper type with increasing elevation.

The mountain browse type, which includes Gambel oak habitat, is only exceeded by the aspen and riparian types in vegetative productivity. This habitat is very important to mule deer in both fall and spring as transition range between summer and winter range types. Many fawns are born in the mountain browse zone. Deer often remain in this type late into the fall until forced to lower elevations by deepening snow. On units where summer range is the limiting factor, that is, on ranges where the extent and productivity of the winter range is greater than that of the summer range, the mountain browse type becomes the primary summer range. On areas where traditional winter ranges have been altered by fire or encroached by development, the mountain browse type again becomes the primary winter range.

The aspen type is a widespread and highly productive Utah range type. It is the most important summer range type for mule deer. The high variety of forbs, grasses, and browse provide the summer nutrition needed to survive harsh winters. However, the aspen type is susceptible to overuse by both big game, according to Chase (1987), and livestock (Bartos and Harness 1990). Overused stands of aspen are composed primarily of old-aged, often dying canopies with little or no aspen reproduction. The young aspen shoots are very palatable and are often browsed to the ground level, preventing aspen regeneration. Conversely, properly managed stands of aspen contain all sizes and ages of trees. Fortunately, over-aged aspen stands, which are clear-cut for firewood or bulldozed for regeneration, will generally vigorously sprout and revegetate the area quickly if ungrazed or grazed very lightly for three to five years. Similarly, aspen areas burned by fire regenerate quickly.

Stands of conifer trees and mountain grasslands are used lightly by scattered deer, except along riparian corridors where use is generally heavy. Riparian habitats are always important for mule deer, in addition to most species of wildlife, but acreage of these habitats is very limited in Utah. Where aspen and/or mountain browse types are limiting, conifer, mountain grasslands and riparian habitats are critical as summer ranges.

Healthy areas of the four most significant habitat types for mule deer must be maintained throughout the state in large acreage. These habitat types are essential for healthy populations and successful harvests of mule deer in Utah.

Migration

Deer population movements between summer and winter ranges occur on most units during spring and fall. However, in some areas or subunits, resident deer herds remain in the same locations year around.

Resident herds occur along riparian zones in valley bottoms and in agricultural areas. Since the winter of 1983–1984 resident herds have become established in some urban areas. Examples are along the Logan River in Cache Valley, crop lands between Brigham City and Tremonton, several locations along the Wasatch Front, and in the foothills along the Sevier River. These deer often cause problems with home owners' gardens and farmers' produce. Other resident herds are found on some low-elevation mountain ranges. For example, the Fish Springs Mountains in western Utah contain a small resident population.

Deer migration routes may be divided into two types. The more common type of migration is the movement to winter ranges at the base of the same mountains deer inhabit during the summer. This type of migration is referred to as elevation migration. Many deer units with high mountain summer ranges, such as the Uinta, Wasatch, Fishlake, and Dixie National Forests have primarily elevation migration routes for the majority of the summering deer.

A minority of summering deer may migrate considerable distances in the second type of migration. This secondary type of migration is usually referred to as lateral migration. Unfortunately the number of deer, moving back and forth from summer and winter ranges through lateral migration has been greatly reduced and restricted due to the construction of U.S. freeways and major highways. Lateral migration is generally longer in linear distance, but often with only minor changes in elevation. Sometimes deer will travel over 100 miles in order to arrive at their traditional winter range. In these cases, deer often pass through several adequate winter ranges, sometimes better than the destination winter range. This form of migration is especially common for the Basin and Range topography of western Utah and Nevada (Gruell and Papaz 1963).

For examples, deer from the summer ranges on the Sheeprock Mountains in west central Utah generally move west and as far as the Utah-Nevada border to reach their winter range, a linear distance of about 100 miles. Furthermore, many deer wintering at the base of Blue Mountain in northeastern Utah and on the Crawford Mountains in Rich County, Utah spend their summers in Colorado and Wyoming, respectively.

Behaviorally, deer generally return to the same winter and summer ranges they experienced while fawns. However, occasionally in the initial expansion, male yearlings will wander to new areas, especially during periods of dense deer populations leading to geographic population expansion. These wandering deer generally inhabit less preferred and more marginal habitats. Conversely, as populations decline, rangeland acreage used by mule deer slowly shrinks and deer begin to occupy only the preferred habitats, and the more marginal habitats slowly become uninhabited by deer.

Home Ranges

Home ranges are usually determined by marking specific individuals with telemetry radios, visual collars and ear streamers, or audible bells, and relocating each animal several times during the season of interest. A polygon connecting the outermost mapped locations roughly describes home range.

Size of home range varies considerably by habitat quality. In areas of lush forage resources, home ranges are small compared to the large home ranges on sparsely vegetated desert lands.

For examples, in Arizona, on a semi-desert grass shrub habitat, a mean home range of 751 ha (2.9 square miles) was calculated for five mule deer. The researchers indicated their findings were about average for dry southwest locations (Rogers et al. 1978). In a Colorado mixed mountain browse, grassland, and conifer plant community, researchers determined a mean home range of 217 ha (0.8 square miles) for 22 does (Kufeld et al. 1988). On a high quality summer range, also in Colorado, 11 fawns occupied a mean home range of 130 ha (0.5 square miles) (Geduldig 1981). In Utah, on a typical deer range with mixed vegetation types, researchers determined an area of about 148 ha (0.6 square miles) contained about 92 % of deer movements, and that bucks had a slightly larger home range than does (Robinette 1966).

The influence of deer movement on hunting success is important to management because movements can increase or decrease desired harvests. Deer movements of long or short distances to areas closed to hunting, such as national parks or posted private lands, often result in decreased harvest. In addition, early migration before the fall hunts has resulted in the learning of 'city safety zones' for some wily big bucks and does. Intelligent mule deer have adapted during September and October to the pseudo safety within the city limits of numerous cities including Logan, Ogden, Spanish Fork, Ephraim, and many others. Conversely, movement in open terrain or movement between habitats of heavy cover may result in an increase in harvest.

Surprisingly, hunting generally appears to have little effect on home range size even during deer hunting seasons and hunting normally does not cause deer to initiate long distance movements (Kufeld et al. 1988). Nonetheless, within the established home ranges during hunting seasons, deer tend to move into areas of thicker cover and hence increased protection. Areas of open terrain lacking conifer or other thick cover will usually contain lower deer densities during hunting seasons than habitats with conifer cover or other thick vegetation.

The exceptions to movements sometimes occur in areas where dense cover is limiting or hunter density is extremely high. In these cases deer may quickly move considerable distances to secure locations. As an example on the Cache management unit in areas of high hunter density, radio-collared deer were observed to move overnight from summer range to safe urban habitats in Cache Valley, following the first day of the regular season deer hunt. Interestingly, many of these deer returned to the summer ranges following the end of the hunt.

Chapter 6

Mule Deer Relationships with Livestock, Elk, and White-tailed Deer

The dense population of mule deer in Utah built up chiefly on over-grazed livestock range.

Odell Julander

Grazing Ecology

The composition of a plant community is the total number of individual plants by species within the community. Consequently, plant communities or wildlife habitats are defined by the species present and their abundance or density. Plant community composition is directly affected and altered by grazing animals. All grazing animals both domestic and wild affect changes in the plant composition within their habitats.

All grazing animals prefer some plant species and ignore others. Ungrazed plants receive a competitive growth advantage and gradually increase in vigor and abundance. Because of this, the shift in plant composition associated with grazing is always away from the forage preferences of the grazing animal. Grazing by a single species of animal always results in detrimental plant composition changes of plants preferred by that grazer. Consequently, grazing by two or more grazers with different forage preferences can result in better maintenance of forages preferred by the grazer of primary importance.

The potential of any plant community to produce vegetation remains static unless climate changes or erosion decreases soil depth or productivity. Soils, as influenced by climate and weather, are the basic resources

63

Photo by Dan Miller

Proper sheep grazing can enhance habitat for deer. The rancher and
the wildlife manager should, indeed, be friends.

which define and limit existing plant and animal communities. Even
though plant and animal communities may be abruptly disturbed or
destroyed by fire, agricultural plowing, crop growing, or abusive overgrazing, these communities usually recover in relatively short periods of
five to 100 years, compared to the thousands of years needed to rebuild
lost soil. Therefore, in order to maintain healthy, vegetated lands for
continual productive wildlife communities, it is imperative to maintain
undamaged, fertile soils.

Both the intensity and season of grazing strongly influence the rate of
plant community change. High intensity, year around grazing will cause
rapid shifts in plant composition compared to light use, especially during plant dormancy. Overgrazing for several consecutive years greatly
decreases ground cover and increases the percentage of bare ground susceptible to erosion as well as the distance between surviving plants. Areas
of bare ground, with reduced competition from established perennial
plants, are prime sites for invasion of both native plant species not preferred by the grazer and non-native introduced, especially weedy, species.

Introduced weedy species such as storksbill, bur buttercup, Dyers woad, thistle, gumweed, foxtail, rattlesnake brome and many others are often strong competitors and usually poor, sometimes poisonous substitutes for the native species (Holmgren 1958). Plant communities dominated by introduced species, especially when those species are unpalatable to grazers, are usually slow to decrease and often continue to increase, even with no grazing. In these plant communities, soil disturbance through chaining or plowing followed by reseeding is often needed to restore useful plant community productivity.

Mule Deer–Livestock Relationships on Winter Ranges

Domestic livestock such as cattle, sheep, horses and goats can enhance or degrade habitat for mule deer. Overuse grazing by livestock on mixed plant communities almost always results in decreased habitat values for all grazers, whereas light to moderate use can result in benefits to deer. Heavy grazing by mule deer can also have the negative effects of decreasing total habitat values or shifting the plant community composition toward undesirable species. Excessive use by one or more grazers is rarely beneficial. Similarly, light use by a single grazer, when only the preferred plant species are grazed, will usually cause negative results in the reduction of those preferred species in the plant community.

At least occasionally, light grazing by livestock of understory grasses and forbs in spring and early summer is necessary to maintain productive winter ranges for deer. Livestock grazing should begin at about the same time period when deer and elk move to higher elevation foraging sites, and thus little competition occurs between big game and livestock. Deer use of browse forage in winter with the absence of spring and summer livestock grazing of forbs and grasses provides a growth advantage to the grasses and causes plant communities to shift toward grasslands. Even complete protection of winter ranges from all livestock and wildlife grazing leads to a shift, although slower, toward grassland climax communities.

On areas protected from livestock grazing, the influence of deer browsing on plant community changes is also observable. For example, in one of the earliest grazing research experiments, range professor Art Smith at Utah State University compared adjacent ranges at the lower elevation of the mountain brush zone used by mule deer during winter in northern Utah (Smith 1949). One range was heavily grazed by livestock in spring and summer, while the second had been protected from livestock during the previous 11 years. Perennial forbs and grasses were more abundant on the range protected from livestock, but shrubs, primarily big sagebrush, were much less abundant due to heavy deer browsing. The trend of decreasing shrubs on the range protected from livestock grazing continued through 1982 (Austin and Urness 1998), and as observed in 2000 the range protected from livestock grazing was devoid of all shrubs. In about 60 years a highly productive deer winter range was reduced to one of very limited value for big game simply because of the lack of livestock grazing. Research in Colorado and other states reported similar results (Riodan 1970; Thomas 1970; McKean and Bartmann 1971).

The elimination or major reduction of livestock grazing on ranges where the level of prior use was excessive or abusive, initially results in the recovery and increase of all plant classes—grasses, forbs, shrubs, and trees. For example, by 1905, two comparable, adjacent watersheds dominated by Gambel oak habitat, Red Butte and Emigration Canyons, east of Salt Lake City, Utah, had been heavily overgrazed by livestock for about 30 years. Between 1905 and 1935 Red Butte was protected from all livestock grazing while Emigration received continued heavy use. By 1935 plant canopy cover in Red Butte had recovered to the condition during the pre-settlement period, and was about double that found in Emigration Canyon with all plant classes in greater abundance (Cottam and Evans 1945). Grazing by livestock was gradually reduced and eliminated in Emigration Canyon in 1957. By 1983 the production of all plant classes in Emigration Canyon had increased and was comparable to Red Butte Canyon (Austin et al. 1986). These studies indicate 30–50 years are required for vegetation within the Gambel oak habitat to recover from previous long-term excessive grazing.

Similarly, research on ranges in the Great Basin desert by Rogers (1982) indicated that where previously heavy livestock grazing was eliminated, the succession of plant communities, accelerated by deer use in winter, would alter communities to more grasses and forbs and fewer desirable shrubs. Other studies reported similar results except that palatable shrubs sometimes showed an initial increase in productivity followed by a long-term decrease (Costello and Turner 1941, Robertson 1971).

Fortunately livestock grazing can also be used to improve deer winter range (Urness 1990). For deer to survive extended periods of deep snow, browse plants, especially big sagebrush and Utah juniper, must be available on winter ranges (Austin and Urness 1983). However, without at least some intermittent livestock grazing of grasses in spring and summer, grasses will gradually out-compete and replace shrubs. Under complete grazing protection from livestock and wildlife, big sagebrush may be completely replaced in less than 50 years (Costello and Turner 1941). Generally, properly managed livestock grazing can have a positive effect on deer winter ranges first by increasing productivity of browse forage species critical to deer, second by increasing the nutritional quality of the forage, and third by changing the plant species community composition in favor of deer. Livestock grazing was demonstrated to improve winter ranges for mule deer in these research examples:

(1) Deer diets on snow-covered Utah winter ranges were generally determined to improve on Gambel oak ranges when domestic goats grazed the range during the previous summer. However, grazing by goats made no difference on deer diets under snow-free conditions (Riggs et al. 1990).

(2) Summer sheep grazing in Oregon resulted in improved fall forage quality and increased forage quantity in spring on upper-elevation deer winter ranges (Rhodes and Sharrow 1990).

(3) At the Hardware Ranch in northern Utah, summer grazing by horses increased production of antelope bitterbrush for winter use by deer and elk (Reiner and Urness 1982).

(4) Several studies, also conducted at the Hardware Ranch, showed cattle and sheep grazing in spring increased productivity of antelope bitterbrush, big sagebrush and other browse species by applying grazing pressure to the competing herbaceous vegetation (Smith and Doell 1968; Jensen et al. 1972; Smith et al. 1979). These studies also determined that the timing of cattle and sheep grazing was critical. Grazing needed to be terminated before about July 1 when the herbaceous vegetation lost its lushness and livestock diets began to shift toward bitterbrush and the other browse species palatable during summer.

The combined recommendations from decades of research by numerous researchers, such as Anderson and Scherzinger (1975), should be heeded by land managers having the goal of optimizing big game habitat values on winter ranges. These recommendations for managing livestock grazing for mule deer on winter ranges in the Great Basin are summarized and adapted from Austin's (2000) synthesis:

(1) *Graze livestock between May 1 and June 30.* Livestock grazing should be conducted during spring only. During years with early green-up, grazing may begin as early as April 1, and grazing may be extended into early July during years of high precipitation between the May 1 and June 30 period. Grazing must be completed when livestock begin to switch diets from grasses and forbs to shrub species.

(2) *Alternate between classes of livestock.* Sheep and goats consume higher proportions of forbs, while cattle and horses consume higher proportions of grasses. By shifting classes of livestock between years or by simultaneously grazing two or more classes of livestock, a better balance of grasses, forbs and shrubs can be maintained.

(3) *Use a rest-rotation grazing system, yearly grazing about 2/3 of the available rangeland.* Because regrowth in fall and new growth of grasses in spring are important components to deer diet and nutrition, each year part of the winter range should be rested from spring/summer livestock grazing. Consistent yearly, heavy grazing of perennial grasses reduces productivity and creates space for invasion of weedy species. The exception to this recommendation occurs on ranges largely dominated by annual grasses and weedy forbs, and/or ranges highly susceptible to fire, where livestock should annually graze the entire winter range.

(4) *Graze livestock at an intensity to remove 50 percent of the understory grasses and forbs.* A grazing removal of about 50 percent will maintain a mixed community of grasses, forbs and shrubs and greatly reduce fire risks. Grazing at more than 70 percent removal will increase the proportion of shrubs, while grazing at less than 30 percent will slowly shift many winter range plant communities toward more grasses and forbs. Forb and grass utilization is controlled by restricting livestock numbers.

(5) *Balance deer browsing in winter and livestock grazing in spring.* Excessive utilization of browse by deer in winter over several years will gradually reduce shrub vigor and result in decreasing shrub density, regardless of the intensity of livestock grazing. Effects of drought or wet cycles confound the issue. However, to maintain browse vigor, winter utilization by mule deer should be restricted to 50 percent use of big sagebrush and other non-deciduous shrub species, and 65 percent use of antelope bitter-brush and other deciduous species. Browse utilization is controlled by restricting deer numbers.

(6) *Monitor utilization using permanent plots.* Vegetal utilization and plant community composition should be evaluated using permanent plots on critical or key areas on each deer unit. Spring utilization of grass and forb forages by livestock and overwinter utilization of browse forages by mule deer should be determined yearly. Trends in community composition must be evaluated by detailed sampling at five -year intervals.

Deer–Livestock Relationships on Summer Ranges

Proper management of both big game and livestock numbers on summer ranges results in few conflicts. However, excessive numbers of big game or livestock not only leads to forage conflicts, but often range deterioration and reduced carrying capacities (Julander 1955). The general principals of grazing on summer ranges are:

(1) Proper use of perennial grass and forb species, palatable to cattle or sheep, limits maximum livestock stocking.

(2) Proper use of forb and browse species, palatable to deer, limits maximum deer stocking.

(3) Proper use of grass, forb and browse species, palatable to both livestock and deer, limits maximum combined livestock-deer stocking.

Because summer diets of mule deer and livestock, particularly cattle, overlap by less than 10 percent (Mackie 1981), competition between deer and livestock is usually minor (Skovlin et al 1976). High mobility of deer increases potential forage selectivity, and few conflicts between deer and livestock occur in properly managed areas (Lesperance et al.

1970). However, to maximize deer productivity, livestock grazing should be restricted on important fawning summer ranges during parturition, from about June 1 through July 15 (Pac et al. 1991).

For examples, in British Columbia on a northern deer range in the Douglas fir habitat type, researchers reported that deer diets between areas grazed and not grazed by cattle were generally not different (Willms et al. 1980). However, researchers on a southern deer range in Texas showed a small shift in deer diets toward more browse and grass and fewer forbs on cattle-grazed ranges (McMahan 1964). Deer use of aspen and riparian areas in Utah usually has been shown to decrease under increased cattle grazing (Loft et al. 1991). These researchers reported that for adult mule deer the size of summer home range either stayed about the same or slightly increased in size in cattle-grazed areas.

I intensively studied the effects of cattle grazing on mule deer summer diets and area selection on the Sheeprock Mountains in Utah (Austin and Urness 1986). By monitoring deer in areas moderately grazed or not grazed by cattle, research determined few changes in the dietary, nutritional or habitat preferences of the mule deer.

The conclusions derived from the Sheeprock Mountains study are applicable to most summer ranges in Utah. Specifically, the grazing effects of cattle, or livestock in general, on mule deer diets, nutrition and habitat selection are minor when the intensity of livestock grazing is controlled and moderate, and livestock primarily graze only understory vegetation. Negative effects on mule deer would only be expected when the intensity of livestock grazing increases to the point of heavily over-utilizing the understory grasses and forbs with noticeable use of the canopy vegetation.

Deer–Elk Relationships

Elk compete more directly with mule deer than any other wildlife species, especially on winter ranges. Elk and deer have somewhat similar dietary and habitat preferences. However, because elk are about three and one-half times larger and heavier than deer, elk have a direct competitive advantage. That advantage is increased because elk can use a greater variety of habitats, and their diets are much broader and more flexible (Mackie 1981). One major dietary advantage for elk is that they can successfully graze dry grasses where mule deer cannot.

For examples, deer and elk selected similar habitat types and forage classes on open forest, dense forest, and grassland in Oregon (Edgerton and Smith 1971). In Colorado, year-long diet overlap between deer and elk ranged from 3 to 48 percent (Hansen and Reid 1975). In Montana, researchers determined that although elk required higher security cover, both deer and elk preferred similar clear-cuts on forested summer ranges (Lyon and Jensen 1980). In Utah's Uinta Mountains, forage preferences and habitat selection were similar between deer and elk, except that elk strongly preferred wet meadows and deer preferred clear-cut forests (Collins et al. 1978, Deschamp et al. 1979). In the Wasatch Mountains of Utah, because elk were determined to be less selective for forage and could utilize lower quality forages, they were considered better adapted to the available habitats (Collins and Urness 1983).

Even though most competitive factors favor elk, which have the potential for directly reducing deer population, studies indicating direct population trade-offs—that is, elk replacing deer—are limited (Keegan and Wakeling 2003). An early report suggested that because elk reduced available browse on winter ranges in Oregon, deer mortality was greatly increased during a severe winter (Cliff 1939). At Utah's Hardware Ranch the low number of deer observed was presumed to be caused by the dominance of elk (Bayoumi and Smith 1976). Also, browse on Cache Valley's big game winter ranges, which includes Hardware Ranch, has been greatly reduced with heavy elk use. Nonetheless, comparisons on the Cache unit between the buck deer and bull elk harvest between 1968 and 1989 showed no inverse relationship, suggesting other factors, such as climate, were more important in controlling deer population numbers than deer-elk competition.

Where both deer and elk numbers are moderate and below carrying capacities of the range, it is unlikely that elk competition would significantly affect deer numbers or harvest. However, it is most certainly true that in areas where populations of both deer and elk are high, elk will replace mule deer, especially where total use exceeds the carrying capacity of the winter range. For examples, I observed elk displacing deer on preferred winter ranges in the Blacksmith Fork drainage in the early 1980s and in the lower south-facing slopes in Logan Canyon in the mid 1990s. Elk are a dominant and direct competitor, can eliminate critical winter forage needed by deer, and may cause a decrease in deer use of the most desirable winter habitats. Under some conditions where deer and elk

Photo by Mitch Mascaro/The Herald Journal

The first verified white-tailed deer in Utah leaps a fence in North Logan. White-tailed deer have continued to expand their range.

occupy the same winter range, elk competition could possibly lead to a decrease in deer numbers. These competitive effects would usually be slow and subtle, and may take several years for the results to become evident.

Mule Deer–White-tailed Deer Relationships

White-tailed deer have resided in Utah since 1996 (McClure 1997). The geographic range of the white-tailed deer overlaps that of the mule deer in all western states. The white-tailed deer has expanded its range from coast to coast and is found in all continental states. Where both species are found, competition for resources occurs because forage preferences for the two species are similar. However, habitat preferences and behavior are significantly different, and consequently interspecies competition is low.

White-tailed deer are more likely found in lower elevations in riparian habitats along rivers and streams, within agricultural zones, and in dense moist mountain browse and woodland habitats. Mule deer are more often associated with higher elevations and more open terrain. Conifer and aspen forest, scrub oak, dry sagebrush-grass, desert shrub and logged-over forests are common preferences for mule deer. White-tailed deer are occasionally found in more open terrain and mule deer migrate to riparian and agricultural areas when high quality, upper elevation ranges are limited by snow and cold, or summer drought conditions.

According to Hall (1984), white-tailed deer have survival advantages over mule deer and present three distinct problems for maintaining mule deer populations: increased adaptability, increased resistance to diseases and parasites, and one-way hybridization.

Increased Adaptability

White-tailed deer have been extending their range and increasing populations since at least 1985, whereas the range and populations of the mule deer have been shrinking (Geist 1990). Although white-tailed deer do not displace mule deer through manifested aggression, the higher adaptability of the white-tailed deer to man-made changes upon the environment is the leading reason for the success of the white-tail and the decline of the mule deer. Unquestionably white-tailed deer are replacing mule deer throughout many areas of the West. On some ranges, in Montana and Colorado, and possibly Idaho, where 50 years ago only mule deer were found, white-tailed deer now outnumber mule deer.

Examples of differences in adaptability between white-tailed and mule deer abound: white-tailed deer are more nocturnal than mule deer making them less susceptible to hunting; white-tailed deer generally reside in habitats having denser vegetation, which also makes them less susceptible to hunting; white-tailed deer have a broader range of habitats, including most mule deer habitats, in which they can successfully maintain populations; white-tailed deer can more successfully raise fawns in riparian habitats adjacent to agricultural lands; in non-mountainous areas whitetails are more successful at avoiding predators due to their increased running speed; white-tailed deer fawns are often born a week or more earlier than mule deer fawns; white-tailed deer have higher reproductive rates; and white-tailed yearling does often bear fawns, whereas that is extremely rare in mule deer yearlings.

Increased Resistance to Diseases and Parasites

The white-tailed deer has co-evolved for at least four million years with a number of parasites and diseases whereas the other deer species of North America are relative newcomers (Davidson 1981). White-tailed deer are resistant and tolerant of many diseases and parasites which can cause illness and mortality in mule deer. The deadliest and most common parasite is the meningeal or brain worm *Paraelaphostrongylus tenius*. The adult stage of this roundworm lives in the cranial venous sinuses and causes neurologic disease of which the white-tailed is mostly tolerant. Partially due the intermediate larval stage snail host, this worm may have been one of the major causes for the ecological separation of the two deer species. However, this parasite is known to be lethal for caribou, elk, and probably moose, and is apparently often debilitating and possibly lethal when transmitted to mule deer. Additional parasites, carried by white-tailed deer and problematic for other cervids, include ticks, *Dermacentor albipictus*, and the giant liver fluke *Fascioloides magna*. Although studies on diseases are scant, it appears likely the white-tailed deer is better adapted in most cases than the mule deer.

One-way Hybridization

Where white-tailed and mule deer ranges are sympatric, one-way hybridization will invariably lead to reduced mule deer reproduction. Hybridization with white-tailed deer may be the most significant factor in the long-term decline and possible long-term extirpation or even extinction of mule deer (Geist 1990).

Breeding between mule deer bucks and white-tailed does rarely occurs, because the breeding behavior of mule deer bucks and white-tailed does is mostly incompatible. White-tailed does often run when approached by a buck, and mule deer bucks are adapted to mule deer does that usually allow a buck to approach and either make little movement or sometimes trot in small circles. Furthermore, if the mule deer buck pursues a running white-tailed doe, in many habitats the buck has little chance of keeping up. The fawns resulting from this hybridization are usually poorly adapted, weak individuals, which usually die within a few months of birth.

Conversely, breeding between white-tailed bucks and mule deer does is much more common. The resulting hybrid fawn from this union is usually healthy with high survival. However, because of the incompatible combination of white-tailed and mule deer predator avoidance strategies, hybrids are highly susceptible to predation and rarely survive for more than a year. Because of the loss from hybrid fawns, white-tailed bucks breeding mule deer does can result in a direct and significant loss of reproduction in mule deer populations.

Mule Deer–Other Wild Ungulate Relationships

Other wild ungulates in Utah, including moose, bighorn sheep, pronghorn, mountain goat, and bison, often use rangelands within the home ranges of mule deer. However, little competition for resources occurs. Generally preferred habitats are different between species as are diet preferences. Only during periods of severe forage shortages or during periods of extreme winter weather would competition potentially become significant.

Chapter 7

The Influence of Predators on Mule Deer Populations

Predators–Mule Deer Interactions

The common native predators of mule deer currently found in Utah and placed in the order of their effectiveness in affecting or controlling mule deer populations are the coyote, cougar, bobcat, black bear, gray fox, and some raptors. On rare occasions a badger may kill a fawn within a few days of parturition. Wolverine and lynx are extremely rare if even extant in Utah. Domestic and feral dogs and possibly the red fox are introduced species but effective predators, whereas the grizzly bear and the gray wolf have been extirpated from Utah. However, as a result of re-introductions in the Greater Yellowstone Ecosystem and population expansion southward into Wyoming and southern Idaho, the gray wolf, after an absence of many decades, is slowly returning to Utah in the first decade of the twenty-first century.

The gray wolf is atop the hierarchy of wildlife predators as depicted in my simple graphic, Figure 7-1. The smaller predators include many more than are listed on the bottom line of the graphic. This graphic is presented only to illustrate some of the general order of predator dominance; it is not intended to show the entire scope of predator interrelationships or competitions, most of which are, at best, poorly understood. For examples, at least occasionally otters probably affect mink, coyotes probably affect bobcats, and interactions among the smaller predators are numerous. Often, but not always, an upper-hierarchy predator will exert dominance over several other predators of lower rank, such as the coyote affecting not only red fox but skunk and weasel. In addition, sometimes

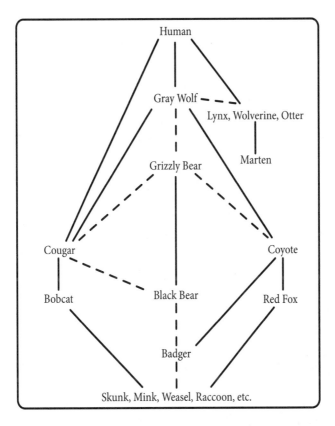

Figure 7-1

dominance may be temporarily reversed, as for example a black bear killing cougar kittens. Unquestionably, predator interactions are variable and complicated. Humans, of course, can affect the entire spectrum of predators. Nonetheless, some relationships of hierarchy between predators are strong and well-defined (represented in the graphic by solid lines). A clear example is the wolf dominating and at least sometimes controlling populations of the coyote, and the coyote having the same potential effect on red fox. A second example is the fluctuations of bobcat populations as influenced by the density of cougars. However, most relationships are poorly understood or weak (dashed or no lines). Examples include grizzly bear and cougar, badger and raccoon, or wolverine and skunk.

Predators can affect mule deer population dynamics and therefore influence hunter harvest. The three dynamic predator-prey interaction factors usually considered as affecting deer populations are mule deer populations, predator populations, and alternate prey populations, including small mammals, birds, other wild ungulates and livestock. The effects of predators on mule deer population dynamics, or causing changes in deer population numbers, are minor when deer numbers are high and near carrying capacity, predator numbers are low, and populations of alternate prey species, such as elk, grouse, squirrels, and mice, are also high. Clearly and almost independent from other factors, the number of mule deer killed by predators sharply declines as populations of alternate prey species, especially rabbits and hares, increases.

Whenever deer numbers are high, even though predators may be harvesting numerous deer, the losses are generally unrecognizable because of the high density of deer. Also, the effects of predators are especially difficult to detect during periods of increasing deer numbers. When deer numbers have become excessive and above the carrying capacity of the winter range, the effects of predators are usually positive and beneficial due to the effects of reducing deer numbers closer to the carrying capacity of the winter range.

Conversely, the effects of predators on mule deer populations can be major when deer numbers are low and considerably below carrying capacity, predator numbers are high, and populations of alternate prey species are low. Under these conditions, predator-caused mortality, especially when combined with other mortality factors, often limits deer population growth and can lead to further declines in the deer population.

In addition to the three predator-prey interaction factors referred to above, the fourth predator-prey interaction factor is weather. Weather conditions favorable to mule deer reproduction and survival greatly lessen the effects of predators, whereas weather conditions unfavorable to mule deer reproduction and survival can greatly increase the effectiveness of predation. Weather factors favoring mule deer and lowering predation include warm, wet spring conditions, late summer–early fall precipitation, and mild winters without extremes in weather conditions. Weather factors favoring predators and increasing predation include delayed spring green-up, summer drought, fall drought, harsh winters, and deep and continuous winter snow cover.

Even though predators often kill smaller, older, and weaker deer, they also kill mature and healthy does and bucks. Reduction in predator numbers can directly lead to increased hunter harvest when predator-killed mule deer would have survived to the next hunting season. Nonetheless, it is important to note that when deer populations are managed at numerical levels above maximum sustained yield or carrying capacity on the summer and/or winter range, the effects of predators on hunter harvest are negligible or even beneficial.

The effectiveness of a predator control program is often significantly influenced by the control of all major predators, especially cougar and coyotes. If, for example, only one of these two major predators is controlled and the other receives little or no control, the potential positive results of the control efforts are often much reduced compared to the potential beneficial effects if both were controlled. Because predator populations respond to prey base availability, the predator not being controlled will take advantage of the increased availability of prey and the decreased competition with the other predator. Indeed, the potential positive effects for deer population dynamics from cougar control may be completely negated by the potential increase in the coyote population. The old adage holds true: "If a cougar doesn't kill it, a coyote will."

A question often asked in wildlife management is whether predator control is economically justified. Quantifying the factors associated with this question is very difficult. However, generally because of high costs of professional private or government trappers, predator control solely to enhance mule deer populations is not economical. Another concern is the difference in predator control effectiveness between eliminating individual predators actually affecting the deer population as opposed to randomly removing predators, many of which may not be preying upon mule deer. Control by recreational hunters and trappers, nonetheless, often yields benefits to herd management. Notwithstanding, in conjunction with the reduction in livestock losses, professional predator control is sometimes cooperatively and economically justified, but only when deer populations are below carrying capacity, and where the increase in deer numbers can be harvested by hunters. Although increasing and maintaining deer numbers through predator control often has additional social and aesthetic values, generally the control efforts and associated costs will still exceed total gains.

One management key in deciding whether to initiate a predator control program is to critically evaluate the deer population with respect to carrying capacity. I suggest the following applied rule. If the deer herd is within 75 to 100 percent of carrying capacity or above carrying capacity, do not initiate predator control. If the deer population

Photo by Larry McCormick

Mule deer bucks must negotiate fences in crossing the fields within
their range. Many are annually killed when the back legs become
entangled in the top two wires.

is between 50 and 75 percent of carrying capacity, the decision must
be based on the recent deer population trend, range trend, probability of the predator control being effective in improving deer population dynamics, available personnel, costs, and funding availability.
Generally as the population declines from 75 to 50 percent of carrying capacity, the likelihood of effective control increases and the factors favoring initiation of the program increase. If the deer population
is less than 50 percent of carrying capacity, predator control programs should almost always be initiated, provided funding and other
resources for success are available.

When a predator control program is initiated and funds are limited, usually the most effective predator control can be accomplished
from about February through mid June on known fawning locations.
Under snow cover conditions, aerial gunning is generally more cost
efficient, and under non-snow cover conditions, trapping is usually
more cost efficient.

Harvest Interactions with Predator Control

From the viewpoint of hunting harvest, generally control of predators is ineffective in increasing deer herd numbers or hunter harvest when deer populations are slightly below to slightly above rangeland carrying capacity. Conversely, predator control is often effective in decreasing deer mortality during periods in which deer populations are below carrying capacity, and positively contributes to increased deer numbers and harvest. Certainly, the further the deer population is below carrying capacity, the more potentially effective are predator control efforts in positively contributing to hunter harvest.

Under low deer populations, should hunter numbers be reduced and predator control initiated simultaneously? Under buck-only hunting and maintaining an adequate number of bucks after the hunts, hunters have limited effects on deer populations because the reproductive (doe) segment of the herd is unaffected. The effects of hunting only become significant on deer herd dynamics when the reproductive segment is influenced negatively, such as with illegal kill or possibly harassment during the breeding season. Therefore, the questions of initiating predator control and reducing hunter numbers should be evaluated separately.

Comparing Predator Mortality with Other Mortality Factors

Generally over the course of a year, predators do not account for the majority of mortality in mule deer. Predators may account for mule deer mortality ranging from near zero percent to more than 50 percent. The percentage of the total mortality attributed to predators and all other mortality factors will vary greatly over time and geographic unit. However, predator control is often emphasized in management simply because the effects of predators can be addressed and reduced. Most other mortality factors are much more difficult to address and usually cannot be actively or directly managed. For examples, managers have little input into mortality resulting from car collisions, or disease and parasites, and no influence on fence line mortality or weather. The inputs by managers on other factors such as poaching, unretrieved kills, illegal kills, free-ranging dogs, or human harassments are also limited. Furthermore, the nutrition of the doe is a primary concern in raising fawns, but managers are mostly limited to managing the forage resources on rangelands owned by the Division of Wildlife Resources.

Coyotes

Coyotes are the most important predator of mule deer and probably kill more deer than all other predators combined. In early summer individual coyotes take significant numbers of newly born fawns until the fawns reach about 8 weeks of age, when predation significantly declines. It has been estimated that individual coyotes kill an average of 4 fawns between parturition and October (Robinette et al. 1977). In winter small packs of coyotes, often four to six individuals, regularly kill adults and fawns. There have been multiple studies of coyote predation on mule deer, which are presented here as examples.

In a study in Oregon using radio-collared fawns, coyotes accounted for 55 percent of the summer mortality and 79 percent of the winter mortality. Other predators, disease and other causes accounted for the remaining losses. In this study coyotes killed 15 percent of the total fawn crop in summer and 39 percent in winter, leading to the conclusion that poor fawn survival was caused by predation (Trainer 1975). Similar results were found on Utah's Oak Creek range where intensive coyote control resulted in increased fawn survival rates during summer (Robinette et al. 1977).

In a two-year study in Colorado, 120 white-tailed and mule deer fawns were captured and monitored with radio collars for 30 days. During the first 30 days following parturition 48 percent of the fawns died, and 46 of the 58 mortalities, or 79 percent of early fawn mortality for both species, were attributed to coyotes (Whittaker and Lindzey 1999).

An 11-year study was conducted in the Harmony and Pine Valley Mountains in southwestern Utah using 270 captured and radio-collared fawns. The annual mortality rate was determined at 36 percent and predator mortality rates were 1.7 times as great as non-predator mortality rates. Coyote predation was the largest cause of fawn mortality (Beale 1992).

In a winter study in Utah's Uinta Basin, fawn-to-adult deer ratios were the same on two adjacent areas in early December. However, by April the fawn-to-adult ratio had fallen to 29 fawns to 100 adults on the area without predator control, but had remained at 59 fawns to 100 adults where predator control was intensive. Over the three years of this study

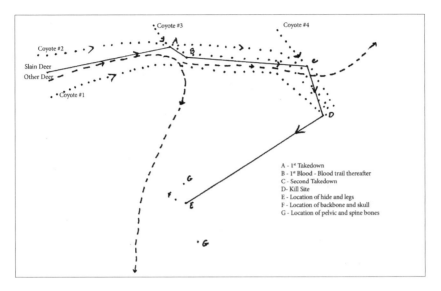

Figure 7-2

on the area where predators were not controlled, predators were effective in removing about half of the fawn crop between November and May (Austin et al. 1977).

> *Note:* To illustrate the cunning of the coyote, the following account was taken from my 1975 morning field notes. See original drawing, Figure 7-2.
>
> I was retracing yesterday's footprints, over the day-old snow on a mule deer winter range on Blue Mountain near Vernal, Utah, and walking toward a weather instrument shelter, when two golden eagles and several magpies took flight from the base of small, juniper-covered hill. I investigated and found a trampling of coyote tracks and the scattered remains of a predator killed mule deer yearling buck, with the fresh, bright red blood clearly indicating the deer had been slain and consumed since dawn.
>
> I backtracked the deer and coyote trails and unraveled the event:
>
> Four mule deer had been chased by two coyotes with one on either flank across a big sagebrush flat toward a low hill containing scattered juniper trees. About twenty feet within the juniper stand a third coyote, which had been lying under a tree,

surprised and attacked one of the deer knocking it to the snow covered ground. Near the point of first attack, two of the other deer, presumably behind the target deer, abruptly changed direction away from the hill, while the fourth deer, presumably in the lead, continued over the hill. About five feet from where the target deer had been overpowered, I found the first sign of fresh blood. From the point of first attack, the target deer regained its feet and ran another twenty yards when a fourth coyote who had similarly been hiding and waiting under a juniper tree attacked and again knocked the target deer to the ground at the point of second attack. The deer began bleeding heavily, but regained its feet and struggled another 15 yards before being overpowered by the pack at the point of third attack. The carcass was slowly dragged down the hill while being torn apart and devoured.

Four months later following snow melt, I returned to the kill site. Only unbleached bones and hair remained to identify the carcass as predator-killed. Interestingly, within a few feet of the recent kill, I found four scattered distinct carcasses with various degrees of bleached and decaying bones from deer taken during previous years. Several years later I returned and again found deer carcasses in various degrees of decomposition, clearly indicating the coyotes were still using the same successful "kill site."

Cougars

Although cougars kill elk, moose, pronghorn, and smaller prey species, in addition to cattle and sheep, the primary prey and dietary year-round food of the mountain lion is the mule deer (Hornocker 1970). In most diet studies of cougar, deer comprise 60 to 90 percent of the diet. Although fawns and older individuals are taken more often than breeding age adults, lions kill mature bucks and does relatively easily. Buck deer are usually taken in a somewhat higher proportion compared to the buck-to-doe ratio in the population.

From numerous studies, it is estimated that individual adult lions kill between 25 and 125 mule deer per year, with the usual estimates ranging between 30 and 50 deer killed per cougar per year. In some areas of high cougar populations and low deer populations, cougars may take more deer over a year's time than are harvested by hunters

Photo by Becky Blankenship

Cougars are highly dependent on deer populations. Cougar numbers
need to be balanced with the deer population.

during the fall hunting seasons. High cougar populations may control population growth of deer herds in areas of low deer numbers. However, mountain lions are not a danger as far as extirpating big game populations (Hornocker 1992).

The potential impacts of high cougar populations are illustrated in the following simplified example. Consider a typical, healthy deer unit in Utah having a range carrying capacity of 10,000 wintering deer and composed of 1,000 bucks, 4,000 fawns and 5,000 does. Without additional adult mortality and the same reproductive success, an additional 4,000 fawns at 80 fawns/100 does would be added to the population by the following winter. Consequently in this example, 4,000 deer would be available for harvest and/or other mortality causes during the course of the year, and the population would still be maintained at 10,000. If the unit contained 50 cougars, which is probably about average for Utah units, and each cougar killed 40 of these deer, total cougar-caused deer mortality would equal 2,000 deer per year. Essentially, half of the available deer mortalities over an entire year could be accounted for by 50 cougars!

An often-asked question is: How many cougars should be maintained on an average Utah deer unit? From the view of mule deer management, I recommend that cougar populations be maintained at levels where cougars are allotted no more than 20 percent of the annual reproduction from the deer population. Referring to the above example with a population of 10,000 wintering deer, and a cougar kill rate of 40 deer per year, a population of 20 cougars would kill 800 deer per year, or 20 percent (800/4,000) of the reproduction. Using these figures, the cougar-to-deer ratio is 20 cougars per 10,000 deer, or 1 cougar per 500 deer. This appears to be a good ratio for management when deer populations are in balance with habitat and reproductive success is good. The ratio of 1 to 500 is similar to the ratio reported by early ecologists in areas of low hunter harvest (Leopold 1933). However, when deer populations have increased above carrying capacity, or other mortality factors such as hunter harvest have declined, allowing the ratio to decrease to as low as 1 cougar per 250 deer may have significant benefits to the deer population dynamics. Conversely, when deer populations have decreased, the cougar-to-deer ratio may be increased to 1 cougar per 1,000 deer or higher in which case cougars would be harvesting only about 10 percent of the deer population's reproduction. For general reference, the outside boundaries for game management of the number of cougars and the number of mule deer appear to be between 1 cougar per 200 to 2,000 deer. Clearly, cougar populations must be managed in concert with deer populations.

Cougars occasionally scavenge deer killed by vehicles or caught in fences, particularly in winter because cold temperatures prevent the meat from spoiling (Robinette et al. 1959). Cougars are opportunistic predators, and realize that potential injury results from capturing live prey. Nonetheless, cougars generally prefer to feed off their own kills.

Occasionally a cougar will select a small area on deer winter range and establish an overwinter 'campsite'. Cougar campsites are usually located in the lower portions of high-quality deer winter ranges where deer movements and density are high. During the winter an adult cougar may kill 15 to 30 deer within a small area, often less than 10 acres. Cougar campsites are evident in spring by the density of the mostly consumed deer carcasses.

> *Note:* My first observation of a cougar campsite was made during early spring in the late 1960s while hiking up a small south-facing drainage near Temple Fork in the Mill Creek Canyon drainage east of Salt Lake City. The small area contained at least 15 scattered carcasses. More recently, cougar campsites on the Cache unit have been reported on the Millville Face, Green Canyon and Woodruff Creek.

Some examples of studies of cougar predation on mule deer follow:

In a diet study in southeastern Arizona using scat analysis, 48% of the overall cougar diet was deer, with rabbits, cattle and javalina comprising most of the rest of the diet. However, based on biomass deer contributed only 40 percent of the diet (Cunningham et al. 1999).

Control of the mountain lion population was considered one of the major factors leading to the eruption of deer numbers followed by decimation of the winter ranges on the North Kaibab deer unit in Arizona (Mitchell and Freeman 1993). Conversely, in a Texas study no benefit to mule deer populations was observed with predator control (Cooke 1990). I consider little or no control of the cougar population on the Utah-Nevada Deep Creek Mountains to be a major factor controlling deer population size and growth.

In a central Utah study on the Oak Creek unit, with the deer population maintained at or slightly above carrying capacity, reduction of half the cougar population, estimated to be less than 10 cougars, was calculated to increase the hunter harvest by only four percent (Robinette et al. 1977). In a study using radio-collared cougars near Escalante, Utah, researchers found that 81 percent of the cougar diet was mule deer (Ackerman et al. 1984). They also reported older deer were more likely to be killed but all age classes of deer were taken.

> *Note:* I was 16 years old hiking the Baker's Fork trail in Millcreek Canyon east of Salt Lake City about midnight during a November weekend when I heard my first "mountain screamer." Under an overcast, blackened sky, with snow-laden tree branches overhanging the trail, and only a weak-beamed flashlight in hand, the close, unknown and terrifying shriek ripped my teenage invincibility while peaking my wildlife interests.
>
> Many years later, after having heard cougars scream on two more occasions, my wife Annie, our five little cherubs, and I were tent camping along a small, isolated tributary stream near the Snake River just south of Yellowstone National Park, when I was awakened by the infrequent screams from a roaming cougar. At first the screams were far away, perhaps half a mile, and muted by conifer trees and the sounds of flowing water. I thought the silent kids and my sweetheart were all asleep. They weren't. When I whispered, "Is anyone awake?" everyone abruptly sat up in their sleeping bags, and once again I realized kids are often more alert than parents realize.
>
> Each "mountain scream" grew louder and more intense as the lion approached our now vacated family tent. With the family in the van, I stepped outside and aimed a flashlight beam into the nearby bushes and small openings along the steam, catching the pair of diamond-like reflecting eyes from the cougar, staring directly at us. Above, a Clark's nutcracker, following the cougar from the tree tops and occasionally uttering its raspy call, paused in the moonlight at the top of a fir tree. The moment was Nature's gift to our family. The cougar gradually moved on, accompanied the Clark's nutcracker, and the "mountain screams" faded into memories. Five-year-old Micah, now finishing his graduate studies, clearly remembers the eyes staring back, and even three-year-old little Mary-Marie, now a medical student at the University of Utah, remembers the screams, as well as sleeping the night in the van beside Mom.

Bobcats

Although the primary foods of bobcats are rabbits, hares, and rodents, they prey on mule deer fawns year-round. Bobcats are particularly successful in killing fawns less than two months of age, and may kill 2 to 20 fawns per year per bobcat. My reasonable estimate is six deer killed per bobcat per year. Most bobcat predation occurs within eight weeks following deer parturition. During the first weeks following parturition, coyotes and bobcats are about equally effective in killing fawns.

Black Bears

The omnivorous black bear is usually found in scattered low density populations. Although deer comprise only a small fraction of the bear's diet, the bear is an efficient predator. Deer are killed primarily in early summer. In local areas fawns may comprise up to 50 percent of the diet for a very short time interval. However, during most of the year, deer contribute less than 5% of the bear's diet. Similar to the bobcat, it is estimated individual bears may kill 2 to 20 deer, mostly fawns, per year. My reasonable estimate is four deer killed per black bear per year. In Utah in the early 1980s it was believed black bears were controlling deer population growth on the LaSal Mountains.

Foxes

Gray and red foxes feed primarily on rodents, and occasionally kill mule deer. Both foxes are very effective predators on mule deer fawns early in the summer. The red fox expanded its range throughout Utah beginning about 1970, substantially increased its numbers to about the mid-1980s, and since then has been commonly observed in most habitats. This newer predator has added extra losses to mule deer fawn mortality, and in some locations may be affecting population dynamics.

Dogs

Domestic and feral dogs kill deer primarily during winter, when snow cover limits deer movement and reduced food availability has weakened deer. Although dogs do kill deer directly by fang and claw, most damage is done indirectly through harassment and chase. When deer are forced to run from dogs in winter, they must use vital fat and energy reserves. When weakened deer are chased by dogs, even though they may escape, they become more vulnerable to winter weather and increased overwinter mortality. The effects of free-ranging dogs can have significant mortality effects on recruitment rates of deer populations.

Raptors

Golden eagles are known to occasionally kill mule deer fawns, but only when fawns are only a few weeks old. Large hawks, such as red-tails and Swainsons, occasionally kill fawns during the first few days after birth. Eagles and hawks more often scavenge deer after being killed by some other means, such as highway mortality. Bald and golden eagles are capable of killing not only young fawns through about six weeks of age, but also fawns weakened near the end of the wintering period. Nonetheless, the effects of all raptors on mule deer populations should be considered very minor.

Chapter 8

Understanding
Population Dynamics

Few deer biologists have recognized that management of a deer
population at maximum sustained yield inevitably results in
lowering of the standing crop under high numbers of deer in
field . . . This factor has several ramifications for the individual
hunter. First, the number of deer in the field will be lower and
the probability of seeing deer will be reduced. Second, the effort
expended per deer killed will increase.

Dale R. McCullough, 1979
The George Reserve Deer Herd

The dynamics of any wildlife population can be simply defined by reproduction, mortality, and movements in and out of the geographic area.
However, these apparently simple factors can almost never be defined or
even accurately measured for wildlife populations. Consequently, indices such as fawn-to-doe ratios, age structure of the harvested population,
and overwinter mortality surveys are used as estimators for population
dynamics analyses.

Understanding the dynamics of any hunted wildlife population is critical
to the proper setting of the hunting seasons, bag limits, and projected total
harvest of the population. Hunting is the major management option influencing most hunted wildlife populations, and hunter management strongly
influences population numbers, age structure, and sex ratios. These three
factors—population numbers, age structure, and sex ratios—directly control the rates of natality and mortality. Therefore, the application of population dynamics is imperative to successful population management.

91

Basic Concepts in Mule Deer Population Dynamics

(1)   Generally, an equal number of male and female fawns are born.

(2)   In populations not hunted, survival rates are similar between males and females.

(3)   Since reproductive rates are relatively high in mule deer, hunting systems have broad flexibility in harvest regulations.

(4)   Because mule deer are a polygamous species where permanent mates are not selected, and in consideration of reproduction, the dynamics of the female segment of the population are much more important than those of the male.

(5)   A cohort of mule deer is a group of deer born the same year. Often the sexes are separated. The cohort is the basic unit of population dynamics, and following birth, is subject only to mortality reducing the size of the cohort until all members have died.

(6)   On ranges where harvest is critical, the highest sustained hunter harvests over several years are not achieved at the highest population densities, particularly under buck-only hunting. Highest sustained harvests are achieved by harvesting both bucks and antlerless deer at population densities below maximum, long-term, rangeland carrying capacity.

(7)   The long-term average number of bucks harvested cannot be increased by adjustment of the post-season buck-to-doe ratio. Buck-to-doe ratios are directly determined by hunting regulations.

(8)   On most mule deer ranges containing adequate summer and winter habitat, an approximate average deer population would be three to five deer per 100 acres, or 19 to 32 deer per square mile. A wide general range of 0.3 to 15 deer per 100 acres, or between 2 and 96 deer per square mile, may be maintained with very marginal to extremely good habitat. On ranges that consistently measure less than 1 deer per square mile, the rangeland is usually not considered deer habitat. The upper density of mule deer within ideal summer and winter range habitats over an entire year is about 100 deer per square mile.

A mule deer fawn is observed in a residential yard. Permanently resident urban deer often cause damage to landscaped yards.

Reproduction

Since the total number of fawns being born into the deer population cannot be counted, two indices can be used to assess yearly reproduction rates. In spring, between February and May, the number of fetuses per doe can be determined by examining does killed along highways and from other accidents. Occasionally a few does are harvested by biologists and researchers for specific studies, or to address local problems. Researchers count number of fetuses and determine the does' ages to determine reproductive rates by age classes.

Mean reproductive rates, or fetuses per doe, based on numerous samples from several locations were as follows: 0 fetuses per fawn, 0.7 fetuses per yearling doe, 1.4 fetuses per twoling doe, 1.6 fetuses per mature doe (aged three to seven years), and 1.5 fetuses per old doe (aged eight or more years). About half of all fetuses were males and half were females (Connolly 1981). Provided habitat is adequate, these reproductive rates are very consistent between years and over different geographical locations.

Nutritional status of the doe preceding parturition, or the process of giving birth to offspring, strongly affects reproductive rates as well as male-to-female sex ratios. Under poor nutritional status, reproductive rates may decrease by half compared to rates during times of good nutrition. In such cases the fetuses are aborted or absorbed in the womb, are stillborn, or die within a few days following parturition. On ranges with good habitat and nutritious forages, surviving fawns may increase to about 56 percent females and 44 percent males, whereas habitats with very low nutrition and poor range conditions show a distinct reversal in the percentage of surviving females, down to as low as 34 percent females and 66 percent males (Verme 1969; Robinette et al. 1977). However, even though the percentage of males is increased under low nutritional conditions, the actual number of males produced and available on the range is greatly reduced.

The second index of reproduction is field observation of the fawn-to-doe ratio. Unless a specific problem needs to be addressed, fawn-to-doe ratios are not collected immediately after parturition in mid-June to mid-July due to the difficulty in obtaining a reliable sample size. Similarly, data are no longer obtained prior to the rifle hunt due to the difficulties in obtaining an accurate and representative sample of bucks, does, and fawns, as well as personnel time constraints. Fawn-to-doe ratio data are normally collected in Utah during two periods: after the rifle hunt and in spring following green-up. During spring classification, fawn-to-adult ratios are obtained, which may be 3 to 25 percent lower than fawn-to-doe ratios depending upon the number of bucks in the sample. Spring counts are usually adjusted using the post-hunt buck-to-doe ratios. Spring counts are usually considered the most important counts concerning population dynamics because they indicate recruitment into the adult herd.

All fawn-to-doe and fawn-to-adult ratio classification counts are variable and require large sample sizes. However, in Utah a minimum sample size of 200 does for each herd unit has been determined to yield reasonably accurate estimates. A sample size of 1,000 deer or 400 does per management unit yields very accurate classification data.

Interestingly, almost all counts of fetuses per 100 does exceed 100 and average about 140, but only occasionally do classification counts of fawn-to-doe ratios reach that level. The decrease in the number of fawns between fetus and classification counts is mostly due to high mortality during birth and in the first two months following parturition. As a general rule, fawn-to-doe ratios during the post-season classification period may be rated on the following scale: poor is less than 50 fawns per 100 does, fair is 51 to 70 fawns per 100 does, good is 71 to 90 fawns per 100 does, and excellent is greater than 91 fawns per 100 does.

Mortality

Mortality or the more commonly used term survival rate is defined as the proportion of deer surviving from the beginning to the end of any specified year or time period and must remain in approximate balance with reproduction and recruitment rates to generate population stability. When deer populations are not controlled by hunting, they will usually increase rapidly in number with few negative effects for one or more years. However, when deer populations decrease to low numbers, due to reduced reproduction, over-harvest, or an increase in other mortality factors, hunting success also decreases. A decrease in hunter pressure usually follows the decrease in hunting success and, over time, a re-balancing in the number of sustainable deer occurs until the mortality factor(s) are altered. In areas of low deer densities with adequate forage resources, fawn-to-doe post-season ratios usually exceed 70 percent and adult doe mortality is usually less than 15 percent per year. Under these conditions, and in the absence of other major mortality factors, deer herds will double in size every three to four years, regardless of the buck hunter pressure or the extent of the buck harvest.

Mortality is usually measured by determining age distribution of the hunter-harvested population and making assumptions on important population issues, such as constant mortality and natality rates for several years prior to the time of sampling (Wolfe 1976). Age-specific harvest data numerically estimate survival rates of individual cohorts. Buck deer generally have much higher mortality rates than does primarily because of hunter harvest, however, survival rates are a result of all combined mortality factors. Buck data from the Vernon unit 1980–1982, shown in Table 8-1, and doe data from the Oak Creek unit 1947–1956, shown in Table 8-2, are examples of high buck and doe mortality rates in Utah.

Table 8-1. Vernon unit age class harvest data for bucks, 1980–1982.

Age Class	Deer Alive at Beginning of Year	Deer Harvested by Hunters	Mortality Rate
1	603	480	.796
2	123	83	.675
3	40	28	.700
4	12	9	.750
5	3	3	1.000
Totals	---	603	.784

Table 8-2. Oak Creek unit age class harvest data for does, 1947–56.

Age Class	Deer Alive at Beginning of Year	Deer Harvested by Hunters	Mortality Rate
1	1165	312	.268
2	853	267	.313
3	586	163	.278
4	423	91	.215
5	332	83	.250
6	249	48	.193
7–17	201	201	.345
Totals	---	1165	.266

During periods of optimum reproduction and maximum harvest, the mean annual mortality rate for bucks would be about 0.50 and for does about 0.25 (Robinette et al. 1977). This means about half of the bucks and a quarter of the does were harvested or died from other mortality factors each year. If all other mortality factors could be eliminated, maximum annual harvest would be about 50 percent of the bucks and 25 percent of the does. However, when hunting mortality is combined with all other mortality factors, total mortality is usually increased at variable rates for both bucks and does, but interestingly, more often the increase was higher for bucks while survival rates were better for does. Mortality rates for bucks generally increased when regulations changed from either-sex to buck-only hunting, as the above example from the Vernon unit showing very high mortality rates illustrates. Buck mortality rates on limited-entry units and CWMUs are greatly decreased.

Always an interesting question in wildlife management is whether mortality from two or more factors is additive or compensatory (Mackie et al. 1990; McCullough et al. 1990; Pac et al. 1991; Bartman et al. 1992; Gasaway et al. 1992). Additive mortality simply adds the losses from each factor and assumes each factor operates independently, whereas compensatory mortality assumes each factor is somewhat dependent on the other mortality factors. Survival rates are always somewhat higher when compensatory mortality is assumed.

To illustrate, buck survival from hunters may be 50 percent and survival from predators may be 80 percent on an assumed deer herd. Under additive mortality, the combined survival rate would be 40 percent, or 50 percent times 80 percent. Therefore, the mortality rate is 60 percent, calculated as (100 percent of the buck population minus the 40 percent that survived). Under compensatory survival theory, one or both survival rates—survival from either hunter harvest or predation—would increase due to a decrease in the number of deer killed by the other mortality factor. The theory is that with each deer that is killed, the remaining deer have a slightly improved chance of survival. Under compensatory survival theory, the combined survival rate may be expected to increase from 40 percent to anywhere up to 50 percent. Although data are insufficient to define the combined effects of mortality on any unit unless specific research is being conducted, additive mortality is the safe and conservative approach usually considered in setting hunting regulations to prevent over-harvest by hunters.

Results from numerous studies provide mixed support for both theories. Simple ecosystems with only one or two mortality factors tend to generally support additive mortality, whereas compensatory mortality, in which each mortality factor is affected by all other mortality factors, is usually the theory present in more complex ecosystems.

Moreover, with evaluation and comparison from many studies, it appears highly probable that at low deer population levels, mortality factors are mostly additive. That is, no change in the predator mortality rate on deer would be expected from changes in the hunter mortality rate on deer. To survive, predators would continue to kill the same number of deer even if the number of deer harvested by hunters were greatly increased. Consequently at low deer population densities, control of one or more mortality factors, such as predation or decreased hunter harvest, would result in an increase in deer survival. Thus, control of mortality factor(s) becomes increasingly important as the population declines.

Conversely, at deer population near or above carrying capacity, mortality factors appear to be mostly compensatory. That is, if hunter harvest is increased, the losses due to other mortality factors would be decreased.

Movements

Mule deer, usually individuals, move into and out of geographic areas or units arbitrarily defined for management purposes. Most of the movement is almost always by yearling deer establishing new home ranges. Travel out of a management area and normal home range is usually caused by a population increase and is normally density dependent. Outward movements usually result in an increase in the number of deer using poorer quality and more marginal ranges. Sometimes deer move into areas that previously did not support a permanent deer population. Movement into another area and increased deer density can also be caused by improved habitat and forage conditions, water development, decreased human harassment, and decreased predator density.

Conversely, as populations decline, rangeland utilized by deer will shrink inward. Higher quality habitats usually retain about the same density of deer during periods of declining populations, whereas marginal habitats may again become sparsely populated or vacated.

While migrating between summer and winter ranges, portions of some deer herds travel across or between units. Some migrations occur over long distances and a few deer may even travel completely through one or more units along the migration route. Fortunately large migrations between units are rare. Management of the segments of migrating herds is greatly complicated when portions of deer herds cross state lines. Generally with bordering states, agreements must be obtained to maintain the herd at the desired level and avoid double hunting and over-harvest. For example, a deer herd summering and hunted in Idaho in the fall, may migrate into Utah during the late fall, and could again be subject to hunting, perhaps leading to over-harvest. Technically, both states may act independently and pass regulations which could eliminate the migrating herd. Furthermore, if the migrating herd was impacting a winter range already at carrying capacity from the in-state deer herd, that state may consider eliminating the migrating out-of-state herd.

> *Note:* If state boundaries had been established on watershed drainages, as was proposed by early surveyors and ecologists in the late 1800s, this problem would not exist and deer management today would be more effective.

Population Trends

Because counts of total deer populations are very difficult to obtain and rarely accomplished, deer biologists must rely on trend data. Indices of population trends can be grouped into three categories: sample counts, indirect population estimates, and harvest data (Wolfe 1976).

Sample Counts

Sample counts attempt to count a representative part of the population. This may be done by vehicle, aircraft or on foot. Sample counts are usually precise if counting periods are consistently repeated with respect to exact locations, time of day and year, weather conditions, and equal ability between observers. A simple example would be a landowner annually climbing to a ridge top where an entire draw could be observed, and then by shouting and using other noise devices, scare, flush, and count all the deer as they depart out of the draw. Using several observation draws, I successfully used this technique in the early 1980s on the Sheeprock Mountains of western Utah. The most commonly used sample counts by state wildlife agencies involve helicopters on snow-covered deer winter ranges and annually cover the exact same geographic area.

Indirect Population Trend Estimates

Probably the most commonly used trend index of population estimates, used extensively in the 1960s and 1970s, is the pellet group count. Pellet groups are counted and removed in the spring from usually permanent plots marked with steel stakes. The usefulness of the technique is limited by winter deer use patterns as affected by weather, deer density, and desirability of alternate foraging sites.

Browse utilization transects can also be used as population trend indicators and are subject to the same limitations as pellet group counts with the additional problem of relative palatability for the browse species being sampled. Except for specific studies, the use of both pellet group counts and browse utilization transects have greatly declined.

Indirect population estimates can also be derived from the change in ratios of bucks to does before and after a hunting season. Data required are pre- and post-season classification counts and harvest data from the hunting season. The method is exact and only limited by the accuracy of the classification and harvest data. However, small errors in the collected data, especially harvest, can lead to gross errors in the population estimate. The following example in Table 8-3 represents numbers typical of Utah's buck-only hunting units and assumes zero antlerless harvest and zero other mortality. The percentage buck harvest in the two examples is heavy at 85% and moderate at 50%. Landowners and hunters choosing to apply this method simply need to replace the numbers shown in Table 8-3 with their estimates and make the simple calculations.

Table 8-3. Simple change in ratios population estimator
from a buck-only unit.

	Classification ratios of Bucks:Does:Fawns:	
	85% Buck Harvest	50% Buck Harvest
Pre-hunt	20:100:75	20:100:75
Post-hunt	3:100:75	10:100:75
Harvest:	680 bucks	400 bucks
Proportion of bucks harvested:	(20-3)/20 = .85	(20-10)/20 = .50
Pre-hunt buck population:	680/.85 = 800	400/.50 = 800
Pre-hunt doe population:	100/20 x 800 = 4,000	same
Pre-hunt fawn population:	75/100 x 4000 = 3,000	same
Pre-hunt total population:	800 + 4K + 3K = 7,800	same
Post-hunt total population:	(800-680) + 4K + 3K = 7,120	(800-400) + 4K + 3K = 7,400
Percentage of the herd harvested:	680/7800x100 = 8.7%	400/7800x100 = 5.1%

Although hypothetical, the data given in this example clearly argue against buck-only hunting, unless the population is considerably under carrying capacity. For a population at or near carrying capacity, even under intensive buck harvest of 85 percent removal, less than 10 percent of the total herd can be annually harvested, and under a 50 percent removal of the available bucks, only about 5 percent of the total herd is harvested.

Harvest Data

Harvest data, the total number of bucks and/or antlerless deer harvested, are also used to index population trends. Harvest data and trend over years are relatively precise under fairly constant conditions of laws and regulations, hunter numbers, weather, and sampling technique.

A second harvest measure occasionally used is the total harvest per hunter day, or harvest per unit effort. For example, in Utah in 1989 during the regular deer hunt, 735,063 hunter days were used to harvest 53,101 bucks, for a mean of 13.8 hunter days per buck harvested (Utah DWR 1951–2008).

Checking station harvest data also offer a quick index to changes in population. However, checking stations must be operated consistently, on the same days and during the same hours of operation, for the data to have trend application. For example, the checking station at the mouth of Logan Canyon in the Cache unit had been run between 9:00 am and 7:00 pm on the opening weekend of the rifle hunt between 1996 and 2009. The data shown in Table 8-4, presented as the number of bucks checked each year, represent the potential population trend, which seems rather steady, but declines slightly from 1996 to 2004 with an abrupt decline during 2005 to 2009.

Table 8-4. Bucks checked at the Logan Canyon station, 1996–2009.

Year	Bucks Checked	Year	Bucks Checked
1996	74	2003	58
1997	79	2004	61
1998	47	2005	40
1999	72	2006	35
2000	66	2007	40
2001	70	2008	28
2002	59	2009	32

For a second example, the checking station at the mouth of Blacksmith Fork Canyon in the Cache unit was run consistently from 1980 to 1997 as shown in Table 8-5. In contrast, these buck harvest data show an extreme decline in population over the years, as well as abrupt declines, such as during 1992–1993, followed by gradual increases.

Table 8-5. Bucks checked at the Blacksmith Fork station 1980-1997.

Year	Bucks Checked	Year	Bucks Checked
1980	386	1989	104
1981	505	1990	181
1982	126	1991	258
1983	223	1992	237
1984	57	1993	16
1985	102	1994	31
1986	134	1995	65
1987	279	1996	64
1988	248	1997	49

A third example comes from hunter records at the East Canyon Resort in Morgan County. This unique resort, containing almost 9,600 acres with adjacent public land and livestock management, has required hunters to annually check harvested deer, as shown in Table 8-6. Although some years of data are missing before 1998, data from this private resort are a good example of how private land ranchers may obtain and maintain harvest trends. In addition to harvest, private land ranchers may also choose to record antler data of harvested bucks in order to assess the trend in quality or size of bucks harvested. Table 8-7 indicates that the recent trend has been toward harvest of larger bucks, since the data show an increased number of bucks with antler tines in the 4x4+ class.

*Table 8-6. Bucks checked at the East Canyon
Resort 1998–2009.*

Year	Bucks Checked	Year	Bucks Checked
1998	23	2004	62
1999	53	2005	54
2000	50	2006	95
2001	44	2007	90
2002	41	2008	17
2003	52	2009	26

*Table 8-7. Percentages of harvested bucks by antler classes from
East Canyon Resort 1987–2009.*

Years	Sample Size	Antler Classes							
		1x1	1x2	2x2	2x3	3x3	3x4	4x4	4x4+
1987-1991	169	13	02	28	05	23	02	21	05
1998-2005	365	07	01	33	08	16	11	16	08
2005-2009	184	03	04	26	08	14	08	21	16

Population Recovery

Given the long-term downward trend in mule deer populations, the question often asked is: Can the massive mule deer herds of the mid-twentieth century in Utah be revived? This question is not readily answered in direct terms. However, the four factors controlling trend and required to optimize mule deer numbers and population dynamics may be described as population growth especially the Three Rs, mortality causes including the Three Cs, competitors, and critical habitats.

Population Growth

The primary factors of natality and potential growth are the Three Rs - reproduction, recruitment, and the ratios of breeding males to females. The primary goals are early doe conception during the first estrus cycle, high conception rates, high percentages of mature does ages two to seven in the population, short breeding period in the fall followed by a short fawning period in spring, and high fawn survival until the following spring green-up period when surviving fawns aged about 10 months are recruited into the adult population. The question is not only to define management strategies which produce the highest number of fawns, but even more importantly, to maximize the number of 10-month-old yearlings recruited into the herd the following spring.

Reproduction begins with breeding activities beginning about November 1, with most does being bred during November. The breeding midpoint, when about 50 percent of the does are bred, is about November 15 to 20. A short breeding season leads to a short fawning period. This is important due to the decrease in time in which the fawn crop is most vulnerable to predation.

In my opinion, human harassment during the breeding period may significantly delay or lengthen the breeding period. Mule deer bucks and does need freedom from harassment to settle into breeding activity behaviors. As human activity on winter ranges increases from hikers, dog walkers, ATV riders, snowmobilers, and others during the breeding period, it seems reasonable that additional stress from these users may be placed on deer, potentially affecting reproduction, recruitment, and overwinter survival. To protect deer and winter ranges, the Division of Wildlife Resources has closed many state-owned big game wildlife management areas to human traffic during winter.

The ratio of bucks to does is important in accomplishing the breeding quickly. The Utah Division of Wildlife Resources has adopted a post-season minimum ratio of 15 bucks to 100 does. Although the ratio of bucks to does needed to successfully accomplish breeding has been shown to be less than three bucks per 100 does, the breeding period may have been lengthened. For examples, in 1973 I classified three bucks to 100 does during post-season counts on a portion of the Blue Mountain area in the Uinta Basin, and in 1982 and 1983 I classified four bucks to 100 does (40 percent of bucks were spikes) on a portion of the Sheeprock Mountains on the Vernon unit. In both areas I observed that the fawning period was delayed. However, in both areas reproduction counts of fawns per 100 does the following fall in the same areas were about average: on Blue Moutain, 74, and on the Sheeprocks, 75 fawns to 100 does. Numerous other examples are extant, such as on the Heber deer unit in 1989 two bucks per 100 does were classified, and the following fall 88 fawns to 100 does were recorded. The fawning period was not observed. In all three examples, as well as many others, it remains unclear if the breeding period may be lengthened under low buck-to-doe ratios. Also, the potential effects of a delayed or lengthened breeding period on reproduction and recruitment rates remain undefined, regardless if caused by increased human activities or wide buck-to-doe ratios.

Clearly, mule deer managers need additional research and data analysis on the number of bucks needed to obtain optimal reproduction and recruitment results. While the 15 bucks to 100 does ratio is a reasonable first approximation, the optimum ratio remains undefined and is probably highly variable.

One critical factor in fawn survival is the constant association with the doe. Research is needed on this subject to define the survival of fawns when separated from the doe at various time periods. In my opinion, separation from the doe before September 1 leads to increased fawn mortality. It is certain that the longer the association with the doe, the higher the survival rate of the fawns.

Herd population increase or decrease is almost entirely dependent upon recruitment in the spring. To maintain the same herd population, recruitment must equal the total adult mortality which occurred during the entire previous year. Recruitment is determined as the number of fawns per 100 adults in late spring, generally after green-up has begun. Once green-up is established, fawn mortality from winter stress and predators is greatly reduced, and the fawns become yearling adults.

Mortality Causes

The interactions between mortality, natality and habitat are seldom well-defined and usually complex. Furthermore, the ubiquitous need for adequate habitat and the associated limited carrying capacity must always remain paramount in defining parameters of population size and dynamics. Nonetheless, the effects of the major mortality factors are usually critical to deer populations and are also of high human interest. Although greatly simplified in this section, discussion of mortality factors simply because management can make effective changes becomes one of the key issues in mule deer management.

Aside from the health of the doe and fawn(s) following birth, the primary mortality factors are the Three Cs - coyotes, cougars, and cars. Each of these factors can effectively reduce mule deer numbers, individually or collectively. The effects of disease, starvation, fawn abandonment and other minor factors are undefined, but usually have limited population influence. However, under unusual environmental conditions these factors may also cause significant effects on populations.

Simply stated, predator control can increase deer survival. However, it should be noted that other mortality factors may somewhat compensate for increased survival due to predator control. For example, if 100 more deer survive due to the removal of two or three cougars, a percentage of those survivors may be killed by other factors, such as coyotes or increased highway mortality. Nonetheless, with the possible exception of deer populations allowed to grow beyond the carrying capacity of the range, compensatory mortality rarely approaches the increases obtained from predator control. Furthermore, predator control becomes increasingly important as mule deer populations decrease.

Although fawn mortality occurs from the time of birth to spring the following year when 10-month fawns are recruited into the adult population, the most critical period is the first eight weeks following parturition. It is estimated higher fawn mortality occurs during this short period than during the following eight months of the fawn's growth period. Mortality causes in the first eight weeks are primarily predators, followed by disease, malnutrition, and abandonment. Maximizing fawn survival during this period through predator control and healthy range conditions will have the highest positive effect on herd recruitment.

Coyote predation can control growth of mule deer populations. Coyotes prey on deer fawns throughout the summer, but especially during the first eight weeks following birth. Hunting in packs, coyotes also prey on fawn and adult deer during deep snow conditions and when deer are weakened near the end of winter. Control of coyote numbers through the U.S. Fish and Wildlife Service, hunters, and trappers should be encouraged.

Although cougars are almost always found in the vicinity of mule deer herds, the recent abrupt rise in cougar numbers was a relatively new factor in wildlife management. The increase in cougar numbers in Utah apparently began in the mid-1980s. Changes in policies by many Western states, such as the restrictive cougar hunting initiative in California, and presumed decreases in illegal harvest due to law enforcement efforts in Utah and other states, probably led to that increase. It is estimated an adult cougar kills almost one deer per week or 30 to 50 deer per year.

For example, on the Cache Unit, cougar numbers have been controlled by limited-entry permits. Under this system about 15 to 25

2009-04-24 7:06:00 AM   M 3/5   P. Cramer UDOT-USU-UDWR   O   42°F

UT 8991 MP14 R37

Photo by P. Cramer, UDOT, USU

Three wintering deer pass through a culvert under US 89-91 near
Logan. Fencing, underpasses, and overpasses allow deer to maintain
traditional migration routes.

cougars were annually harvested by hunters and miscellaneous losses
between 1995 and 2003. In 1994, I estimated the number of cougars on
the Cache unit to be between 100 and 120 animals. Maximum cougar
harvest was obtained in 1999 when 36 cougars were legally harvested
by hunters. Miscellaneous losses include highway mortality and depredation harvests. Careful control of the number of cougars is critically
important during periods of low deer populations. To a lesser degree,
and in decreasing importance, bobcat, black bear, red fox, and golden
eagle are occasional but effective predators of mule deer fawns.

As far as car mortality goes, several alternatives are available to manage vehicles for mule deer. The simple solution is to reduce traffic speed
to 35 miles per hour. At this speed few deer are hit and killed, and vehicle
damage is minimal. I have estimated that reducing speed from 55 or 65
mph to 35 mph would reduce highway mortality by 90 to 95 percent. For
example, if the speed limit throughout Logan Canyon were reduced to 35
mph, the travel time from Logan to Garden City would only be increased

by about 10 minutes and numerous deer, elk and moose, along with birds and small mammals, would avoid highway mortality. Reducing speed limits particularly along defined migration routes is an effective solution, but is often met with major opposition from many highway users as well as bureaucracies.

Fencing is the most common solution of action. Fencing highways with a tight eight-foot-high fence using small mesh wire and secure gates will prevent deer access. The use of common four-inch mesh wire fence often proves inadequate and repairs are often needed. Once deer break through the fence and are trapped on the highway, they are extremely vulnerable to vehicle collisions because of their inability to locate a safe passage back through the fence.

For example, following fence construction, almost 100 deer were killed yearly on US 89-91 through Wellsville Canyon despite fencing with four-inch mesh eight-foot high fences. The underpasses located at the Wellsville spring and by the sleigh riding hill near Mantua are being used by an unknown portion of the migrating deer herd. It has been suggested that two additional underpasses, one on the Wellsville and the second on the Mantua side, are needed to allow deer a reasonable chance to maintain migration patterns.

Sturdy fences with adequate sized underpasses can be effective in preventing highway mortality. I have observed that fences built taller and with heavier materials almost eliminate vehicle collisions with deer along highway and freeway stretches of road in several western states. This is an issue where wildlife management, public safety, and transportation officials certainly find common ground.

Competitors

Species A, B, and C, need to use the same critical habitat H. Each of these species could completely use the space and resources in the habitat. Generally, one species will dominate, while the other two species will receive only minor benefits. Species A, B, and C could be the mule deer, elk, and recreation people, and habitat H is the winter range.

Elk compete directly with mule deer for forage resources. Elk may displace mule deer. Displaced mule deer may be forced to move to less preferred habitats and survival can be decreased. Mule deer managers may consider that competition with elk should be minimized by issuing hunting regulations which separate the two species on winter ranges.

In terms of carrying capacity on browse-covered winter ranges, I have estimated that five to eight mule deer are equivalent to about one elk. For example, if the winter range between Green and Logan canyons on the Cache unit can maintain an estimated 200 deer, those deer could be displaced by 25 to 40 elk.

Elk feeding programs at Hardware Ranch and the Millville face on the Cache Unit are effective in minimizing competition. Elk simply remain near the feed grounds and provide little competition to mule deer on surrounding areas. However, managers must also consider the negative aspects of establishing elk feeding grounds, including but not limited to disease vectors, habitat degradation, associated costs, predator conflicts, behavior modifications, and perpetual reliance on supplemental feed which may lead to an increase in depredation.

With a maximum population objective of 2,300 wintering elk on the Cache unit, for example, hunting strategies become important management tools to reduce competition. As a case in point, deer and elk populations in Logan Canyon are being separated by allowing liberal antlerless elk hunting opportunities. Specifically, from the mouth of Logan Canyon to the Woodcamp Bridge in the Beirdneau hunt area, heavy late-season hunter pressure is being applied to the elk population. This strategy allows the lower portions of the Canyon to be primarily used by deer. Above the Woodcamp Bridge, at higher elevations where snow depths often preclude wintering deer, elk may enjoy adequate habitat throughout the winter without hunter pressure.

As white-tailed deer become established in Utah, competition with the mule deer will occur, and the white-tailed deer is a better competitor than the mule deer in many habitats (Geist 1990). In my opinion, the white-tailed deer will, without question over time, displace and replace mule deer in significant numbers in many, perhaps most, locations. The potential urban and agricultural problems, such as increased vehicle collisions and crop depredation, should not be ignored. However, numbers of white-tailed deer have not increased through 2009 as rapidly as I had originally projected in 1996.

The competition between human recreation and mule deer is a difficult problem for mule deer managers because recreation almost always wins. Recreational snowmobilers and ATV users displace mule deer on winter ranges such as the Hardware Ranch Wildlife Management Area on the Cache unit, among others. Walkers, skiers, bird watchers, and hikers, enjoying Utah's wintry outdoors, use the foothill ranges and displace wintering mule deer. How much displacement is harmful? The answers remain mostly social and political. Biological data are scarce and research studies are needed. However, on most of Utah's wildlife management areas, wildlife is considered the primary user and recreation is secondary. As a result, many wildlife management areas supporting mule deer in Utah are closed to all public access between January 1 and April 30 to protect wintering wildlife.

A major form of mule deer competition with people involves the use of crop lands. Wildlife managers are often forced to reduce mule deer numbers to minimize conflicts with crop land production or urbanization. Mule deer numbers may be reduced below carrying capacity to address these problems. Utah needs legislation that safeguards the producer but also requires landowner tolerance of reasonable mule deer depredation.

Critical Habitats

As highlighted in several places in this book, mule deer numbers are decreasing in the long-term primarily as a result of decreasing quality and quantity of winter range habitat. Without adequate winter range habitat, the mortality factors discussed above—coyotes, cougars, cars, and competitors—have limited impact. Clearly, maintaining large mule deer herds is directly dependent upon maintaining large acreage of quality winter range.

Based on forage production of shrubs, I have estimated that five acres of fair to good quality winter range are needed to support one deer over the winter. Thus a full section, 640 acres, of average winter range could maintain about 128 deer. For example, the 1,000 acres of critical winter range acquired by the Division of Wildlife Resources in 1999 on the west slopes of the Wellsville Mountains may be able to maintain about 200 wintering deer.

Quality of Critical Habitats

The three primary methods for enhancing and maintaining quality, useable winter ranges are seeding depleted ranges, fencing, and managing livestock grazing.

Seeding rangelands with appropriate plant species is most commonly attempted within the year following a wildfire. Immediately after a fire soil nutrients are high and weed competition is low. Rangeland fires

typically destroy established shrubs, such as big sagebrush, antelope bitterbrush and most other browse species and result in stands of grasses
and forbs. Seeding with both seeds and seedlings is also attempted on
ranges depleted of shrub species. Successful seeding is highly dependent upon soil moisture and precipitation immediately following the
seeding. For example, the seeding completed on the Woodruff Wildlife
Management Area in fall 1997 was successful primarily due to very favorable moisture conditions. Conversely, the seeding effort at the Richmond
Wildlife Management Area in fall 1994 was almost a complete failure due
to extremely dry conditions immediately following the seeding.

Because of steep slopes and rocky terrain, only some portions of deer
winter ranges can be treated mechanically and the remainder must be
hand-seeded. Mechanical seeding is much more successful and much
larger acreage can be affected. Nonetheless, seeding projects need to be a
yearly activity to maintain the production and values of winter rangelands.

Fences are good solutions where mule deer winter ranges on private
lands may eventually become urbanized developments that extend to the
boundary of the wildlife management area or other public lands. Eight-
foot-high fences can maintain deer within wildlife management areas,
which helps control depredation of landscaped ornamental plants. Fences
are also needed to mark the exterior boundaries and subdivide management areas for control of livestock grazing and motorized vehicles.
The chain-link fence at the now-defunct Mule Deer Research Wildlife
Management Area near the mouth of Green Canyon provided an excellent example of the effectiveness of fences separating winter range from
urban development.

Proper livestock grazing is the long-term key to maintaining quality
winter ranges. Excessive utilization of browse by deer in winter will gradually reduce shrub vigor and result in decreasing shrub density regardless of the intensity of livestock grazing. To maintain browse vigor, utilization by mule deer should be restricted to 50 percent use of the current
annual growth of big sagebrush and other non-deciduous and evergreen
species, and 65 percent use of antelope bitterbrush and other deciduous
browse species.

Quantity of Critical Habitats

High acreage of habitat must be secured to maintain deer populations on
all units. Each unit has its unique requirements for securing permanent

habitat. However, few if any units will ever secure the habitat acreage required to maintain optimum deer populations.

For example, on the Cache unit, to secure the optimum potential for future mule deer populations, I suggest that the following minimum acreage of winter range would need to be secured with conservation easements or acquisition purchases from private landowners. On the east foothill benches between Logan Canyon and the Utah-Idaho state line, 10,000 acres or about 15 sections would be the optimum acreage. On the benches between Logan and Blacksmith Fork canyons, along Blacksmith Fork Canyon, and around Hardware Ranch, large deer populations would need 8,000 acres or about 12 sections. Around the Wellsville and Clarkston mountains, 10,000 acres or about 15 sections would maintain optimum deer populations, as would 2,000 acres or about three sections along Woodruff Creek and east of Randolph. In addition, on the east side of Bear Lake and around the Crawford Mountains, where migrating mule deer herds from Idaho and Wyoming winter, an additional 10,000 acres or 15 sections are needed to secure these herds. A total of 50,000 acres of rangeland is needed to secure the optimum future for mule deer and associated wildlife species on just the Cache unit! Economics make obtaining this massive amount of acreage an impossible task.

However, the Utah Division of Wildlife Resources has acquired seven wildlife management areas containing mule deer winter range on the Cache unit up through 2004. These wildlife management areas total 23,800 acres and include Hardware Ranch at 16,000 acres, Millville Face, Richmond, and Woodruff all at 2,000 acres, Cold Water Canyon at 1,000, Swan Creek at 600 acres, and Mule Deer Research at 200.

Lessons Learned from White-tailed Deer and the George Reserve Deer Herd

Since 1928, white-tailed deer populations have been uniquely studied on the Michigan George Reserve deer herd (McCullough 1979). The population dynamics of white-tail deer are very similar to mule deer. The 464 hectare, 1,146 acre area is completely enclosed by an 11.7-foot-high deer-proof fence. Many of the concepts in deer population dynamics come from studies on the Reserve. No comparable studies on mule deer have been conducted, although in the 1940s Utah established a similar reserve in central part of the state to conduct research. Unfortunately, the entire area, including fence lines, burned the year following construction and the research effort was abandoned.

In 1928, four female and two male adult white-tailed deer were introduced in the George Reserve. After seven years of no hunting, the herd had grown to 222 deer! This experiment was repeated in 1975 when the herd was reduced to 10 deer, mostly fawns, and after six years the herd numbered 212. In both experiments yearly growth rates were about 0.51, or a doubling of the population in less than two years. One important finding was that the maximum rate of population growth was a doubling every two years. Perhaps the most important finding of the experiments was that population growth rates decreased as the population increased. Stated differently, when resources per individual deer were more abundant, reproductive success and survival were higher.

Maximum sustained yield (MSY) is defined as the highest number of deer which can be harvested yearly on a sustained basis. MSY is limited by habitat quality and quantity, and is determined by using the post-hunting season's residual population. MSY does not occur at low populations because the number of reproducing does is too low, even though population growth and recruitment rates are likely near maximum. Similarly, but perhaps surprisingly, MSY does not occur at high populations because population growth and recruitment rates decrease.

On the George Reserve MSY occurred at a post-hunt population of 99 and a harvest of 48 bucks plus antlerless deer. Post-hunt deer density was calculated at about 9 deer per 100 acres (57 deer per square mile) with a harvest rate of about 4 deer harvested per 100 acres (26 deer per square mile). When the post-hunt population was decreased from 99, the harvest declined, even though reproduction and recruitment rates increased. The harvest also declined when the post-hunt population was allowed to increase above 99, but the reproduction and recruitment rates decreased.

Because of the bell-shaped curve of deer population dynamics, the same harvest can be obtained at two population points, on the high and low sides of the MSY point. The same harvest could occur at slightly below MSY, or under carrying capacity on the up-slope of the bell-curve, or slightly above MSY, or over carrying capacity on the down-slope of the curve.

Mule deer managers generally agree with the bell-shaped curve of deer dynamics, but most believe that the curve is somewhat different from that of the white-tailed deer. The rather even bell-shaped curve for the white-tailed deer has a short MSY plateau with gradual slopes from both sides of the plateau. The mule deer curve has a much broader MSY plateau, an even gradual up-slope on the low population side, but importantly, a much more rapid decline in the slope when populations become excessive.

The major advantage in managing deer populations on the low population side of MSY is that the deer population has low potential for habitat destruction during harsh winters compared to higher populations. However, hunter effort per deer harvested is increased at the lower population level. The major advantage of managing populations at higher levels above MSY is that hunters and other observers will see more deer, which is a major factor in hunter satisfaction. On the other hand, managing deer at the lower population side of MSY increases the size of bucks harvested. Larger bucks were harvested on the George Reserve during periods of low population density (Haverstrom and Cambrum 1950). Simply stated, more resources are available for individual deer at low populations. Most conscientious managers try to manage deer population on the low side of MSY, whereas most hunters and other wildlife observers, without the knowledge of population dynamics or habitat balance, prefer the higher population.

A common question regarding MSY is whether a shift in sex ratios can increase harvest. Many hunters and some managers believe that by having a low buck-to-doe ratio in the post-season population, more fawns will be recruited and an increase in harvest will follow. The fact is, even though recruitment is determined by the number of females and no relationship exists between recruitment and the number of males, MSY cannot be increased by adjustment of the sex ratio due to female-to-female competition for habitat resources. Nonetheless, at low population levels where female-to-female competition is greatly decreased or is not a factor, population increase may be accelerated if the sex ratio were adjusted in favor of females.

Utah data support these findings. During 13 years (1961–1973) of either-sex hunting in Utah, 64,719 bucks were annually harvested when the post-hunt buck-to-doe ratio was moderate (15 to 20 bucks per 100 does). Similarly, during 13 years of buck-only hunts (1974–1986) 63,339 bucks were harvested annually when the post-hunt buck-to-doe ratio was much lower (5 to 10 bucks per 100 does). In Colorado, one study showed no change in the harvest of bucks with either 0 or 15 percent harvest of adult does (Bartman et al. 1992).

Because harvest at MSY cannot be increased by sex ratio adjustment, once a population reaches the point of MSY, there is no advantage in hunting discrimination between the sexes. Thus the harvest of antlerless deer where populations are at MSY is necessary to achieve maximum harvest. For example, in Utah between 1961 and 1973, under either-sex hunting, hunters harvested 37,796 antlerless deer yearly, compared to 6,088 antlerless deer under buck-only hunting with control permits during 1974–1986.

Even at very low populations, from the viewpoint of deer population dynamics, complete closure of hunting has little justification. Buck-only hunting is almost always preferable to hunters and useful to mule deer population recovery when populations are low compared to available habitat and below maximum sustained yield. Nonetheless, managers who wish to decrease illegal antlerless kill, which aids in population recovery, or to increase the size of harvested bucks during the following season may choose to close some units.

When hunting is restricted to buck-only, deer numbers will usually increase unless other mortality factors have significant effects. Illegal kill and crippling losses, highway mortality, predators, poaching, disease, and accidents; mortality factors can be significant and tend to maintain population size. However, despite these mortality factors, under buck-only hunting, many populations remain high and often above carrying capacity. When populations exceed carrying capacity and MSY, mortality factors are usually beneficial and can increase the sustained harvest of bucks as well as keep herd numbers below the habitat destruction level.

A Final Note on Dynamics

Between about 1999 and 2005, the western states and southwestern Canada experienced many years of drought. These drought years reduced the potential MSY due to reduced forage availability and habitat quality. Throughout the West mule deer numbers declined. In addition to the drought clearly affecting population dynamics, other mortality factors have also become more salient and important. The increase in vehicular traffic and highway speed has accelerated the number of deer killed on highways. It is estimated that on some units, highway mortality exceeds hunter harvest, and most of the highway mortality is the reproductive female segment of the herd. The highway factor cannot be ignored. Other

Photo by Mark Elzey

A deer is pictured in the shade of rich aspen habitat. Summer ranges
provide the high quality forage needed to build fat stores necessary
for winter survival.

factors acting negatively on population dynamics include the continual
urbanization of winter ranges, increased human harassment in summer,
long and continuous hunting seasons in fall and winter, increased use
of snow machines and other human activities on upper winter ranges,
increased restrictions on predator control, problems associated with depredation, wildfires decimating winter ranges, lack of planned livestock
grazing on winter ranges, and many others. These combined factors leading to increased mortality and decreased natality, even under buck-only
hunting with zero legal antlerless harvest, appear to me on many Utah
units to be curtailing and controlling population growth since about
1993. To allow deer populations to return to MSY, managers need to initiate aggressive programs that will greatly reduce the mortality factors
and enhance natality.

Hunters, Hunting, and Harvest

Mature does that are healthy in the fall have very high overwinter survival rates.

Chapter 9

Profiles and Preferences of Hunters

Utah Resident Hunter Profile

More than 90 percent of Utah resident deer hunters are male, over half (55 percent) are between 25 and 44 years of age, and the majority (61 percent) have 11 or more years of experience as licensed Utah deer hunters. Except for the youngest age class (14 to 25 years) the percentage of participating hunters decreases with increasing age. That is, as a hunter cohort ages, fewer hunters continue hunting. However, most hunters who are active at age 25 continue hunting at least until their mid 40s. After age 45, participation percentage in the Utah deer hunt rapidly decreases. Since most hunters begin hunting before age 25, the youngest age class would be expected to have the highest percentage of hunter participation (Decker and Connolly 1989). However, in recent years this age class was not the highest, and the data suggest that a declining percentage of young people will hunt. The mean age of Utah deer hunters is about 40 and increasing (Austin et al. 1992).

The number of Utah deer hunters remained somewhat constant between 1994 and 2008 after Utah limited the number of buck hunter permits during the general rifle season to 97,000. That number was reduced to 95,000 in 2005, but the reduction had only minor effects on the number of Utah deer hunters. Prior to 1994, buck permit sales were not limited.

Annual and continuous participation by hunters indicated by the number of years of deer hunting experience represents the sustained interests and continued activity of most veteran deer hunters. However, many younger hunters quit deer hunting after only a few seasons. Indeed more than one-fifth, or an estimated 22 percent, of Utah hunters who had hunted deer over a period of 1 to 15 years had quit hunting before the sixth year of field experience. The loss of interest is likely due to lack of success as a young hunter, accompanied with a change in motivation and competition with other recreational activities. Since wildlife management is supported mostly by the license buyer, it is important for wildlife agencies to recruit new hunters during the later teenage years and retain the activity of these hunters for at least 10 years. After 10 years of experience, hunters are considered veterans, and the hunter drop-out rate is much lower.

Most hunters, almost 70 percent, had household incomes of less than $50,000 per year and about 15 percent had incomes of less than $20,000 per year in the early 1990s (Krannich et al. 1991). Although income levels have increased considerably in recent years, hunters continue to come from mainstream citizens. Hunters as a group generally have incomes slightly lower than the average for their location. Regardless of income level, deer hunting is very important to most hunters, especially to those who have 10 or more years of experience (Austin and Jordan 1989). Very few hunters, especially veterans, would be eliminated because of increased license fees. One study determined that about 80 percent of these hunters would continue to hunt even if license fees were doubled (Keith et al. 1991). In my work with hunting groups, it is apparent that relative income levels and interest in deer hunting, especially for veteran hunters, has not changed.

Nonresident Hunter Profile

Almost all nonresident hunters, more than 95 percent, are male; combined with the similar percentage of male resident hunters, these data support the idea that hunting is only moderately important to women (Krannich et al. 1991; Austin et al. 1992). Conversely, in recent years a slight increase in the number of female hunters has been linked with higher social and economic classes of some participating women.

Age classes of nonresidents followed the same pattern as for resident hunters. However few nonresident hunters, less than 10 percent, were represented by the youngest age class. Compared with resident hunters, more nonresident hunters were represented by the older age classes, 45 years and older. These differences between resident and nonresident hunters are probably in part due to higher monetary and time costs associated with nonresident hunting.

Participation by experience classes is very different between resident and nonresident hunters. An amazingly high percentage, almost 60 percent, of nonresidents had only one to five years of Utah deer hunting experience. This finding suggests that important reasons cause nonresidents to discontinue hunting in Utah, including travel costs, hunting opportunities in other states, low success in the Utah deer hunts, high hunter density, and interests in alternative outdoor activities. Since the older experience classes with six years or more experience were about the same between resident and nonresident hunters, a much lower rate of nonresident hunters quit hunting after five years of deer hunting experience in Utah.

Boundaries for Rules and Regulations

Any combination of hunting regulations which does not drive the deer population toward extinction or toward excessive overpopulation is generally biologically acceptable. These are the outside boundaries for regulations. Simply stated, as a result of hunting neither the species nor the habitat is endangered. Annual overkill of deer herds in excess of the annual recruitment, including hunting and all other mortality factors and partly caused by excessive hunter pressure and liberal regulations, will gradually eliminate populations. However, no known populations of free-ranging mule deer have been extirpated through hunting. Nevertheless it is well-documented that many local populations of gray wolves, grizzly bears, river otters, beaver, pine marten, elk, and other species have been extirpated by unregulated or excessive harvest. Conversely, excessive overpopulations of mule deer, resulting from a reduction in the sum of the mortality factors, including hunting, have been periodically problematic on most of Utah's deer units.

To be successful from both the hunter and the manager perspective, hunter management must meet the harvest objectives as well as the post-season residual population expectations of the management plan. If both criteria are not met, the management plan or the harvest must be adjusted. Because of high reproductive rates and habitat adaptability by mule deer, management plans have wide flexibility, and deer populations can rapidly adjust to any changes. For example, in 1973 and 1974 deer populations in Utah were greatly reduced due to a combination of several factors, including over-harvest and weather. The resulting Utah buck harvest of 43,734 in 1975 was the lowest since 1946. However, following two years of normal recruitment, under buck-only hunting and with very limited antlerless permits, by 1977 most deer herds had recovered and the buck harvest returned to the pre-1973 level. Only two years were needed for Utah's buck harvest to fully recover from the lowest buck harvest recorded in almost three decades! Nonetheless a few deer herds in southern Utah recovered much more slowly, probably as a reaction to drought and other factors increasing fawn mortality.

Comparison between the Three Major Hunt Types

In Utah, rifle hunting seasons were first established in 1894 and re-established in 1914, archery hunting seasons were first authorized in 1942, and muzzleloader hunts in 1973. Both archery and muzzleloader hunts were established in response to hunters desiring a hunt using improved primitive weapons. Archers harvest deer in late August and early September, the muzzleloader hunt currently occurs in late September and early October, and the rifle hunt occurs in late October and begins on the Saturday closest to October 20. Requests for other separate deer hunting seasons, such as those limited to pistol, crossbow, live and kill trapping, use of dogs, deadfalls, blow-gun, poison baiting, spear-throwing, and voodoo have been denied by the Wildlife Board.

Generally primitive weapons require increased hunter skills and result in lower success rates. In Utah during the 1980s, archery hunters had a success rate for buck deer of about 11 percent, muzzleloaders about 22 percent and rifle hunters about 33 percent. Rifle hunters were about three times more likely to harvest a buck than archers, and muzzleloaders were about twice as successful as archers. In terms of harvest, only about four percent of bucks were harvested by archers, four percent by muzzleloaders, and most bucks, about 92 percent, were harvested by rifle hunters (Utah DWR 1951–2008).

Since the muzzleloader season was moved to the late September through early October season, and with the improvements in technical efficiencies in archery bows and muzzleloader firearms, those success ratios have significantly shifted. Between about 2000 and 2005 hunter success rates for the general season rifle hunt have average about 30 percent, for the muzzleloader hunt about 40 percent, and for the archery hunt approaching 20 percent. Although these success rates are variable, the success rates for archers and especially muzzleloader hunters have increased. The increase in success for muzzleloaders can be attributed to moving the muzzleloader season before the rifle hunt, thereby allowing muzzleloader hunters the opportunity to hunt before deer are significantly harassed by rifle hunters.

Because of the lower success rate with archery weapons, managers trying to reduce buck harvest often recommend regulations which encourage more hunters to use archery equipment. Conversely, an increased harvest would be obtained by encouraging the number of rifle or muzzleloader hunters.

In Utah before 1993, hunters could generally hunt during all three seasons with the same Utah deer license. The philosophy to maximize hunter opportunity had been in place since at least 1951. However, with undesirable hunter crowding and yearling bucks comprising the large majority of the harvest, the management philosophy changed to reduce some hunting opportunity and to provide a higher quality hunt. A major change in wildlife management policy began in 1993 when hunters were restricted to hunting during only one season.

Comparisons between Types of Rifle Hunts

Utah has had four basic rifle hunts since 1951, with each hunt type having a variable number of antlerless permits. Either-sex hunts dominated from 1951 to 1973 and buck-only hunts dominated from 1974 to 2008, as well as before 1951. From 1985 to 1990 hunts restricting the number of hunters (limited entry and high country) were adopted, and from 1984 to 1989 antler-restrictive hunts (three point and better) were established on some units. Limited-entry hunts have continued on some units through 2009.

Either-sex Hunts

During 23 years of either-sex hunting (1951–1973), the statewide total buck harvest averaged 66,992 and the antlerless harvest was 39,228. Using the estimated mean for unretrieved deer (eight deer per 100 hunters) and the mean number of rifle hunters afield (153,666) the yearly loss of unretrieved deer comes to 12,293, bringing the mean total annual hunting mortality to 118,513 (Austin et al. 1989; Stapley 1970). Hunter preference for buck-only versus either-sex hunting has never been addressed.

Antler-restrictive Hunts

Three-point-and-better antler restrictive hunts were available on some units between 1984 and 1989. In comparison with buck-only hunts, three-point-and-better hunts showed a reduction in hunters afield, buck harvest, and hunter success (Utah DWR 1951–2008; Utah DWR memo 1990). These hunts also showed a small increase in the post-season total buck-to-doe ratios but a large decrease in the number of post-season mature bucks counted. On these areas, they also showed a large decrease in the small buck (two point or less) to doe ratio between pre-season and post-season classification counts. Small bucks (two point or less) were killed illegally during the hunts.

Questionnaire surveys confirmed those negative results with the highest number of unretrieved deer, reported at 39.6 deer per 100 hunters. The 39.6 deer included 21.7 bucks (Austin and Jordan 1989; Austin et al. 1990, 1991, 1992). This number of bucks, mostly two point and less, can be compared to 4.6 unretrieved bucks per 100 hunters on buck-only areas. However, hunters on antler-restrictive areas were moderately satisfied with mean index of 4.8 on a 0-to-10-point scale, and mean hunting party success of 55.6 percent suggests that a large number of hunters per party participated on these hunts. During 1989, the last year of three-point-and-better hunts, 40 percent of Utah resident hunters had hunted at least once on a three point and better hunt, but only 27 percent of them preferred to continue this type of hunt. Indeed, less than half, 48 percent, of hunters who chose to hunt these units in 1989 preferred to continue them.

Even though antler-restrictive hunts were not successful over entire deer management units, on private lands and ranches selection of conscientious hunters to avoid high unretrieved deer losses may lead to successful antler-restrictive management. In such situations, management could adopt incentive or penalty options for hunters who may mistakenly shoot small bucks restricted by the private land management plan. Also because of phenotypic selectivity by hunters and potential negative effects on deer size, the best restriction may be to harvest three-point-and-better as well as spike bucks. If antler restriction hunts are adopted in the future or by private ranchers, I would recommend to occasionally hunt 2x2 point bucks to remove those old but genetically small bucks from the breeding population. Consequently, at least once every three to five years only 2x2 and smaller bucks should be hunted.

For a case in point, at the East Canyon Resort (10,000 acres) in northern Utah, where a restricting harvest of 2x2 point bucks with voluntary fines for mistakes was implemented, the mean number of total antler tines prior to restrictions (1985–1987) was 4.5 with more than 60 percent of the harvested bucks being 2x2 or smaller. In the three years (1988–1990) of restrictions, the mean number of total antler tines increased to 6.1 per buck, and only 35 percent of the harvest was 2x2 and smaller bucks. During the three years before restriction, none of the bucks checked were larger than 4x4, compared to eight large bucks checked under restrictions.

Hunter-number-restrictive Hunts

Limited-entry hunts have been in place on some units since 1985. In comparison with buck-only hunts, they provide higher hunter success and satisfaction, but no difference in percentage of unretrieved deer, averaging about 18 unretrieved deer per 100 hunters with about nine buck and nine antlerless deer. Hunting party success is much higher and usually exceeds 50 percent. By 1989, 23 percent of resident hunters had hunted deer on limited-entry areas, and most, 66 percent, agreed the increased fee was fair. While most hunters favored the same or increased number of limited-entry units, hunter preferences for various draw options for permits and landowner hunting opportunities are unclear. The largest problems associated with limited-entry hunts are the shifting of additional hunters to areas open to general hunting and the loss of hunting opportunity on limited-entry units due to a reduced number of hunters. Also, the loss of opportunity for landowners to hunt on the unit in which they own lands can be a negative factor if the landowners fail to draw permits.

A second type of hunter-number-restrictive hunt was the high-country hunt. This uncrowded, high-quality hunt, which harvested bucks that consequently were not then available during the October rifle hunt, surprisingly received positive support from most, 60 percent, of Utah hunters.

Buck-only Hunts

Between 1974 and 1990, total buck harvest in Utah averaged 63,250 per year with 8,633 antlerless harvest and 181,235 hunters afield. The number of unretrieved deer reported per 100 buck-only hunters in four check station surveys ranged from 15.9 to 21.7 with a weighted mean of 17.9 unretrieved deer per 100 buck hunters. Total unretrieved deer for this period was 32,441 deer per year and mean total annual hunting mortality was 104,324 per year. Mean hunter satisfaction (1987–1990) with zero representing the worst hunt and the 10 the best hunt was 4.4. Hunting party success was 45.8 percent.

Subsequent to 1990, generally hunter harvest and satisfaction have declined. Harvest has declined to less than 40,000 bucks, hunter license sales have been limited, previously open private lands are mostly closed to the public hunter, and special interests have often prevailed over common interests. However, CWMUs have offered limited but high quality public hunting on private lands. The trend of buck-only hunting since 1991 has been toward establishing increased hunter restrictions.

Too Many Hunters, Too Few Bucks

Complaints by hunters before the mid 1960s were few because deer numbers were high, deer hunter numbers were relatively low, and deer hunting was very good with hunting success percentages often exceeding 50 percent. Most hunters who hunted diligently bagged a deer, and if a buck could not be harvested, a doe filled the freezer just as well.

However, since the change from either-sex to buck-only hunting in the early 1970s along with the rapid increase in the number of hunters beginning in the late 1960s, and newer restrictions in the 1990s, the number of complaints from Utah deer hunters increased (Krannich and Cundy 1989). Two issues of complaints are always in the forefront: overcrowding of hunters during the rifle hunt and especially on opening weekend, and excessive hunting pressure on bucks. This is simply stated as too many hunters and too few bucks. The third complaint is usually too few big bucks. The fourth complaint, which is increasing in frequency and will likely move to third in importance, is problems associated with private lands. The fifth most common complaint was the hunters' becoming too old or physically impaired. Sixty-six additional factors were listed by one study (Austin et al. 1992). However, the four major complaints as listed above, over which management regulations have significant input and control, have continued to dominate even though Utah has limited the total license sales to 95,000.

Finding solutions to these two major problems—too many hunters and too few bucks—such that hunter satisfaction is increased and deer populations are maintained at carrying capacity, while revenues for wildlife agencies are maintained, continues to be the key issue facing Utah deer management into the twenty-first century.

Hunter Preferences

Hunter preferences for deer management changes are often difficult to define, and the results usually vary by the hunters sampled, the time period of sampling, as well as the manner and exact wording in which the questions are written. Consequently, when results agree between independent surveys, much more confidence can be placed upon the results.

> *Note:* When hunters or wildlife biologists gather in discussion groups, I have observed on numerous occasions that the outcome and resolve usually follows the opinion of the most forceful individual. Despite large differences of opinion at the beginning of the meeting, by the end everyone seems to agree. However, I have also observed the same groups of hunters and biologists meeting again, perhaps a year later, beginning again with diverse opinions about the identical topic, and coming to a totally different conclusion from the first meeting!

Deer hunting as a sport is very important to Utah hunters, and almost all hunters anticipate hunting yearly. Surveys consistently agree that the most important aspect to deer hunting is annual participation. Hunting deer on alternate years or most years, as has been suggested on numerous occasions, is not acceptable to a high majority of hunters. Only those hunters with marginal interest seem to agree with the concept. However, in controversy, the majority of hunters believe deer hunting pressure and opportunity should be reduced to increase the quality of the hunts. The question invariably becomes, what hunter opportunities should be sacrificed for increased quality, and which hunters are going to make those sacrifices? Each hunter generally feels entitled to higher quality hunts, but doesn't want to be the one to change. Such is the manager's dilemma.

The decline of mule deer numbers is a long-term trend that began at least as early as 1970, and deer herd numbers will continue to decline for many decades due to habitat changes, human encroachment, competitors, exotic species of forage, and numerous other factors. One experienced biologist apparently suggested that within the next 100 years or by about the year 2100, mule deer may become so scarce as to preclude any hunting. Hunters clearly desire management to make every effort to limit this decline. These efforts will surely include habitat management, but must also include controlling predators, wildlife competitors, and human encroachment and harassment.

Options for improving quality of the hunt have received mixed responses. Changes in the length of the rifle season or splitting the hunt into two or more hunts are not favored by most Utah hunters, with numerous hunters indicating they may quit hunting because of too short a season length. Most hunters preferred to keep the hunts as currently managed. Years ago most hunters were generally satisfied with the 11-day October rifle hunt, and many hunters were displeased when the season was shortened to nine days in 1993.

The proportion of mature bucks, defined as bucks three-and-a-half years and older, is a major concern by hunters. Almost 10 percent of hunters indicated that they may quit hunting in Utah specifically because of too few big bucks in the harvest, especially on public lands. Surprisingly, a majority of Utah hunters would even prefer to harvest a mature buck less frequently as opposed to harvesting a smaller buck more frequently (Austin et al. 1992).

The decline in the proportion of mature bucks in the harvest is an accurate perception by hunters. Before 1950 the proportion of mature bucks in the harvest was about 50 percent. During the years of either-sex hunting, 1951 to 1973, mature bucks comprised about 25 percent of the buck harvest. Beginning with the buck-only hunting era, 1974 to 2000, the proportions of mature bucks was only about 10 percent. Since 2000 with increased hunter sales restrictions, the establishment of Cooperative Wildlife Management Units, the goal of 15 bucks to 100 does post-season with five of them being mature bucks, that proportion has increased considerably. For example, from the Blacksmith Fork checking station on the Cache unit, 59 percent of the bucks were mature in 1946; that percentage dropped to 25 percent between 1962 and 1966, and greatly decreased to six percent in 1986–1988, but has risen to about 33 percent since 1996.

Hunters generally supported high-country hunts, and continue to support limited-entry hunts. However, most hunters rejected three-point-and-better-hunts. Although they were attempted on several management units, they were only successful in limited areas. The Wellsville Mountains on the Cache unit and the LaSal Mountains were marginally successful as observed by myself and the area conservation officers, and some private lands, such as the East Canyon Resort with 10,000 acres, were also marginally successful. These hunts mostly failed because too many bucks having two points or less were harvested or killed by hunters. One unpublished field survey estimated that for every legal buck harvested on these units at least one illegal buck was harvested and usually left in the field.

One effective way to reduce hunter crowding was to require hunters to choose and hunt only one season. This rule was adopted in Utah in 1994 and has been reasonably successful. However, shortly after its passage, dissatisfied hunters petitioned the state to allow a special interest group of hunters, willing to dedicate time or money to the state, to hunt all three hunts. The Board approved the application for the Dedicated Hunter Program. This program has been enthusiastically supported.

Hunter access to at least some private lands has shrunk since 1993. Access to some public lands surrounded or partially blocked by private lands has similarly become unavailable. However, with the advent of the CWMU program, some private ranches, formerly unavailable to public hunting, now maintain limited-by-permit public access. Although access to private lands is difficult to obtain at any level of private or governmental effort, hunters have repeatedly stated that access to all public lands for hunting is a high priority.

In summary, hunters prefer management options that would reduce hunter crowding, increase buck harvest success, improve the proportion of available mature bucks, open private lands, and insure access to all public lands to hunting. Practical options hunters clearly prefer include limiting license sales, choosing only one season to hunt, and perhaps choosing to harvest only one animal yearly. Hunters generally agree on current license fees, but may be willing to pay additional costs for improved quality.

Future Hunter Management

As hunting and hunters evolve, management philosophy must also change. All management scenarios evaluate existing data as the major sources of information for planning strategies. Because hunter numbers greatly exceed the total harvest by a ratio of at least three to one, hunter numbers are always more than adequate to accomplish the need to maintain populations within carrying capacity, via buck and antlerless harvest, and to meet management objectives. Surprisingly, annually about five percent of hunters who buy licenses do not hunt during that year. Heavy hunter selectivity of larger bucks within age classes after several years can lead to smaller bucks in carcass weight and decreased number of antler points (Austin et al. 1989). Similar to most other biological systems where selectivity occurs, future management must not only work to insure adequate numbers of deer, but also must maintain genetically healthy deer herds.

Unquestionably, the most difficult decisions in deer management involve how to manage hunters. The future management of Utah's deer hunters will be determined at several levels of influence. The first determining factors are the political issues as established by the state legislature, especially with respect to license fee revenues, flexibility in available management options for the Division of Wildlife Resources, and private land issues. The second level deals with cooperation between the Division of Wildlife Resources and private landowners, Utah trust land managers, and federal land managers in sharing and utilizing the benefits of our natural resources among several interests, including wildlife, livestock, recreation, and watershed uses. The third level deals with legal conflicts with private organizations, the one side working for increased hunting opportunities and on the opposite side proponents for almost total wildlife protection and anti-hunting. Because few biological arguments to perpetuate a species can be made for hunter harvest of game animals other than deer and elk, anti-hunting factions may have increasing influence into the future. Finally the preferences of responsible hunters will have influence, but this seems to be gradually decreasing due to the shrinking proportion of hunters in Utah's population, and especially since the argument for 'feeding a family' currently bears almost no weight.

Chapter 10

Hunter Ethics

Hunting opportunities for future generations depend upon the development of strong ethics by today's hunters.

Basic Hunter Ethics

Hunter ethics is the set of written and unwritten rules of hunting behavior based upon respect for the land and water resources, all wildlife species, and other hunters. It is likely that the number and types of big game hunters, as well as the number of available upland game, waterfowl, and furbearer species available to hunters, by the middle of the twenty-first century will largely depend upon the quality of ethics developed and practiced by hunters in the early part of this century. The various numerous, and often wealthy organizations which mildly or vehemently oppose hunting as a sport are a serious threat to hunting. They will certainly utilize observed poor hunter ethics as arguments and weapons against hunting.

The ethical deer hunter of the early twenty-first century must exhibit and teach the next generation not only the joy and lure of hunting, but even more importantly the highest hunting ethics. High ethics must be continuously practiced not only on hunting trips, but during each outdoor activity, including camping, fishing, birding, sightseeing and other trips.

Many of the basic concepts of deer hunting ethics are listed below. The list is not complete, as each hunting situation is unique and requires adapting individualized ethics. However, these concepts may serve as guidelines. Although few hunters have observed the highest level of hunter ethics during all hunting trips, and most hunters have broken at least a few of these concepts, all hunters should adopt a higher standard of personal ethical behavior rules.

Photo illustration by Dan Miller

A poacher is caught in his headlights. Over the decades, the objective
of the poacher has changed from obtaining venison to
acquiring trophy antlers.

Common concepts of ethical deer hunting:

(1) Never litter, including empty casings.
(2) Report all hunting violations to the local law enforcement
     authority.
(3) Always respect private property.
(4) Always obey all hunting rules and regulations.
(5) Always be able to visually identify the game animal(s) being
     hunted.
(6) Never be under the influence of alcohol while hunting.
(7) Never destroy habitats by driving a vehicle in closed areas.
     Drive only on designated roads.
(8) Never carry a loaded firearm in any motorized vehicle.
(9) Always check for a wounded animal every time a gun is fired,
     even if a miss was a certainty.
(10) Always clean the carcass immediately after the kill.
(11) Never waste nor allow venison to spoil.
(12) Never leave a carcass in the field, even if you accidentally killed
     an illegal deer.

(13) Always instruct new and young hunters in proper hunter ethics.

(14) Never aim a gun at anything you do not intend to shoot.

(15) Never use a rifle scope in place of binoculars.

(16) Always assist other hunters who need help.

(17) Never allow companions to hunt illegally.

(18) Always condemn unethical behavior.

(19) Practice with your weapon before hunting, know your skill level, and make "clean" kills.

(20) Never take a shot in which you are not absolutely positive about safety or the target.

(21) Always respect other hunters.

(22) Never criticize the valiant efforts of law enforcement.

(23) Never "party" hunt.

(24) Never harvest more game than you can or will consume.

(25) Diligently work to never leave a wounded animal in the field.

(26) Never hunt just to kill.

(27) Never hunt on a bet or a dare.

(28) Always hunt safely.

(29) Always hunt within your physical capabilities.

(30) Know what to do in case of an emergency.

(31) Always hunt in the style of "Be Prepared."

(32) Be knowledgeable and well-read about mule deer biology and management.

Not all acts of poor hunter ethics directly affect the biological management of mule deer. Littering, for example, has no effect on deer numbers. However, whenever deer are wasted or illegally taken, or habitat is negatively impacted, population dynamics and management options are decreased.

Three Frequent Ethical Problems

Party Hunting

Deer are often observed in groups throughout the year, and "bachelor" buck groups with or without one or more does are not uncommon, especially at the beginning of the rifle hunt. Consequently, hunters spotting deer often find two or more bucks together. Party hunting results when one hunter illegally harvests two or more deer which are then tagged by another hunter or hunters in the party. Party hunting results in a lowering of success rate for the ethical hunter and hunting parties, and often leads to a few hunting parties having all the 'luck'. Party hunting is commonly observed by a male hunter placing the tag of his spouse or mother on the deer. Both the hunter and the owner of the tag are subject to a wildlife citation.

Illegal Kill and Wounding Loss

Occasionally, a hunter may mistakenly kill two deer. Examples are killing two deer standing side by side with one bullet, or shooting at a second deer in a group after the first was, unknowingly, mortally wounded. In such cases, the second deer should be cleaned, but not transported, and then immediately reported to the local conservation officer.

Far too many deer are killed, wasted, and left in the field. On the average, a hunter will find one or more deer shot and left by the end of the rifle hunt every five or six years under buck-only hunting. Although wounding loss may be decreasing, about 18 percent of rifle hunters find a wasted deer yearly (Austin and Jordan 1989; Austin et al. 1992; Stapley 1970). Solutions are ethically simple: if a hunter kills an antlerless deer on a buck-only tag, the deer should be cleaned, and the hunter should immediately report the violation. Every time a hunter shoots at a deer, even a probable miss, the area should be carefully checked for a blood trail. On buck-only hunting units, illegal kills usually involve antlerless deer, and wounding losses consist mostly of unretrieved bucks.

Poaching

The purposeful, illegal, out-of-season, harvest of big game is significant, but fortunately decreasing in frequency. Poaching simply decreases success for ethical hunters. Furthermore, since poachers often select only the largest antlered bucks, trophy bucks become more limited to ethical hunters.

Hunters must report poachers. In Utah, day or night, call 1-800-538-DEER. Other states have similar hot lines. Significantly more poaching cases are processed by tips from ethical hunters and other concerned citizens than are directly observed by conservation officers in the field.

The number of deer poached yearly in Utah is not known. Most poaching activity takes place at night with a spotlight and is rarely reported. For example, I conducted research studies into depredation by spotlighting and counting deer using alfalfa and wheat fields. In over 100 nights of observations, only on one occasion was the activity questioned or reported to authorities.

Estimations of combined losses from party hunting, illegal kill and wounding loss, and poaching range from 2 percent to over 50 percent of the annual legal buck harvest. As a rough mean estimate, in my opinion, 10,000 deer, but possibly as few as 5,000 or as many as 20,000 deer, may be annually lost to these unethical and unlawful activities in Utah.

Chapter 11

Successful Mule Deer Hunting

Be Prepared.

Boy Scouts Motto

Since only about one in three hunters, or fewer, are successful in harvesting a deer in Utah in any year, it seems reasonable that hunters who really desire to be successful would place considerably more effort into preparation. Most hunters anticipate the annual Utah deer hunt with the hope of success, but far too often, hunters return home with feelings of too many hunters and too few deer. Although being prepared is no guarantee of harvest success, it is a guarantee to a more enjoyable hunt and likely will increase the chances of success.

It is interesting to note that about 20 percent of Utah deer hunters really have minimal desire to harvest a deer. From my observations, these hunters use the deer hunt more as an opportunity to get out into the woods and share social time with family and friends than to harvest a deer. Hunting is only of secondary importance to these hunters.

Note: My early pre-teen and teen experiences with deer hunting began the night before the beginning of the hunt when my uncles would furiously try to pull all their gear together in an hour for the three day camping-hunting trip. Their only preparation prior to the evening before was to decide what time to leave and where to go, and to let my aunts know that "deer hunters' widow for the weekend" shopping was okay.

Invariably, some important item was always forgotten. One year an uncle had brought a new 270 Remington rifle but had remembered to bring only three shells, leaving the unopened boxes in the family car. On another trip one uncle forgot a sleeping bag and had to borrow my extra bag, which my dad had insisted I bring due to the extra cold weather. My family never practiced aiming and shooting, and I fondly remember sitting on a hillside in the Strawberry Reservoir area watching as my uncle and four friends, with almost uncontrolled excitement, emptied their iron-sight lever-action 30-30 rifles of about 25 total rounds at a group of standing bucks less than 100 yards away, and while the hunters frantically reloaded, the unscathed and, to me, smirking deer, slowly walked into the timber.

One year I was "brushing" deer up a draw to the ridge line and the awaiting family hunters. Several times I had noticed a deer just staying out of my clear visual sight and slowly moving in front of me up the draw. Upon reaching the last stand of conifers, the doe saw the hunters on the ridge and me below, panicked, bolted down the slope, crash-slammed into a downed log, and, as I watched between the trees, somersault-flipped in the air and landed on her back with a broken neck. It is the only deer story I have ever heard where a deer was harvested without a shot being fired.

To my extended family, any deer—buck, doe, or fawn—was a good deer, antlers were essentially worthless, a single deer harvested by the party meant a successful hunt, all deer tasted the same, and we always shared the venison.

Factors of Success

Two factors which would appear to be, but are not, highly important in determining hunting success are the hunter's age and the number of years of hunting experience (Austin et al. 1992). When these two factors were compared with buck hunter success during the rifle hunt they were only weakly correlated. In only two of four years was the number of years of hunting experience significantly related to buck hunting success, and in only a single year was age significant. Consequently, much of the success in harvesting a buck depends upon plain "hunter luck" and other factors. However, it is likely these two factors would show a higher relationship for archery and muzzleloader hunters, due to the generally higher levels of hunter dedication and necessary skills.

The majority of bucks that are harvested during the rifle hunt are harvested on opening weekend (Utah DWR 1951–2008). Long-term averages indicate about 40 percent, 15 percent, and 10 percent of the harvested bucks are taken on Saturday, Sunday, and Monday, respectively. About 10 percent are harvested the second Saturday. Harvest on all other days is about 5 percent or less. Because opening weekend pressure is high and deer are moved in and out of cover by hunter presence and especially the bangs from rifle shots, it seems reasonable that hunter location being in the right place at the right time may often prove to be a more important factor than past experience combined with hunting skill. Almost every hunter has a story of how a deer just happened to walk out of the cover when the hunter just stopped momentarily, or how the hunter jumped a nice buck, could not get a shot, and the buck ran straight into the guns of another party who were simply visiting, often by their vehicles. Nonetheless, the well-prepared hunter increases the chance of a satisfying experience and perhaps for harvest success, particularly following the opening weekend.

Most hunters believe the patriarch buck is also the smartest buck, and research supports this claim (Maguire and Severinghaus 1954). If all bucks, regardless of age, had the same degree of hunter wariness, there would be no change in the proportion of younger to older bucks in the harvest as the hunt progressed. However, if older deer are indeed more intelligent, a lower proportion of older bucks would be taken at the start of the hunt, and the proportion of older bucks in the harvest would gradually increase as the younger deer "wised-up." The latter is the case. For example, on opening day in 1977 from the Current Creek deer unit, 81 percent of the bucks harvested were yearlings. On the second day 73 percent were yearlings and by the third day 69 percent were yearlings. It has generally been observed that after the second or perhaps third day of the rifle hunt, the differences in wariness between older and younger deer become minor and wariness is about equal.

Nonetheless, hunters should not wait several days before hunting that big buck because most bucks, even most big bucks, are harvested during the opening three days. Another factor to consider is that daily hunter success decreases from about 10 to 20 percent on the opening three days, with opening day being the highest daily hunter success, to less than 10 percent during the rest of the hunt.

Hunt Preparation

Physical Fitness

Most of us vividly remember hiking to the mountain peaks with little effort just a few years ago, followed by the memory of the struggling effort involved in climbing the smallest hill during last year's hunt. With most hunters employed in sedentary jobs, few are physically ready for marching up a mountain with a five-pound gun, ten pounds of hunting gear, two apples, four candy bars, water canteen, and too many pounds of excess body fat. Too many current hunters rely almost solely on ATVs and four-wheel drive trucks to do all the work. However, for the hunter who is in good shape, the hunt becomes many times more enjoyable, regardless of available transportation or success.

Getting in reasonable shape does not take a lot of time and really not much work. Your spouse will be delighted, you may prevent a heart attack, and you will just plain feel better. However, shaping up does take several weeks of consistent effort (Krantz 1992). Labor Day in early September may have a double meaning for the rifle hunter and is a great time to begin exercise training. Archers should consider July 1. Remember, a check-up with a doctor is a prerequisite necessity.

Daily, or almost daily, walking, increasing to fast walking, and then to a slow jog, is the cornerstone to slowly and properly improving fitness. Fast walking means walking a mile in about 15 minutes or a pace of 4 mph. A daily fast walk for 15 to preferably 30 minutes, after two to three weeks of effort, greatly improves muscle tone and the cardiovascular system. Additional strenuous exercise through activities such as jogging, swimming, cycling, tennis, hiking, even heavy yard or housework will help to improve fitness even faster. However, with increased physical activity, the risk of injury such as tendinitis, lower back problems, swelling in the joints, and pulled muscles is greatly increased, especially if the conditioning is not approached gradually.

> *Note:* Many years ago I set a personal goal of getting into shape every year for at least a short period of time. For me, year-round training simply led to too many injuries. My goal was to be able to run at an eight-minute-per-mile pace for at least 24 minutes or for three miles, and for two months of the year. Although my goals have changed and decreased in the last few years, this was

a reasonable goal for me that I maintained for almost 30 years, past 55 years of age. I suggest every hunter set a similar personal yearly goal.

It has often been said that exercise is king and nutrition is queen. A well-balanced diet is the second factor in obtaining and maintaining good physical condition. Every hunter should establish good dietary habits and weight limit goals and stick to them.

Firearm and Bow Preparation

Practice with a well cared-for weapon. Too many hunters fail to practice shooting before the hunt, and many more do not practice enough. Almost all hunters have personal stories like, "It was an easy shot, but I just missed."

I recommend archers spend five to eight sessions in practice before the hunt and firearm hunters two to three. Sessions do not need to be long. Importantly, by the end of the sessions, the hunters should feel very confident in being able to hit a target. As a general guideline, a hunter should be able to hit an eight inch circular pie plate in the field at 25 yards with two out of three shots using a rifle or muzzleloader, whereas archers and pistol shooters should be able to hit the pie plate at 15 yards.

When rifles are sighted in at 25 yards, which is the common distance, the bullet is centered at both 25 and about 200 yards, depending upon the ballistics of the gun and ammunition. At about 100 yards the bullet will be about one to four inches high. Because of the variability in muzzleloaders, they should be sighted in at the distance the hunter anticipates to shoot, usually between 50 and 100 yards. After a hunter becomes confident with the accuracy of the weapon at these short yardages, I recommend setting the pie-plate targets at 100 or more yards for rifles and 75 yards for muzzleloaders and practicing until the plate can be hit with two out of three shots. Archers should practice at distances ranging from about 10 to 40 yards.

With my 30-06 iron-sight rifle, I often have checked the rifle's accuracy and my ability by setting out three aluminum cans at 100 to 120 yards. Hitting two of three cans at that distance in sitting position or with a solid rest assures the hunter of a high level of shooting accuracy.

Although scopes on rifles allow the hunter to more easily see the target, scopes do not make holding the rifle steady easier. Also sometimes hunters fail to get off a shot because of not being able to find the animal in the scope. Another problem with using scopes is the potential of the scope being bumped or jarred out of the true alignment without the hunter knowing. Nonetheless, scopes are a very valuable addition to effective hunting, and most deer hunters currently use scopes on their rifles. Indeed, the rifle without a scope is rapidly becoming a rarity. However, scopes are certainly not necessary to be successful as evidenced that very few hunters used scopes in the early 1960s or before.

Another important element of hunter preparation is a clean and cared-for gun. Cleaning a firearm requires a cloth, ramrod, solvent, oil, and about 15 minutes. When hunters fail to clean their guns, their value is reduced and often the guns become unusable and must be discarded. A well cared-for firearm, even if used very often, will easily last a lifetime.

Basic Deer Hunter's List

The items a hunter can carry by personal choice are many, but only a few, mostly lightweight items, are necessary:

Clothing: Always carry enough clothing to keep warm in consideration of the current temperature and weather conditions. Appropriate for the weather, well-conditioned, and comfortable boots are extremely important. An extra pair of stockings, which can double as mittens, is a good idea. A clean handkerchief, which has many practical and first aid uses, should always be included. When weather conditions are cold and snowy, it is also a good idea to carry a pocket size emergency blanket. Hunter orange outer clothing that covers the head, back, and chest is required by law.

Compass and area map: Every year hunters get lost. Regardless of a hunter's experience in an area or outdoor expertise, getting lost or disoriented, particularly during heavy fog or blizzard weather conditions, is always possible. Using a compass and map is easy to learn and a skill that every hunter should acquire. The readily available Boy Scout Handbook is an excellent source for learning. GPS units, which require batteries, are rapidly replacing the compass and map.

Water: Carrying a quart of water, not soda pop, in a canteen or water bottle may seem like a lot of extra weight, but even on very cold days, body liquids are lost and need to be replaced. Physical efficiency decreases rapidly with body dehydration. Eating snow will help. Also, when snow is available, start out with a canteen full of hot water and replace the water in the canteen as it is consumed with snow. The warm water will melt enough snow to stretch the canteen water to about one-and-a-half quarts.

Matches: Always carry strike-anywhere matches in two different containers, such as a plastic bag or match case. Butane lighters or other fire-starting materials may substitute for one container of the matches.

Knife: A sharp pocket knife or dagger with a straight blade three inches or longer is a necessity.

Rope and String: Most hunters should plan on using a nylon rope, about eight feet in length, for dragging the carcass to the road or in some cases hanging the carcass from a tree overnight, and a string, about two feet in length, to attach the tag.

License and Shells: Beware as these are the most commonly forgotten important items. Double check for the license. How many shells should a hunter carry while hunting? In an unpublished survey of Utah hunters, I determined less than one percent of hunters ever shot more than 20 rounds during the hunting day at deer, and almost all hunters who were successful in harvesting a deer used five or fewer shells. I suggest hunters carry 20 shells or one box plus a few bullets in the magazine, not chamber, of the rifle. Only a few hunters will use the shells from the box. For hunters using more than one caliber of rifle, make certain the bullets match the rifle.

Food: If a good breakfast is eaten, very little if any food is needed. However, most hunters enjoy eating a couple of chocolate candy bars and an apple during the day.

Reading the Regulations

Understanding the proclamation and especially any special regulations associated with one's particular hunting unit is not only a preventive measure to avoid making an inadvertent violation, but it will also raise the hunter's level of confidence and add to the overall hunting experience.

Most wildlife citations issued to deer hunters are a result of negligence. Hunters rarely purposefully violate regulations. In Utah, 5,000 to 6,000 wildlife citations are issued per year for all violations. About one-fourth are related to deer hunting activities. Less than one percent of Utah deer hunters receive a citation in any year, and most hunters never receive a wildlife citation of any kind over a lifetime. The most common violations associated with deer hunting are failure to properly tag, failure to wear hunter orange, hunting without a license, loaded firearm in a vehicle, shooting from a vehicle or road, and trespassing.

Hunter Safety

Deer hunting in Utah is a very safe sport with few accidents. Since the beginning of the hunter education program in 1958 and the required wearing of hunter orange in 1973, the mean number of total Utah accidents and fatalities related to all kinds of hunting per year has averaged about 11 and 3, respectively, with about three of those accidents and one fatality associated with deer hunting. In recent years these figures have continued to decrease. Before 1958 when neither hunter education nor hunter orange was required, over 100 accidents and about 20 fatalities occurred yearly from all hunts combined. Compared with many other outdoor recreation activities, such as downhill skiing, hunting has become a relatively safe sport.

General Hunting Techniques

Using Binoculars

Probably the number one change the majority of hunters could easily make to become more successful would be to carry and use a good pair of binoculars. The use of a pair of average 6x30 to 10x50 binoculars will greatly aid in finding deer. Every ten or twenty minutes and especially every time a new draw or landscape is approached, the area within view should be searched carefully. It is really amazing how many additional deer and other wildlife can be found when using binoculars.

One technique, uncommonly used, is for the hunter to climb to the top of a ridge or other high point and search the area carefully for 15 to 20 minutes or until a deer is located. The area searched should extend for a mile or more in one to several directions. The hunter then determines the best, hidden approach to the deer where the hunter may expect to obtain a good shot.

Too often hunters use the scopes on their rifles as binoculars. Most scopes have a very limited field of vision, and it is very frightening as well as maddening to see a fellow hunter on a distant ridge with his scope on you. Scopes should only be used when the firearm is to be fired!

Hunting Time

On the morning and evenings of the four primary and most successful hunting days during the rifle hunt, the first three days and the second

Saturday, hunters intent on bagging a buck should be in the field. Since deer are crepuscular, most active in the early morning and late afternoon-evening hours, hunters should be hunting during these times. The most successful hunters will be in the field at the chosen hunting location at first light, and will return to camp only later in the evening, often using a flashlight. A small flashlight and fresh batteries are basic items.

Besides hunting the primary four days, all other days when the hunter can plan to hunt will increase the chance for success. Many bucks are harvested near the hunter's home town when the hunter leaves work early, about 2:00 to 3:00 pm during mid-week, and returns home after dark. Sunday afternoons often have most hunters returning home and usually offer a more relaxed and uncrowded hunting opportunity.

Daily Planning

Each day's hunting scheme will be more successful if thought out in advance of the hunt. It is always a good idea to decide which area or draw will be hunted if you are familiar with the larger area. Much time is wasted in trying to decide when to stop the car or ATV and begin hunting. A good rule is to plan hunts in locations where deer were harvested or at least observed on previous hunts. If hunting an unfamiliar area, spend at least part of a day driving and scouting before the season to decide upon a promising area with good habitat. Each hunting party needs be willing to adjust the next day's hunting plan based on the experiences of the day.

Always decide on the size of the buck you are willing to harvest before stepping into the field. Far too often hunters shoot a small buck and are disappointed with the size. Hunters sometimes ignore, waste, and leave the small buck in the field. Occasionally a hunter will harvest, clean a small buck, hang it in a tree, and then hunt for a larger buck. This practice of "high-grading" is not only especially illegal, but disturbingly unethical. If a hunter really does not want to harvest a small buck, especially at the beginning of a hunt, the gun or bow should not even be removed from the resting position anymore than if a doe or fawn was sighted.

Habitat Selection

Hunt only where deer are found. Very often hunters spend considerable time in empty habitat. If few or no fresh tracks or pellet groups are observed in the area, simply hunt elsewhere.

On the mornings and evenings of the four primary harvest days during the rifle hunt, look for deer on the edges of openings near adequate cover. After the opening weekend, deer spend most of their time in heavier cover but usually within their home ranges. Habitats preferred by deer after having been pursued by hunters on opening weekend include mixed stands of conifer and aspen, mixed stands of conifer and mountain browse species such as Gambel oak or maple, and areas of mixed, patchy habitat such as clumps of aspen, Douglas fir, mountain mahogany or Gambel oak. Few deer are found in open habitats without visually protective cover. These habitats include low-growing big sagebrush and mountain meadows. Intermediate habitats include large expanses of aspen, conifer or Gambel oak and riparian areas.

Hunters should not spend the majority of time hunting canyon bottoms and ridge tops, except on the mornings and evenings of the four primary harvest days. Outside of these times, hunters should spend most of their time hunting at mid elevations between the canyon bottoms and ridge tops, because that is where the majority of deer will be hiding.

Using Intuition

Few hunters with considerable experience have not had the feeling of being watched by game animals, or the feeling that game animals are very close. Hunt quietly. Our sixth senses sometimes detect animals before our regular senses can verify. Never hesitate to look back over the shoulder or retrace a few steps when a "feeling" comes. Never hesitate to stop for a few minutes and listen to an unknown soft sound. Also the common sound of the bounding gait of running mule deer is unmistakable. This form of running, called stotting, where all four legs leave the ground simultaneously, is a very unusual form of running and adapted to mountainous terrain to escape from cougar predation.

Carcass Care

Shot Placement

Only after the shooting ends and the carcass is examined does the realization of the importance of good shot placement become apparent. Deer which have been shot through a major part of the hind quarters with even one bullet will have a significant portion of the meat destroyed. As much as seven to eight pounds of meat can be damaged with each shot.

Only expert shooters should aim for the head because the target is only about four inches in diameter and is usually moving. Neck shots are equally difficult. However, head and neck shots provide the cleanest carcass for butchering. The best place to aim is in the middle of the body cavity just behind the front shoulder. Any shot in that area is fatal and provides a quick death as the bullet must pass through the heart, lungs, or, if the shot is high, the backbone. Shots placed in the body cavity but nearer the hind quarters will likely pass through the rumen. Most "gut shot" deer will die, but they may travel several miles before lying down. Never shoot at a deer moving directly away from the hunter because the chances of hitting the deer in the rump, and thereby destroying a good portion of the meat, are very high. Furthermore, the wounded deer will often continue to run for a considerable distance and the chances of the deer being lost become very high.

Whenever a conscientious hunter shoots at a deer, even if the hunter was almost positive or even certain of a miss, the vicinity where the deer was standing when the shot was fired should always be carefully searched for blood, even though this may involve significant hiking effort. Many deer carcasses are wasted because hunters failed to check. Often deer shot through the lungs will not appear wounded and may run over 100 yards or further into nearby cover before dropping and dying.

Checking the Kill

After having shot a deer, which is observed lying on the ground, approach cautiously. Wounded deer, especially bucks, have injured many hunters. If the deer is observed to be alive, carefully fire a shot into the head, or if the hunter has a personal preference for saving the buck's head, into the neck at the base of the head. If the animal is not moving and to make certain the deer is dead, reach out and tap the head with a stick, or, with the rifle action on safety, tap the head with the barrel. Just to be safe, and regardless of whether the deer appears alive or dead, many hunters shoot the deer in the head or neck before approaching.

Validate the Tag

Before cleaning the carcass, be sure to detach and validate the tag. If the hunter waits to validate the tag until after cleaning, the tag will be more difficult to cut with the then duller blade. In Utah the tag should be "immediately and securely attached to the carcass." However, the validated tag may be carried in the pocket to avoid being lost while the deer is being dragged to a road or vehicle. However, as soon as the road or vehicle is reached, immediately secure the tag to the carcass.

Cleaning the Carcass

Cleaning the carcass should usually take less than 15 minutes, and must be completed as soon as possible to insure the highest venison quality. The following steps are suggested:

(1)   Cut the throat at a few inches under the jaw, deeply, and through the windpipe. Allow a few minutes for the carcass to bleed out.

(2)   Using the rope, tie the head to a tree or bush. Position the deer with the head uphill. If possible tie each back leg, spread apart, to trees, bushes, or boulders. When hunting in a group, a companion can hold the legs.

(3)   If a buck, tie off the end of the penis with a few inches of string to prevent urine from getting on the hunter and the deer.

(4)   At the anus, cut completely around the large intestine until it is loose from the hide, and also loose for a few inches inside the anus cavity. The end of the large intestine at the anus must be cut completely free from hide and other tissues.

(5)   With the deer on its back, cut the hide along the middle of the body cavity from the pelvis to the rib cage. Cutting should start in about in the middle of the belly with an incision and cut in both directions. Avoid cutting into the intestines or rumen.

(6)   On the inside of the body cavity, cut the lung-protecting membrane away from the rib cage.

(7)   With the deer on its side, reach inside the body cavity under the rib cage and firmly grasp with both hands the windpipe and esophagus. A strong, steady pull will severe the few remaining connected tissues in the upper chest and neck. Finally, firmly grasp the large intestine inside the pelvic girdle and pull, again severing the few remaining connected tissues in the girdle. The viscera will be pulled out in one piece. Sometimes the large intestine is not easily removed, and an extra strong pull or even a little more cutting around the anus may be necessary.

(8)   Clean out any excess blood or other materials from the body cavity.

(9)   If the deer is to be dragged more than a quarter of a mile, the four legs should be cut off at the knee joint. This will make the job of dragging just a little easier.

(10)   If the heart and liver are undamaged, they should be cut from the viscera, cleaned, and placed in a heavy duty plastic bag.

(11)   Clean the blood and hair from the knife and hands, using snow, if available, or a few swallows of canteen water.

Skinning the Deer

As soon as the deer is hung in camp or when the deer is hung in the garage or back yard, whichever is first, the hide should be removed immediately. Leaving the hide on the deer, even overnight, is the most common way of decreasing the value and palatability of the meat. The hide will rapidly increase the undesirable gamey flavor of the venison.

Judging the Size of a Buck

Very few hunters will ever harvest a deer that will make the Boone and Crocket record book (Warren 1988). Less than 100 Utah bucks have been entered into the record. Only about one out of every 56,000 bucks harvested in Utah are large enough. This means that less than one buck harvested in Utah each year will make the record book. The highest scoring typical buck, bucks having 4x4 antler tines, ever taken in Utah had a Boone and Crocket score of 202⅛, and was harvested in San Juan County in 1973. The highest scoring atypical buck taken in Utah was the second largest buck in the record book with a score of 330⅛ points. This buck was shot on the Wellsville Mountains in 1943.

A good lifetime goal for most hunters seeking a trophy buck is to harvest at least one buck with an outside tip-to-tip antler measurement at or above 28 inches. A few bucks of this size are harvested off almost every mountainous unit every year. The desert units typically have smaller deer and only rarely grow a 28-inch-plus trophy buck.

Conscientious hunters and landowners can learn to approximately judge the size of a deer in the field. For examples, buck deer with antler spread less than 15 inches are almost always yearlings. In the field, if the antler spread is less than double the spread between the raised ears, the deer is probably a yearling or in some cases a twoling. Bucks with two tines on one or both antlers are also mostly yearlings. Trophy bucks can be judged in the field as having an antler spread of at least three times the distance between the raised ears and with at least four tines on each antler, excluding brow tines. Many old bucks become 'roman-nosed', with a pug, often wrinkled, nose. When observed in the field, these bucks, usually with heavy antlers at least at their base, are usually trophy sized, but may be in decline in both antler development and body size.

For the purpose of judging the size of a harvested buck in general terms, I recommend using hog-dressed weight, antler spread and the number of tines as presented in Table 11-1 (Austin 1991). Almost all bucks in the small class will be yearlings. Twolings will make up most of the medium class, large bucks are mostly three to five years, and trophy bucks are usually six or more years. In some cases the measurements of a buck may fall in two classes, and the hunter should, of course, select the larger class. For example, sometimes twolings and occasionally older bucks of the medium class may weigh over 100 pounds, (medium class), have 2x2 antler tines (small class), but have an antler spread over 14 inches (medium class). Note that some antler tine classes fall in two categories and the class depends on the weight and antler spread. About 50 percent of Utah's harvested bucks fall in the small class, 30 percent in the medium, 18 percent in the large, and about 2 percent will fall in the trophy size class.

Table 11-1. Judging the size of hunter-harvested buck mule deer.

Class	Small	Medium	Large	Trophy
Hog-dressed weight (lbs)	100 or less	101-149	150-199	200+
Antler Spread (inches)	13 or less	14-20	21-27	28+
Number of tines 1" or longer, no brow tines	1x1	2x3	3x3	4x4
	1x2	3x3	3x4	4x5
	2x2	3x4	4x4	5x5+

Antlerless Deer Hunting

The hunter who is serious about harvesting a deer for recreational values, table fare, and other purposes, rather than antler pride, should always apply for an antlerless permit. Antlerless permits provide a means for a much higher level of success. The success rate for hunters with antlerless permits in most areas is usually more than double the success rate for hunters with buck-only permits.

Chapter 12

Utah Mule Deer Harvest

To hunt a species to extinction is not logical.

Spock, *Star Trek*

Even though aesthetics and non-consumptive values associated with deer hunting are increasing in importance, hunter harvest remains the most critical motivator for hunting recreation and economic contribution into wildlife management. The many facets of the harvest include numbers of animals harvested by sex and age classes, hunter success and densities, and harvest densities and trends.

Utah Statewide Buck Deer Harvest

No buck harvest data were available before 1896. Although some incidental harvest records were obtained during the year of Utah's statehood in 1896 and throughout the early 1900s, accurate data of the legal harvest were not collected until 1925. Thus the numbers presented in Table 12-1 for the decades beginning in 1900 and 1910 are only estimates, and the data for the decade beginning in 1920, although a bit more accurate, is still only an estimate as data for that decade are incomplete. Data from the 1900s decade includes the four years 1896 to 1899 for all tables in this chapter. Data from the decade beginning with 2000 used the years from 2000-2008. Before 1914 the buck harvest was very low and very few deer were found on Utah ranges. Indeed, deer harvest was outlawed for the six-year period from 1908 through 1913. However, with improved management, regulated hunting, predator control, law enforcement, and livestock grazing, which is favorable to shrub growth on winter ranges, populations of deer and buck harvest constantly increased between 1914 and 1950.

The statewide buck harvest remained amazingly constant and stable between about 1951 and 1992. During those four plus decades, the Utah buck harvest averaged 65,400 bucks. The fact that the buck harvest remained rather constant beginning in 1951, when buck-only hunting ended and either-sex hunting was established, and through the reverse transition from either-sex to buck-only hunting beginning in about 1974, is a strong tribute to successful deer management in Utah during those decades. Despite the loss of many winter ranges to urbanization and other developments, the cutting of migration routes by freeways, highways, and reservoirs, and the general reduction of rural areas with lower human impacts, buck harvest remained high during that 42-year period.

The year of the highest buck harvest in Utah was 1983 when harvest reached 82,552. The second highest year of harvest, 1981, recorded 80,627. The highest consecutive three years of harvest occurred between these two years. A mean of 79,415 bucks were harvested.

Between 1951 and 1992 the years of lowest harvest were 1975 and 1974 when the harvest of bucks was only 41,356 and 45,306, respectively. Similarly the three consecutive years of lowest harvest were 1973 to 1975 with an average of 46,083.

Table 12-1. Mean number per decade of buck deer annually harvested in Utah.

1900s:	500
1910s:	1,000
1920s:	3,700
1930s:	17,000
1940s:	44,200
1950s:	69,900
1960s:	65,000
1970s:	59,700
1980s:	67,000
1990s:	37,800
2000s:	26,700

The differences between the highest and lowest harvest years may appear numerically large, but from a population dynamics standpoint, the differences were very small. For example, consider the extreme weather severity of the winter of 1983–1984 along with the massive overwinter deer losses, and the fact that statewide buck harvest only decreased

Photo by Becky Blankenship

Although bucks of equal rank have serious fights, most sparring is
more like a simple game to establish dominance.

24 percent between 1983 and 1984. These data suggest the resiliency of
deer populations to balance the number of deer with available habitat.

The data also suggest that total deer numbers did not significantly
change between 1951 and 1992. Because buck harvest is more dependent
upon the number of bucks available and less dependent upon the number of hunters, the direct inference is that the statewide deer population
remained rather static.

The prospects for future harvest of buck deer in Utah also appeared
mostly stable in 1992. With critical ranges being purchased and managed by the Utah Division of Wildlife Resources and with adequate summer and winter ranges on federal lands, which will not be developed, the
prospects appeared reasonably good. Nonetheless, a slow decline in the
number of deer and harvest was expected due to urbanization usurping
winter ranges on private lands, state legislation, which could reduce the
flexibility of the DWR in managing, or judicial injunction, which could
curtail hunting.

Beginning with the severe winter of 1992–1993, the major and sustained decline in buck harvest became evident. Buck harvest declined by

more than 40 percent between the 1980s and 1990s, by more than 30 percent between the 1990s and 2000s, and by more than 60 percent between the 1980s and 2000s. As a broad example, on ranges where 1,000 bucks were harvested in the 1980s, less than 400 would be harvested by the mid-2000s. Although the trend in decreasing buck harvest is expected to continue, it appears a wide plateau has been reached and future declines will probably occur at much slower rates. Indeed buck harvest between 1997 and 2008 appears to have reached a long-term stabilization, as shown in Table 12-4.

Utah Statewide Antlerless Deer Harvest

The harvest of antlerless deer in Utah has shown considerably more variability than the buck harvest. The antlerless deer harvest data, followed by the antlerless harvest as a percentage of the buck harvest, are presented by decades in Table 12-2.

Table 12-2. Mean number of antlerless deer annually harvested in Utah and the antlerless harvest as a percentage of the buck harvest.

1900s:	0	0%
1910s:	0	0%
1920s:	0	0%
1930s:	2,600	15%
1940s:	14,700	33%
1950s:	41,100	59%
1960s:	38,900	60%
1970s:	13,200	22%
1980s:	11,800	18%
1990s:	6,200	16%
2000s:	2,700	10%

The first antlerless permits were issued in 1934, and number of permits was generally and gradually increased through 1950. During this period, management and harvest of antlerless deer was considered very conservative.

During the 23-year period of either-sex hunting, 1951 to 1973, the harvest of antlerless deer averaged 39,200. During the following 14-year period between 1974 and 1987, under buck-only hunting with conservative numbers of antlerless control permits, the antlerless harvest averaged only 6,200 deer. From 1988 to 1992, also under buck-only hunting but with a moderate number of antlerless control permits, the harvest averaged about 17,300 antlerless deer. During the 16 years from 1993 to 2008 a mean of only 2,670 antlerless deer were annually harvested. By comparison, where 100 antlerless deer were harvested during the period of either-sex hunting, 1951 to 1973, only about seven were harvested between 1993 and 2008.

Since 1934, the highest harvest year on record occurred in 1962 with a harvest of 55,092 antlerless deer, and the highest three consecutive years were 1960 through 1962 with a mean harvest of 53,439. The lowest number of antlerless deer harvested was recorded in 1976 when only 95 deer were harvested. The three consecutive years of lowest harvest were 1975 through 1977 with an average yearly harvest of 838 antlerless deer.

Compared to the period of either-sex hunting, harvest objectives of antlerless deer under buck-only hunting since 1974 have been lower and management much more conservative. This change in management was partly due to the greatly increased illegal kill, which almost always occurs during the more restrictive buck-only hunts. Illegal kill in this case refers to hunters mistakenly killing antlerless deer on buck-only hunting units.

The antlerless harvest as a percentage of the buck harvest was small before 1951 when either-sex hunting was initiated. During the 1950s and 1960s for every 100 buck deer harvested about 60 antlerless deer were harvested. During the 1970s and 1980s less than 20 antlerless deer were harvested per 100 bucks harvested. During the 1990s that percentage continued to drop to 16 percent, and since 2000 that percentage has averaged less than 11 percent.

> *Note:* When deer herd size is in balance with available habitat, reproduction is excellent, and mortality factors for does are minor, I suggest this approximate rule for maximizing harvest. Buck harvest should remove approximately two-thirds of the available bucks, or about 67 percent of the available bucks on the unit should be harvested. Antlerless harvest should equal no more 50 percent of the previous year's buck harvest. Consequently, over several years one in three deer harvested may be antlerless, or antlerless deer should comprise no more than about 33 percent of the harvest.

Utah Statewide Number of Deer Hunters Afield

The number of deer hunters increased concurrently as the number of deer increased during the first half of the twentieth century in Utah. Total deer hunters afield from all combined hunts where buck deer could be taken increased steadily between 1951 and 1964, decreased for the three years 1964 to 1967, slowly increased from 1967 to 1969, then abruptly increased between 1969 and 1973. After a second three-year period of decreasing hunters afield, 1973 to 1976, hunter numbers fluctuated but remained high through the 1970s and 1980s. During the early 1990s and 2000s license sales were restricted and hunter numbers plummeted. The average number of deer hunters afield in Utah are presented by decade in Table 12-3.

Table 12-3. Mean number of deer hunters afield in Utah.

1900s:	5,000	1960s:	161,600
1910s:	5,000	1970s:	195,900
1920s:	9,200	1980s:	244,500
1930s:	29,200	1990s:	145,600
1940s:	75,600	2000s:	96,400
1950s:	125,200		

The year recording the highest number of hunters afield was 1988 with 248,685 hunters! Between 1971 and 1992, the number of hunters afield exceeded 200,000 during most years. Hunters afield between 1994 and 2008 have been generally restricted to about 100,000. Based on current hunting regulations for Utah, I estimated that if license sales were not restricted, and despite decreased harvest success rates, approximately 150,000 archery, muzzleloader, and rifle deer hunters would be annually afield in Utah. However, because of hunt restrictions, necessary revenue, and limitations on license sales, the number of hunters afield is expected to remain mostly constant near 100,000.

Utah Herd Unit Boundaries Redefined

Utah's deer herds and their boundaries were first established in 1946 with 53 units, and data were first collected on a unit basis in 1951. They were based on the herd unit concept, which assumes that most of the deer found on the herd unit would live year-round within the boundary. The generally small size and high number of units allowed management flexibility in adjusting for increasing or declining populations. However, on some units, such as the Wellsville Mountains unit, the small size prevented some management options and complicated the regulations for other units.

Beginning in 1997, DWR redrew and redefined the boundaries and reduced the number of deer herd units from the then current 56 units to 30. This major change in management was based on previous deer migration and movement studies to better define actual herd unit boundaries, to make the boundaries more easily identifiable by hunters, to separate units based on private or public land ownership, and to provide for potentially more comprehensive data collection and management of deer herds.

The 30 units are distinctly and geographically defined. They are based on migration routes, home ranges, and movements of deer. Although movement of individuals or small groups of deer is not uncommon between herd units, generally, deer units represent distinct populations. Therefore, if the deer population on a particular herd unit is greatly reduced or increased, management decisions can be adjusted to the current population within the unit. Changes in deer numbers due to migration in or out of the unit are usually inconsequential but recur annually. Also, as deer herd movements and ranges become better defined, herd unit boundaries may be further refined to improve the effectiveness of management. The concept of distinct herd units is basic to deer management.

> *Note:* Because of these changes in herd boundaries, restriction in license sales, decreased deer numbers and modifications in hunter management, the year 1997 marked the beginning of a new era in Utah deer management.

Harvest and Hunter Trends Since 1997

Generally since 1997, buck harvest has shown a slightly declining trend. However, this trend was mostly weather related, specifically due to a drought that extended through 2005. Nonetheless, almost 28,000 bucks have been annually harvested during the 12-year period between 1997 and 2008. Although this figure represents a decrease of more than 50 percent buck harvest compared with previous decades, the long-term outlook is hopeful. Table 12-4 presents the statewide Utah deer harvest data beginning in 1997, when the boundaries were redefined and harvest data were first compiled within the 30 new units.

Based on available and perpetual habitat on federal and state-owned lands as well as some private ranches, a statewide mean annual buck harvest near 30,000 may be predicted as possible to maintain indefinitely. This goal appears very practical considering the massive acreage of U.S. Forest Service and Bureau of Land Management lands, important DWR wildlife management areas, State Institutional Trust Lands Administration areas, and an increasing acreage of private lands under conservation easement. Eight of the 12 years between 1997 and 2008 recorded a harvest within 10 percent of 30,000 bucks.

Table 12-4. Utah deer harvest data 1997–2008.

Year	Buck Harvest	Antlerless Harvest	Total Harvest	Hunters Afield	Harvest/ Hunters Afield (%)
1997	29,800	3,200	33,000	112,000	29.4
1998	32,200	2,900	35,100	112,000	31.2
1999	31,500	3,000	34,400	100,000	34.5
2000	33,000	4,500	37,600	103,000	36.3
2001	27,500	4,200	31,700	97,000	32.8
2002	24,400	3,100	27,500	103,000	26.8
2003	22,500	2,500	25,000	91,000	27.6
2004	27,900	2,200	30,200	87,000	34.9
2005	21,500	2,000	23,500	92,000	25.4
2006	30,500	1,900	32,400	102,000	31.8
2007	30,200	2,100	32,300	102,000	31.8
2008	22,900	2,100	25,000	92,000	27.3

Statewide, antlerless harvest during this period (1997-2008) has shown high variability, has averaged about 2,800 deer, and contributed to only about 9 percent of the total harvest. An annual antlerless harvest of up to 15,000 is remotely possible with optimization of deer population dynamics. However, due to many uncontrollable mortality factors, including highway mortality, urbanization, wildfire and other habitat disturbances, and human harassment, which tend to affect the reproductive female segment of deer herds, a more practical goal would be to maintain a mean annual harvest minimum of 2,000 to 5,000 antlerless deer. In the future, harvest of antlerless deer may be considered a hunter bonus resulting from effective management and favorable weather.

The number of hunters afield is now determined by restricted license sales. The cap of 95,000 licenses appears to be a reasonable and working compromise between providing hunter opportunity and maintaining hunt quality. The distribution of the total number of permits within the five regions is a DWR managerial option to equitably distribute hunter harvest, numbers, and success.

Percent hunter success, or percent harvest per hunters afield, has also declined from previous decades. What percent hunter success is needed to maintain adequate hunt quality and retain hunter interest? This question is a perpetual professional debate. In the early 1970s that minimum percent was considered by many professional biologists to be 50 percent. With changes in management and populations, currently I believe most professional biologists and many hunters would consider 25 percent a minimum practical and acceptable goal for buck hunter success. Between 1997 and 2008, a mean of about 28 percent buck hunter success was determined. The number increased to almost 31 percent when antlerless deer were included. Therefore, it appears reasonable that the annual issuance of 100,000 buck permits, my recommendation, which is currently close to DWR's number for license sales, should result in sustained buck harvest and acceptable hunter success.

The trend and size of deer populations may be improved if weather conditions improve, drought and wildfire become less of a problem, and highway, predator, and human harassment mortality are decreased. The trend in buck harvest would follow, and could be further increased by, DWR adjustments of restrictive hunter regulations on some units. The trend in hunter numbers is solely a function of DWR-enacted regulations and limitations on license sales.

> *Note:* Through changes in regulations, hunter numbers afield could range between an estimated 50,000 to more than 150,000 hunters. However, the effects of changes in hunter numbers on the viability and dynamics of Utah deer herds under buck-only hunting would be minor and probably not measurable.

Additional Indices of Hunter Success

Hunter trip success means the percentage of hunters who harvested a deer before returning home. Hunters may take several trips within any hunting season. Hunter trip success ranges from less than 5 percent to more than 25 percent. Limited-entry and CWMU hunts, as expected, have the highest success rates. One reason for the higher success rates on these areas is that hunters usually travel long distances, but once on the unit stay up to several days longer than hunters using units closer to home.

The units close to the major population centers in Utah along the Wasatch Front that contain considerable public land have usually had lower hunter trip success rates. However, units close to the Wasatch Front that contain considerable private lands have better success rates. Hunter trip success has high variability between years, units, and subunits, and is strongly and primarily influenced by number of hunters, number of deer, and weather.

Regardless of the length of the season, the average hunter spends about four to five days hunting deer each year. When season length is shortened, hunters strongly tend to hunt those four to five days in a shorter time interval. When season duration is lengthened, hunters tend to spread out their hunting days. Hunter day success can be calculated as the percentage of hunters who harvest a deer on a daily basis. Hunter day success also has high variability and is extremely influenced by day-to-day changes in weather.

Harvest by Unit 1997–2005

Table 12-5 compares the primary harvest data means from Utah's 30 deer management units from 1997 to 2005. The primary data include buck and antlerless harvest, number of hunters, hunter success, square miles per unit, hunter density, and buck harvest density. The data means from this nine-year period, containing several years of drought, may be considered as manageable harvest objectives on a unit basis. Beginning in 2006 the effects of statewide droughts were decreased.

Table 12-5. Utah mule deer harvest data by herd unit—means 1997–2005.

Unit	Buck Harvest	Antlerless Harvest	Hunters Afield	% Hunters Afield	Miles²/Unit	Hunters /Miles²	Buck Harvest/ Miles²
1. Box Elder	1,289	222	4,638	32.6	9,004	0.5	0.14
2. Cache	1,491	103	8,580	18.6	1,835	4.7	0.81
3. Ogden	583	40	2,874	21.7	641	4.5	0.91
4. Morgan	622	337	3,035	31.6	922	3.3	0.67
5. E. Canyon	924	338	4,226	29.9	631	6.7	1.46
6. Chalk Ck.	828	367	2,344	51.0	617	3.8	1.34
7. Kamas	492	34	2,847	18.5	342	8.3	1.44
8. North Slope	555	15	2,142	26.6	1,221	1.8	0.45
9. South Slope	1,978	390	7,074	33.5	4,427	1.6	0.45
10. Book Cliffs	284	4	335	86.0	3,580	0.1	0.08
11. Nine Mile	392	10	1,224	32.8	2,557	0.5	0.15
12. San Rafael	189	2	591	32.3	5,023	0.1	0.04
13. La Sal	618	12	1,636	38.5	2,682	0.6	0.23
14. San Juan	898	13	2,185	41.7	5,031	0.4	0.18
15. Henry Mtns.	14	0	16	87.5	1,340	0.1	0.01
16. Central Mtns.	4,126	144	15,696	27.2	3,634	4.3	1.14
17. Wasatch Mtns.	2,854	210	13,619	22.5	2,855	4.8	1.00
18. Oquirrh-Stansbury	934	10	3,025	31.2	1,512	2.0	0.62
19. West Desert	823	8	2,725	30.5	10,409	0.3	0.08
20. Southwest Desert	115	1	469	24.7	5,204	0.1	0.02
21. Fillmore	912	80	3,092	32.1	2,855	1.1	0.32
22. Beaver	928	86	3,318	30.6	1,798	1.8	0.52
23. Monroe	822	72	2,525	35.4	693	3.6	1.19
24. Mt. Dutton	178	0	697	25.5	657	1.1	0.27
25. Plateau	1,471	99	4,369	35.9	3,295	1.3	0.45
26. Kaiparowitz	47	0	173	27.2	3,138	0.1	0.01
27. Paunsaugunt	190	142	334	99.4	1,494	0.2	0.13

28. Panquitch Lake	870	81	3,044	31.2	883	3.4	0.99
29. Zion	769	40	2,255	35.9	1,720	1.3	0.45
30. Pine Valley	1,051	35	3,485	31.2	2,603	1.3	0.40
Unidentified	<u>497</u>	<u>2</u>	<u>1,713</u>	<u>29.1</u>	<u>2,272</u>	<u>0.8</u>	<u>0.22</u>
Statewide Totals	27,744	2,897	99,194*	30.9	84,875	1.2	0.33

* Statewide total for hunters afield does not equal sum of the column because some hunters could hunt multiple units.

Buck Harvest

The units of highest buck harvest between 1997 and 2005 were the Central Mountains contributing to about 15 percent of the total harvest, the Wasatch Mountains at 10 percent, South Slope at seven percent, Cache, Plateau, and Box Elder all at five percent, and Pine Valley at four percent. Each of these units maintained a harvest in excess of 1,000 bucks and combined contributed to over 50 percent of the total state harvest. The fewest number of bucks were harvested on the Henry Mountains with only 14 bucks per year and contributed 0.05 percent to the state's harvest. The Henry Mountains unit was followed by Kaiparowits at 0.17 percent, Southwest Desert at 0.41 percent, Mt Dutton at 0.64 percent, San Rafael at 0.68 percent, and Paunsaugunt at 0.68 percent. Each of these six units annually harvested fewer than 200 bucks, and combined contributed less than three percent to the total buck harvest. The average number of bucks harvested per unit was 925, and the Oquirrh-Stansbury, Fillmore, and Beaver units were each close to the average.

Antlerless Harvest

In DWR managerial response to low deer populations over the entire state between 1997 and 2005, antlerless harvest has remained consistently low on almost all units. During this period deer populations were mostly below carrying capacity and additional population growth control via antlerless harvest was not needed on most units. Depredation problems accounted for a large proportion of the antlerless harvest. Annual antlerless harvest varied from zero to a high of 390 on the South Slope. On most units, antlerless harvest was not a significant factor affecting deer management or population dynamics.

Antlerless harvest densities were much lower than those of bucks on all units. Antlerless deer harvested per square mile of available rangeland per unit varied from zero to a high of 0.59 on Chalk Creek. The statewide average was less than 0.04 antlerless deer harvested per square mile.

Hunters Afield

Hunters afield by unit provide a comparative measure of the popularity and importance of the unit to hunters. The two most important units were the Central and Wasatch Mountains. These two units were hunted by almost 30 percent of all hunters. The five units with highest number of hunters were the Central Mountains, Wasatch Mountains, Cache, South Slope, and Box Elder. These five units were hunted by almost 50,000 hunters and provided the hunting locations for about 50 percent of all Utah deer hunters. The average number of hunters per unit was about 3,000, which represents about three percent of all hunters. Morgan-Rich, Oquirrh-Stansbury, Fillmore, and Panguitch Lake each maintained about the average number of hunters per unit.

Hunter Success

Percent harvest per hunters afield ranged from less than 19 percent on the Cache and Kamas units to well over 50 percent on units with limited-entry hunting. Most units with adequate public access maintained hunter success rates of around 30 percent. Success rates lower than 20 percent provide marginally acceptable hunt quality for the average hunter, and success rates exceeding 60 percent are generally indicative of trophy buck hunting units. I consider success rates between 25 and 35 percent as providing a good balance between hunter crowding and hunt quality.

Size of Units

The Kamas is the smallest and the West Desert is the largest of Utah's 30 units. The West Desert contains over 30 times the acreage on the Kamas. The average Utah deer unit contains over 2,800 square miles and is about the size of the Fillmore or Wasatch Mountains units. As urban development, highway construction, and other conversions from deer rangelands continue, the useable size of units will continue to shrink.

Hunter Density

Hunter density or hunter crowding is a very important factor to almost all hunters in determining hunt quality. Hunter densities are simply calculated by dividing the rangeland acreage by the number of hunters afield. Hunter densities ranged from near zero to over eight hunters per square mile. Eight hunters per mile roughly translates to one hunter per 80 acres or about eight square city blocks.

Units with large acreage associated with desert winter ranges, such as the Southwest Desert, generally have low hunter densities. In the western half of Utah low hunter densities over the entire units are common. However, because hunters concentrate on the limited summer ranges contained on these units, actual hunter densities may equal or exceed densities on units having extensive summer range. Lowest hunter densities on extensive summer ranges occur on the North and South Slopes of the Uinta Mountains. Generally, the further away from the Wasatch Front a deer unit is located, the lower will be the hunter density.

Buck Harvest Density

The number of bucks harvested per square mile of combined winter and summer range can provide an excellent comparison between units of overall habitat quality. However, the comparisons become less reliable due to differences in hunting regulations between units and may also be skewed by the influence of variability in management effectiveness. Nonetheless, the buck harvest per square mile provides a useful index to year-round buck density as well as habitat effectiveness for maintaining mule deer.

Many units with limited winter range, such as South Slope or Plateau, show reduced productivity, whereas units associated with vast acreage of desert, such as Box Elder and San Juan, are low in productivity because of the lack of summer range. Some units, such as the Book Cliffs and Paunsaugunt, are low in productivity due to severe limitations of hunters.

In my opinion generally buck harvest density exceeding 1 buck per square mile should be considered excellent, between 0.99 and 0.50 as good, between 0.49 and 0.25 as fair, and less than 0.24 as poor. Units having high density indexes maintain a good balance between available summer and winter range, and demonstrate effective management decisions. Thus, the combined northern region adjacent units of East Canyon, Chalk Creek, and Kamas probably provide the best combination of productive summer and winter range in Utah. The Central and Wasatch Mountains including Monroe and Panguitch Lake comprise the second most-productive combined units. The adjacent Cache, Ogden, and Morgan-Rich units comprise the third most-productive combined areas. Sustaining productive buck harvest on these three large areas must remain a high priority for deer management in Utah.

> *Note:* The Fillmore unit, located in central Utah and close to the center of the range of mule deer in North America, represents the average of Utah's deer units. Buck and antlerless harvest, hunters afield, hunter success, size of unit, hunter density, and buck harvest density are all very near the state average. In terms of buck harvest and hunters afield, the Central Mountains, followed by the Wasatch Mountains, South Slope, and Cache, are the most important units in the state.

Buck Harvest and Hunter Success by Unit, 2006–2008

Probably the most engaging data that the hunter, landowner, or wildlife manager examines all year is the buck harvest data for the area or unit of interest. Each year the data indicate the conclusion of the story of events effecting the deer population that occurred over the past year or years. An observant hunter, landowner or biologist can usually fit the puzzle pieces of weather, natality, mortality and hunting factors together in determining the positive or negative causes leading to the annual changes in the harvest data. Each unit has its own slightly different story, and the story for each unit usually changes from year to year. Generally, many factors are involved annually to define the changes.

Changes in harvest data by about five percent and sometimes up to ten percent may be attributed to sampling error of the harvest data, and generally should not be considered significant. In such cases populations and harvest may not be indicating trends or changes. Referring to the unit harvest data for 2006 to 2008 in Table 12-6, a few very simplified examples of the annual stories of harvest trends follows.

Table 12-6. Utah mule deer buck harvest and buck hunter percent success by unit, 2006–2008.

Unit	2006 Harvest	%	2007 Harvest	%	2008 Harvest	%
Box Elder	1,433	35.3	1,482	41.3	1,059	29.8
Cache	1,410	19.9	1,607	26.0	1,196	19.5
Ogden	624	25.3	603	28.4	463	21.9
Morgan-Rich	701	33.1	1,082	43.6	417	19.7
East Canyon	857	23.4	1,003	29.3	454	14.1
Chalk Creek	887	45.7	872	45.8	466	27.8
Kamas	584	18.7	524	17.1	319	10.9
North Slope	816	32.2	761	25.4	599	19.4
South Slope	2,306	38.4	2,493	37.3	1,809	29.0
Book Cliffs	463	90.0	469	91.4	467	86.5
Nine Mile	472	37.8	463	30.2	391	30.9
San Rafael	215	29.7	265	31.4	214	32.8
La Sal	808	47.6	429	35.1	497	30.9
San Juan	1,358	49.8	818	44.8	1,216	47.7
Henry Mountains	28	100	32	88.9	41	95.3
Central Mountains	4,443	27.2	3,885	25.1	2,599	17.7
Wasatch Mountains	2,799	22.2	2,929	23.4	1,876	15.1
Oquirrh-Stansbury	883	29.5	772	28.8	611	25.1
West Desert	549	28.2	548	30.1	560	27.2
Southwest Desert	169	27.8	114	18.9	131	17.8
Fillmore	713	27.9	1,211	30.8	841	21.0
Beaver	1,142	32.6	1,185	32.8	959	29.2
Monroe	798	31.4	813	35.1	679	30.5
Mt. Dutton	254	36.5	268	35.6	275	31.1
Plateau	1,655	37.0	1,580	32.1	1,394	30.1
Kaiparowitz	73	37.4	76	35.3	48	22.9
Paunsaugunt	160	78.8	157	78.9	172	84.3
Panguitch Lake	1,041	30.6	1,151	31.8	1,052	29.7
Zion	1,019	40.8	962	38.0	749	34.4
Pine Valley	1,575	36.0	1,290	29.0	1,120	28.1
Unidentified	313	27.2	367	30.1	184	21.6
Statewide Totals	30,548	30.5	30,211	30.4	22,857	25.6

Several units responded to the moderately harsh winter of 2007–2008. During that winter on many units fawn mortality losses were significant and adult losses were noticeable, especially on many of the northern region units. Thus the Morgan-Rich and East Canyon units decreased by 61 and 55 percent, respectively, in buck harvest between 2007 and 2008. These units apparently received the heaviest impacts from the winter storms. Adjacent and nearby units showed smaller declines with the Chalk Creek population down by 47 percent, Kamas by 39 percent, Wasatch Mountains by 36 percent, Box Elder by 28 percent, Cache by 26 percent, and Ogden by 23 percent. However, the West Desert just to the south of Box Elder unit showed no decrease in harvest, meaning the effects of the winter were probably negligible, and the data suggest this unit is maintaining a stable population. Many other units showed smaller decreases, mostly resulting from the winter.

The Book Cliffs unit shows a remarkably consistent harvest over these three years as a result of limited entry hunting. The consistent and very high success rates indicate bucks were abundant and hunters were likely very selective in their harvest. Perhaps the few hunters who were unsuccessful simply could not find a buck meeting their expectations. The unit could support a higher buck harvest, but the quality of the harvested bucks and the quality of the hunter experience would decline. The Paunsaugunt and the isolated Henry Mountains have similar stories.

In many cases only the observers in the field may be able to determine the story explaining the changes. Thus, the abrupt decrease in harvest between 2006 and 2007 on the La Sal and adjacent San Juan units and the abrupt increase the following year on the San Juan unit may only be able to be explained by local observers. Conversely, the Fillmore unit followed the opposite pattern with an abrupt increase from 2006 to 2007 followed by a decline the following year. As expected when deer herds are managed on a geographic herd unit basis, populations and harvest may react independently with little influence from adjacent units.

A research deer is shown browsing an apple sapling tree. Apple tree buds and twigs are a favorite winter food of deer. Browsing can lead to significant crop losses.

Determining Management Decisions

Photo by Becky Blankenship

Misshapen and broken antlers are usually the result of injuries.
Occasionally a hunter may miss and shoot off antler tines.

Chapter 13

Management Challenges

Primary Wildlife Responsibilities

The three most important and recurring challenges of mule deer management are:

(1) Maintaining habitat quantity and quality.
(2) Collecting sufficient data.
(3) Balancing deer populations with available habitat.

The Utah Division of Wildlife Resources has expended a significant part of its time and monetary resources available to accomplish these three major goals. Since the 1940s, DWR has acquired more than 450,000 acres of wildlife habitat within the state of Utah for the purpose of wildlife management. Most of these purchases were acquired for winter range to maintain healthy and viable numbers of big game. However, these lands are also important for many other game animals as well as non-game species of wildlife. These wildlife habitats are managed primarily for wildlife survival and harvest, and only secondarily for other uses such as non-consumptive recreation, watershed protection, or livestock production.

Collecting the data necessary to determine population indices as well as the assessment of forages available within the various habitats is a major part of the yearly activity budget of time and money. This challenge and high-priority item is to collect at least minimum information on each deer unit every year. However, sometimes one or more data collections are deleted from work schedules due to heavy workloads in the wide variety of wildlife tasks delegated to too few biologists.

Using data analysis and field observation evaluations, the balancing of deer populations with available habitat remains both a science and an art. Data is essential in understanding population dynamics and range conditions, but management requires subjective judgment with regards to antlerless harvest needed, weather, competition for resources, natality or birth rate, depredation, predation and other mortality losses, public perceptions, missing or incomplete data, political formats and necessary legislation, budget priorities, manpower priorities, and so on.

Besides these three major areas of concern—maintaining habitat, data collection, and balancing populations—many additional problems must be addressed by the wildlife agency. Indeed, most biologists would be overjoyed if their entire job consisted of data collection and habitat and population management. The importance of the various problems that DWR must face changes over time; however, the line-up of conflicts reaching center stage and the biologists' desktop is continuous. This chapter addresses a few of the major concerns and problems.

Hunter Management Strategies

Because resources and deer numbers are limited by habitat, a perfect solution to hunter management, where all hunters are satisfied, simply does not exist. Between the extremes of no hunting and no hunting restrictions, which are both potentially disastrous to deer populations, countless generally workable and biologically acceptable strategies exist. Consequently wildlife managers in Utah favor alternatives which are believed to best serve Utah hunters as a group. The management challenge is to balance hunting opportunity with quality of the experience and still maintain necessary managerial income. Following are listed 11 of the more commonly perceived options available for hunter management along with the probable effects on harvest.

Limit the Total Number of Licenses Sold

Limiting license sales is the most obvious means of improving quality of the hunt, since fewer hunters afield means more bucks available, especially mature bucks, and more deer sighted in general. However, a large majority of hunters oppose the license fee increases that are necessary to offset decreased sales. By restricting license sales wildlife revenue is also restricted, which means fewer dollars for management programs and research. Restricting license sales results in a decrease in hunter harvest, but the decrease in harvest is highly variable and dependent upon many other factors that affect population dynamics. However, a limit on sales establishes a long-term standard for minimum buck hunter success and for hunt quality, places a cap on statewide hunter density, and probably increases the demand for the license. As adopted, the overall effect creates an umbrella for a minimum quality hunting experience under which additional management options are available to further improve quality. Despite the pros and cons of the option, the 11 western states have been forced to take this approach due to declining deer numbers in recent years.

In the late 1980s most hunters believed the total number of hunters in Utah should be restricted by limited license sales at various identified levels (Austin et al. 1992). Almost two-thirds of hunters supported limiting hunter numbers by setting the upper limit at 200,000 total Utah deer hunter license sales. At that time, the current level of license sales was over 200,000 hunters, and the recommendation would have slightly decreased the number of hunters. Almost the same two-thirds majority supported placing limits at 150,000 buck licenses if antlerless licenses were available to hunters not able to obtain buck tags. In response, the Utah Wildlife Board set deer hunter number objectives beginning in fall of 1993 at 40,000 archers, 16,000 muzzleloaders, and 110,000 rifle hunters. Most hunters agreed with those objectives and preferred license sales limitations for each of the hunts. However, subsequently in 1994 the Wildlife Board established a hunter cap of 97,000 for general season deer hunters. That cap remained through 2004 and was changed to 95,000 in 2005.

Number and Types of Hunts

Total harvest as well as hunter pressure is increased with each added hunt. Potentially deer can be hunted from mid-August through December during six consecutive hunts: early depredation, archery, rifle, muzzleloader, post-season and late depredation hunts. DWR has responded to several reasonable hunter requests and gradually added hunting opportunities. Although the effects of hunter harassment on the vitality and health of deer has not been clearly defined, unpublished information from a Utah State University graduate study suggests potentially negative effects on deer physiology.

For example, in Utah I found that buck deer of the same age classes lost two to three percent of body weight between the opening and second weekend of the rifle hunt. In Colorado, hunting pressure resulted in deer moving into denser cover compared to deer in areas where hunting was prohibited (Kufeld et al. 1988). Mule deer harassed by ATVs in fall suffered significant disruptions in their biology. Compared with deer not harassed, deer harassed by ATVs in the fall shifted feeding bouts into the dark hours of the night, more often used dense cover, departed from home ranges more frequently, increased flight distances from approaching vehicles, and showed significantly reduced reproductive success (Yarmoloy 1988). In my opinion, hunting, a necessary component of management, has some potential negative effects on deer physiology. These effects would likely become more stressful and exacerbated later in the fall during the November and December periods because of the decline in forage quality, cold temperatures, and snow cover.

Season Length

Extending the hunting period to longer seasons would have similar negative effects on deer physiology as adding increased numbers and types of hunts. However, extending seasons into the rutting period, beginning in early November, could lead to increased harvest because buck deer are often more interested in the does and less cautious toward hunters during the breeding season. Shortening the hunting periods would tend to have the opposite effect, but depending on hunter intensity may show no change in hunter effort. This was the result when the rifle season was shortened from 11 to 9 days. Hunters generally plan to hunt a certain number of days during the season; shortening the season, in most cases, simply forces hunters into a shorter time period to put in their desired number of hunting days.

Limit Hunters to One Hunt

This option, first adopted in 1993, initially reduced hunter pressure on bucks and resulted in a slightly lower harvest during at least the first two or three years of the program. A small but positive increase in the mean size and age of harvested bucks occurred. This option reduced hunter opportunity. However, since the number of bucks harvested is more dependent upon the number of bucks available and less dependent upon the number of hunters, the effects were not very observable.

Limit Hunters to Harvest One Deer per Year

Also adopted first in 1993, but rejected in 1994, this regulation reduced hunter pressure on bucks. A strong positive point is that hunters choosing to harvest an antlerless deer would have an excellent opportunity to be successful. This option clearly limits hunting opportunity.

Change to a Mid-Week Opening Day

This would probably reduce opening day hunter crowding a little, but more likely, only lead to a five-day opening weekend, Wednesday through Sunday. Little change in harvest would be expected.

Weapon Restrictions

Restricting equipment, such as requiring the use of only sightless re-curve bows, round balls and true muzzleloaders, rifles without scopes, or even limiting rifles to the traditional western lever-action 30-30 caliber, would make hunters less effective and would at least somewhat reduce buck harvest. In an unpublished hunter opinion poll, about 55 percent of hunters favored some units with weapon restrictions, thereby increasing the degree of challenge and difficulty in harvesting a deer. Weapon restriction hunts have not been attempted in Utah.

Increase Fees

Increasing license fees would reduce hunter numbers and have some effect on reducing total harvest. To maintain funding levels for wildlife management, license fees periodically need to be adjusted to maintain pace with the consumer price index.

Access Management

Restricted use of vehicles on public lands to main access roads would provide more areas of escape cover and refuge for deer. The likely result would be a reduced buck harvest on areas with vehicle restrictions. For example, experience with access restrictions at Hardware Ranch has been met with mixed hunter opinions. Many hunters complained initially of the road closures during the rifle deer hunt, but complaints essentially ended after only a few years, and support for the closures has gradually increased. The effects on buck harvest, however, have only been very minor.

Hunter Training

Beyond the required Hunter Safety courses, education of hunters about the management of deer and the ethics of hunting will have mainly positive effects, especially if made mandatory. Among those probable positive effects would be a reduced illegal kill and wounding loss, higher hunter selectivity of harvested animals, and increased appreciation for care, cooking, and consumption of the harvested deer.

Restrict Individual Hunters to Units or Regions

Restricting hunters to certain geographical boundaries provides the best control of hunter density. However, since most hunters tend to hunt in many areas of Utah during the season, this restriction has had negative impacts, especially on families that live in different locations but that prefer to spend the hunting season together. This scheme, by itself, has had little effect on harvest. However, combined with limited license sales, it provides the greatest control for limiting buck harvest and for increasing the quality of the hunter experience and harvest totals.

Every deer manager knows that regulations do not exist that will make all hunters happy, nor do regulations exist that can be totally equitable to all hunters. The deer manager faces the daunting challenge of defining regulations which find a level of acceptable hunter satisfaction and somewhat equal opportunity for all hunters.

Depredation

Depredation occurs when big game animals begin feeding on commercial agricultural products. Damage from depredation happens only when crop production is decreased as a result of the depredation. Crop utilization usually results in costs and crop losses to the landowner, but not always.

Depredation by big game of alfalfa growing in fields during the summer was recognized as a problem before 1930 when deer numbers began to increase rapidly and the use of alfalfa fields, especially in southern Utah, became apparent. Use of winter haystacks in northern and central Utah was similarly first recorded about 1930, as was the use of orchards and other crops during the mid-to-late 1930s. To ameliorate at least part of the problem, the Utah Division of Wildlife Resources, formerly the Utah Department of Fish and Game, began building fences around highly impacted winter haystacks and providing some landowners with the materials to do so themselves.

Cartoon by Alan Gardner Courtesy of The Herald Journal, Logan

Politics of Depredation

As big game populations continued to increase, so did the farmer complaints about the depredation problem. In 1947 the legislature passed Utah's first wildlife damage law. This legislation was designed to reduce the economic losses incurred to farmers and permitted DWR to pay for big game depredation crop losses up to a maximum payment of $100 per year per landowner. More importantly, however, the law clearly indicated that the state of Utah, through DWR, accepted at least part of the responsibility for commercial crop utilization by big game. The maximum payment was increased to $200 in 1953, and abruptly raised to $2,000 in 1977. The maximum payment amount was later eliminated, making DWR responsible for all crop damage which was properly claimed by landowners.

Agency Costs of Depredation

The budget for depredation is significant and rising. Prior to 1977, monetary expenditures and the number of claims from private landowners were small, with the number of claims per year generally less than 15 and total program costs per year less than $30,000. However, since 1977, the costs of maintaining the required depredation program increased over 10 times and annual costs exceeded $600,000 per year.

These costs are about equally divided between direct payments to land-owners, fencing purchases, and personnel costs to address the problems and work with landowners.

Commercial agricultural products which are considered for crop loss payments include alfalfa hay, grass hay that is mechanically harvested, cereal grains, stored crops, orchards, vineyards, tree plantations, row crops, and commercial nurseries. The three major areas of big game agricultural depredation conflicts are field-growing alfalfa hay in spring through fall, green leafy cereal grain grass in early spring and often again in fall, and orchards, especially apple trees, in winter. Almost all depredation activity occurs at night.

Common Depredation Solutions

There are six solutions to the problem of depredation that are commonly used in Utah.

(1) In some cases, the best solution is simply to harvest the animals doing the damage. The preferred option is to issue depredation permits to hunters. A second option is to assign DWR personnel the task of removing the deer. This is usually accomplished most efficiently by wildlife officers using spotlights at night. Landowners dissatisfied with the DWR response may file the required paperwork and kill big game doing damage to their crops. The landowner is required to notify DWR of the harvest, and DWR is responsible for the removal of the carcasses. Although this option often leads to increased conflicts between the state and the landowner, sometimes it becomes the only workable option available to the landowner. In one infamous case in northern Utah, a single landowner killed at least 168 deer in alfalfa and wheat fields over the course of one winter. However, when under a revised DWR depredation program the same landowner began working with the new local biologist and allowed hunters, friends, and family to harvest the deer, the number of offending deer killed by the landowner was reduced to zero within two years.

(2) Sturdy, permanent fences built to a height of eight feet are very effective in repelling deer. The DWR provides some fencing materials to growers who are very susceptible to deer

damage. Such materials become the property of the landowner, and it also becomes the responsibility of the landowner
to construct and maintain the fence. Temporary, lightweight
plastic fencing is also available from DWR to some growers.
Plastic fence is usually used to protect haystacks during winter, and usually the material remains the property of DWR.
Fencing is a viable solution for orchards vulnerable to depredation and other crops at some locations. Fencing provides
workable compromise solutions between wildlife and agricultural interests.

(3) If depredation is expected to be very temporary, sometimes
deer can be kept out of agricultural crops by repellents and
scare devices. Repellents are commonly used in orchards and
include several commercially available sprays, scents, and
human hair. Human hair, usually available at no costs from
barber shops and placed in nylon bags or stockings, has often
been found to work as effectively as commercial repellents.
Repellents usually work well when deer have alternative forage sites available. However, repellents have only minor effects
when deer become hungry.

Scare devices include propane canons and firecrackers. They
will often move deer to nearby, alternative locations if forage
conditions are comparable. Scare devices are effective for only
a few days, at best, and when deer are not limited in choice in
feeding areas.

(4) Occasionally wildlife officers or biologists, working at night,
herd deer away from crops. The use of horns, shotguns, and
lights are effective in moving deer. However, deer usually return
within a few hours after the horns, shotgun bangs, and lights
have departed.

(5) Although deer can be trapped or tranquilized and moved to
other locations, trapping is often unsuccessful because of difficulties in capturing a high percentage of the population,
extremely high costs, and its general ineffectiveness as a long-
term solution. For example, it has been estimated that only up
to about 25 percent of any deer population can be live-trapped,
primarily due to the behavior adaptability. Consequently, live
trapping is only attempted under special circumstances.

(6) When deer depredation cannot easily be controlled and crop
     loss has occurred, the grower can be compensated for the dam-
     age by DWR. Specific guidelines for evaluating crop damage,
     based upon current available research for each type of agricul-
     tural crop, are used by DWR for evaluation (Bartmann 1974;
     Katsma and Rusch 1980; Tebaldi and Anderson 1982; Austin
     and Urness 1987, 1989, 1992; Austin et al. 1998). Occasionally,
     the use of a third party to determine the losses is necessary
     when the landowner and the state cannot agree on a fair settle-
     ment. Although damage to landscaped yards, ornamental
     plants, and non-commercial orchards may be significant, DWR
     is not responsible for those losses (Austin and Hash 1988).

Relationships with Private Landowners

Wildlife advocates and private landowners share the common goal of
appropriate management of rangelands in terms of proper forage utilization, watershed protection, water development, erosion control, animal production, weed control, and many others. Both parties rely on
the resources of the land to produce many products. Private lands are
important to Utah deer hunters as they provide some of the best hunting in the state. Furthermore, an estimated 15 percent of Utah resident
hunters hunt deer on private lands (Austin et al. 1992). Many of Utah's
landowners have recognized the economic values of big game on their
lands and have been incorporating trespass fee hunting for many years,
and sometimes for decades, to take economic advantage of the resource.
Because private lands provide critical forage and habitat for wildlife, the
DWR generally supports private land fee hunting. Fee hunting provides
economic incentives for better wildlife management on private lands and
usually results in livestock practices more favorable to wildlife. On private lands where fee hunting is not feasible because big game are not
available on those lands during the hunting seasons, DWR and landowners must seek alternative cooperative avenues.

In 1986, landowners involved with fee hunting achieved net mean
revenue of $6,649 (Jordan and Workman 1989). Although 18 percent
of landowners experienced a net loss, three percent indicated that more
than 50 percent of their gross income resulted from fee hunting. Fees
for unguided deer hunting ranged from $5 to $2,000 with a mean of

$169. Fees for guided hunters ranged from $132 to $3,000 with a mean of $1,106. By 2009, I estimated that these fees would have at least doubled from those cited in the mid 1980s. Private hunting fees for CWMUs are several times higher.

For most private landowners, fee hunting provides three positive incentives: supplemented income to the ranching operation, control of trespass, and compensation for any damages caused by hunters. Many private landowners involved with fee hunting simply lease their properties to hunting clubs and avoid the problems of liability, hunter management, and insurance costs. My estimated minimum acreage needed to provide fee hunting for big game species, dependent upon the quality of the habitat, is 600 to 2,000 acres or about one to three square miles of contiguous rangeland. It is often more economical for ranches of this size to combine their lands and manage as a CWMU.

Cooperative Wildlife Management Units (CWMUs) were originally known as Posted Hunted Units; the name was changed in 1998, and in 1996 they were added to the list of alternatives for wildlife management for some landowners. However, minimum acreage to be eligible was set at 5,000 acres for deer and pronghorn, and 10,000 acres for elk and moose. Although many restrictions as well as incentives apply, the CWMU program gave landowners, or in some cases landowners with adjacent properties, the opportunity for improved control of the hunting resource, decreased hunter trespass, and greatly increased economic gain. Hunter density is much lower but success rates and hunter satisfaction are much higher on CWMUs. In most cases the landowner receives 90 percent of the buck or bull tags, and public hunters receive 10 percent of the buck or bull tags and all of the antlerless permits. Normally the landowner sells the buck or bull tags to private hunters at market value. Both public and private hunters are required to purchase licenses from the state. The number of Utah's CWMUs has gradually increased to about 80.

Protection of Riparian Zones

Riparian habitats along streams, ponds, springs, and marshlands are the most vegetatively productive of wildlife habitats. They potentially always provide high quality and quantity of forage and cover. Unfortunately riparian areas are often heavily used by livestock, decreased in size by agricultural cultivation, and channeled for agricultural and other purposes. Water is often diverted from riparian corridors, thereby further reducing environmental values. Consequently, potential values to wildlife are often curtailed in riparian zones.

Riparian habitats become critically important during mid-to-late summer under drought conditions. When most other forage sources become dry and decrease in nutritional value and palatability, deer gradually increase use of riparian habitats. Often in late summer, especially during dry years, high numbers of deer can be observed in the evening along water courses throughout the state. Although deer utilize the stream water as needed, the main attraction is the succulent vegetation.

Grazing use of riparian habitats by livestock and big game must be carefully monitored. Riparian habitats must not be degraded or over-utilized. Abused areas must be allowed to recover. Riparian zones also serve as valuable forage reserves for deer during winter and should receive the highest habitat management priority. Fencing of riparian zones has been found to be an effective management tool to maintain balance between productivity and utilization.

The DWR has been purchasing riparian habitat conservation easements from private landowners since the early 1990s. These easements limit the use of livestock, usually provide sportsman access, provide income to the landowner, protect stream banks, decrease erosion, and ensure perpetual wildlife habitat.

Factors Affecting Changes in Deer Populations

Numerous factors have short and long-term effects on deer populations. Unfortunately many of these factors are negative and have long-term effects. State game agencies must deal with both the positive and problematic factors. Although most of these factors are discussed elsewhere in the manual, and many are subjective, they are presented below in summary form as having positive, neutral or negative influences on deer populations. Even though these factors are prioritized within categories from more to less significant, the order could radically be altered over time or between areas. Additionally, and as applied to specific deer herds, some of these listed factors would be eliminated and others added. Although most of these factors have been present for decades, I consider this listing as applicable to Utah's mule deer populations beginning about 1993 and continuing well into the twenty-first century.

Negative External Factors List 1

These factors are not influenced by the Division of Wildlife Resources or by hunter organizations:

- Increases in transportation methods, number of people, and number of vehicles.
- Urbanization of deer winter ranges, increased housing density, fewer or smaller corridors.
- Climatic or weather changes.
- Increase in bald and golden eagle populations.

Negative External Factors List 2

These external factors are somewhat influenced by DWR and various hunter organizations:

- Increase in highway speeds, ineffective highway fences, increase in vehicular mortality.
- Reduced livestock grazing of winter ranges during spring on public lands.
- Decline in productivity of winter ranges on public lands.
- Increased fire frequency on winter ranges on public lands.
- Increase in range problems associated with introduced weeds.
- Increases in recreational harassment.
- Reduced control of coyotes.
- Decrease in the number of effective predator trappers and hunters.
- Changes in depredation legislation.
- Increase in fire frequency of winter ranges on private lands.
- Livestock grazing during fall and winter on private and public winter ranges.
- Effects of chronic wasting disease and other deer-related diseases.
- Increase in populations of red fox.
- Decrease in productivity of winter ranges on private lands.
- Overgrazing by livestock on some winter range riparian areas.
- Overgrazing by livestock on some ranges during summer.
- Since the winter of 1992–1993, overutilization of some winter ranges by big game.

Positive Internal Factors

These internal factors are often controlled by DWR:

- Implementation of livestock grazing plans on DWR winter ranges.
- Revegetation of winter ranges on DWR wildlife management areas.
- Revegetation of winter ranges on private and public lands.
- Closure of DWR winter ranges from all public uses from Jan 1 through April 31.
- Cooperation, contribution, and encouragement for conservation easements of private lands.
- Additional acquisitions of critical winter ranges.
- Law enforcement efforts.
- Increasing effectiveness of range management on DWR lands.
- Effects of winter deer feeding during some years and at some locations.

Neutral Internal Factors

These internal factors are also controlled by DWR:

- Data collection, including fall and spring classification, check station, harvest, and other data.
- Number of management units reduced from 56 to 30.
- Ratio of bucks to does for breeding (DWR minimum goal of 15 bucks per 100 does), increase in trophy bucks.
- Implementation of the Cooperative Wildlife Management Unit program.
- Implementation of the Dedicated Hunter program.
- Requirement of hunters to select region.
- Limitation of deer hunters from 97,000 to 95,000.
- Complicating of the deer hunting rules and regulations.
- Changes in administrative personnel.

Negative Internal Factors

These negative internal factors are often slightly influenced by DWR:

- Increase in disease problems in mule deer.
- Depredation problems, changes in landowner tolerance on farms, ranches, and backyards.

- Decrease in total numbers and in revenues from deer hunters.
- Decrease in applied research.
- Shifts in resources' allocation away from mule deer management to people-related problems and other wildlife species.
- Increase in competition with elk for browse on winter ranges.
- Decrease in annual range assessments, e.g. range rides, browse production and utilization surveys, and pellet group surveys.
- Increase in number and adaptability of cougars and coyotes on some units.
- Increased effects of predation by bobcat, red fox, and other predators on some units.
- Increase in number of dogs harassing deer in winter.
- Continued poaching, illegal kill, and unrecovered carcasses.
- Increase in competition with white-tailed deer.
- Increase in hunter harassment into the breeding period on some units.
- Increased, sometimes negative, influence of public opinion on wildlife management decisions.

Chapter 14

Lessons From the East Canyon and Oak Creek Management Units

East Canyon

Population versus Range Carrying Capacity

Between 1951 and 1968, under either-sex hunting, buck harvest on the East Canyon Unit was relatively consistent, and the total population was considered to be maintained within winter range carrying capacity. Increased population and buck harvest began about 1969, and by 1975 the population was clearly exceeding the carrying capacity as evidenced by very heavy use on shrubs on most of the scattered winter ranges within the unit. However, the winter ranges remained healthy, most shrubs recovered during the summer, winters were moderate, hunters were happy, and deer populations remained high. Winter range conditions were probably gradually deteriorating, but the decline was not visually evident until about 1980.

Between 1980 and 1983 hunting pressure was high on the East Canyon Unit, but deer populations were very high and greatly exceeded the carrying capacity of the winter range. The average number of bucks harvested during these four years was just under 3,000, and over 1,000 antlerless deer were annually harvested, as shown in Table 14-1. In 1982, the area conservation officer and I estimated that over 2,000 antlerless deer would need to be harvested just to maintain the population at the current level with a normal winter, and a harvest of 3,000 antlerless deer was recommended to reduce the herd to be closer to carrying capacity.

Herd reductions were not made and the extremely severe winter of 1983–1984 killed almost all the fawns and a high proportion of the adults, reducing the total herd by an estimated 70 percent. The number

186

of bucks harvested between 1983 and 1984 dropped from 2,810 to 960, a one-year 66-percent reduction in harvest.

However, the most significant result of the overpopulation of deer during the late 1970s and early 1980s was that the winter range was extremely over-utilized, resulting in high mortality and reduced vigor of shrubs, and importantly, a massive reduction of the future deer carrying capacity of the winter ranges.

Nonetheless, the next several years recorded high reproduction and recruitment rates and the herd rapidly recovered to a population again exceeding carrying capacity. The moderately severe winter of 1988–1989 killed most of the fawns, but the adult population was not significantly reduced. The result was a single-year decline in hunter harvest, mostly due to the lack of available yearling bucks, killed as fawns during the previous winter. Buck harvest declined from 1,706 to 800, a one-year 53-percent reduction in harvest.

The herd continued to show high, non-stop population growth following the winter of 1989, and by 1992 was again clearly and greatly exceeding the carrying capacity of the winter range. The severe winter of 1992–1993 killed an estimated 70 percent of the population, and the buck harvest plummeted from 2,916 to 362 bucks, a one-year 86 percent reduction in harvest.

The herd recovered during the next several years, but less rapidly, probably again to the point of exceeding winter range carrying capacity. Another moderately severe winter, 1997–1998, reduced the herd, and the buck harvest dropped from 1,331 to 746, a one-year 43 percent reduction in harvest.

The herd slowly recovered to about carrying capacity or slightly above, until the two mildly severe back-to-back winters between late 2000 and early 2002 reduced the herd through overwinter losses. Buck harvest declined from 1,177 to 912 to 568, during 2000, 2001, and 2002, respectively. This represents a 52 percent reduction in harvest over two years.

Between 2003 and 2007, herd numbers as well as the number of hunters remained rather constant, and within carrying capacity of the winter range. Herd growth had been controlled by antlerless harvest, moderate winters, vehicle mortality, and predators. However, the winter of 2007–2008 was moderately harsh and overwinter losses, especially of fawns, were significant. The 55 percent decrease in buck harvest between 2007 and 2008 reflected that winter mortality.

The main lesson from the East Canyon Management Unit joins that of the infamous North Kaibab and many others that have fallen to the same fate (Mitchell and Freeman 1993). Simply, overpopulation of deer on winter ranges leads to overutilization of shrubs, followed by massive die-offs during severe winters, and results in reduced future carrying capacity of winter ranges.

Balancing Deer Populations with Winter Range

The Utah Division of Wildlife Resources has estimated the deer range for the East Canyon Unit at about 230,000 acres, with about 194,000 acres of summer range and 36,000 acres of winter range. Clearly, winter range is the limiting resource on this unit and comprises less than 16 percent of the total deer range.

The state's goals for the East Canyon Unit are to maintain a winter population of 8,500 deer and a minimum post-season buck-to-doe ratio of 15 to 100. Using these goals, about 1,000 bucks would be expected to be annually harvested on the unit. The five years, 2003 to 2007, of harvests were roughly between 800 and 1,000 bucks, with the mean equaling 879. The antlerless deer harvest averaged almost 300, with the mean equaling 267, and comprised almost one-fourth of the total harvest. These figures suggest a good balance between total population and range carrying capacity, indicate a well-balanced harvest between buck and antlerless deer, and reflect conscientious game management decisions.

Deer management plans are flexible and can be adjusted to increase or decrease deer numbers as additional information becomes available. For example, the estimated balance between winter range carrying capacity and the 8,500 deer is a reasonable approximation. However, based on available winter range and past history, a winter population of 7,000 deer is possibly a better estimate of carrying capacity and greatly reduces the risks of overutilization of the winter range. According to my rule of thumb, with one wintering deer per five acres of average condition and productive winter range, the carrying capacity of the winter range is roughly estimated at 7,200 deer (36,000 acres divided by five acres per deer). Using my rule of thumb for practical and potential harvest percentages, at 7,200 deer, annual buck harvest would be estimated at about 850 (approximately 12 percent of population), and a maximum antlerless harvest of about 425 (approximately six percent of population), but more realistically due to other mortality factors, about 300.

Table 14-1. Number of hunters and deer harvest on the East Canyon Unit 1980-2008.

Year	Number of Hunters	Harvest Bucks	Antlerless
1980	6,423	2,944	1,114
1981	7,109	3,582	1,276
1982	8,057	2,537	1,241
1983	7,413	2,810	1,332
1984	3,007	960	0
1985	3,397	874	182
1986	3,191	1,347	291
1987	2,942	1,596	325
1988	3,665	1,706	1,163
1989	2,740	800	825
1990	9,427	2,580	943
1991	10,459	3,015	940
1992	9,797	2,916	3,008
1993	3,922	362	116
1994	3,017	616	112
1995	3,059	733	42
1996	2,505	824	108
1997	4,938	1,331	433
1998	3,546	746	457
1999	3,537	903	209
2000	4,836	1,177	365
2001	4,387	978	430
2002	4,223	642	290
2003	3,715	875	321
2004	3,618	858	306
2005	5,237	802	231
2006	4,020	857	311
2007	3,662	1,003	166
2008	3,210	454	46

Oak Creek

Located in rural central Utah and near the center of the mule deer range in Western North America, the Oak Creek Management Unit was strategically positioned for intensive studies of mule deer (Robinette et al. 1977). The relatively small size of the study area within the Oak Creek unit, about 53 square miles, along with drainage and topography typical for the Great Basin also made it ideal for studying mule deer, which it was, intensively, from 1946 to 1960. The study area was mostly within the Fishlake National Forest but also contained about four square miles of private lands and one square mile of Bureau of Land Management lands.

The Oak Creek Management Unit was comprised of about 200 square miles. Essentially all deer on the unit were contained year-round on the summer and winter ranges within the study area. Pinyon-juniper, big sagebrush and Gambel oak comprised the major vegetative types.

Harvest Decline

Between 1947 and 1960 the herd size was estimated to be between about 2,200 and 2,400 deer, using the three then available methods of pellet group counts, classification indices, and Lincoln-marked individual ratios. As a research note, winter population counts by horseback, foot, or airplanes were determined to be ineffective and inaccurate in determining total herd population. During the same period slightly over 200 bucks were annually observed at checking stations and a total kill of about 240 bucks per year or about 10 percent of the herd was harvested.

> *Note:* A hunter harvest of bucks amounting to 10 percent of the total herd is a good estimate of maximum sustained potential buck harvest. About 200 does and fawns were also harvested each year from this unit, or about 18 to 20 percent of the herd was harvested per year. A hunter harvest of 20 percent of the total herd is approaching the limit for the herd to be able to sustain constant mule deer populations.

Due to several fires on subunit winter ranges soon after 1960, the population and harvest greatly declined. The same quality and quantity of summer range remained intact. The population was estimated at less than

Fires on winter ranges, such as the High Point burn in Green Canyon,
have a long-term impact on deer habitat. Full recovery of range
vegetation often requires 20 years or more.

Photo by Dick Spencer

1,000 deer in the early 1990s and has remained at about that level or below. Because of limited-entry hunting regulations beginning in 1990, changes in unit boundaries, and a greatly reduced number of hunters afield from usually between 1,000 and 2,000 before 1990 to considerably less than 500 after 1990, direct comparisons of harvest are not possible. However, the buck harvest since 1993 has remained at less than half of that observed in the 1950s, and the antlerless harvest has remained near zero.

The main lesson from Oak Creek is that wildfire destroyed a considerable portion of the winter range, the winter range has not recovered even after 20 or more years, and the herd size remains considerably below the population observed in the 1950s.

> *Note:* Both the East Canyon and Oak Creek units suffered significant losses in winter range productivity. Once that productivity in winter forage quality and quantity is lost, the deer herd will be perpetually reduced until the range productivity is recovered. Depending upon climate, and a number of environmental variables, the recovery period for the winter range may vary from one or two decades to never.

Deer Size

Because of the extraordinary sample sizes obtained with 1,320 bucks, 899 does, 187 buck fawns, and 162 doe fawns, hunter-harvested hog-dressed weights collected at checking stations from the Oak Creek unit between 1951 and 1959 provide a comprehensive age-weight relationship representative of the Basin and Range topography throughout western Utah, Nevada, southern Idaho, southern Oregon, and eastern California. The data may be extended throughout the range of the mule deer with higher mountainous areas having slightly higher weights by 5 to 20 percent and the more desert environments, mostly to the south of Oak Creek in southern Utah, Arizona, New Mexico, and Mexico, having lower weights by 5 to 10 percent.

For bucks, with ages determined as fawns, yearlings, twolings, and mature, the mean weights in pounds were 49, 90, 122, and 161 pounds, respectively (Robinette et al. 1977). Bucks increased in weight to about age seven, remained at about the same weight for three years, and began to decline in weight at about age nine.

For does, similarly aged as fawns, yearlings, twolings, and mature, the mean weights were 46, 81, 92, and 94 pounds, respectively. Does increased in weight to age five, maintained weight for several years, and began to decline at about age 11. During the course of the Oak Creek study the oldest deer was aged at 19 years.

In 1971 and 1972, and again during 1990, 1991, and 1992, checking stations were established on the unit at the same locations as the original study, and weight and antler measurement data were similarly collected. However, sample sizes were much smaller due to the greatly decreased deer population, and because of buck-only hunting regulations, only data for antlered buck deer were available and collected.

Surprisingly, deer weights declined within age classes over the decades. For yearling bucks mean weights declined from 90 to 86 to 78 pounds during the periods 1951 to 1959, 1971 to 1972, and 1990 to 1992, respectively. Similarly, twolings declined from 122 to 113 to 105 pounds, and mature bucks declined from 161 to 155 to 125 pounds, respectively. Changes in weight between 1951 and 1959 and between 1990 and 1992 were statistically significant with declines of 13 percent for yearlings, 14 percent for twolings, and 22 percent for mature bucks, as shown in Table 14-2.

Data from the 1951 to 1959 period indicated that antler size reached maximum at six years of age and declined slowly after that age. The average percentage of total bucks harvested by antler classes represents 1x1 as 16 percent, 1x2 as 5 percent, 2x2 as 33 percent, 2x3 as 9 percent, 3x3 as 15 percent, 3x4 as 7 percent, 4x4 as 11 percent, 4x5+ as 1 percent, and miscellaneous as 2 percent. These figures represent expected hunter harvest of bucks by antler classes throughout the Great Basin, including the dryer desert environments. These harvested antler classifications would be expected to improve on higher mountainous units.

Although antler data from 1971 to 1972 are not available, the number of antler points also declined between periods as shown in Table 14-3. Between the periods 1951–1959 and 1990–1992, the mean number of antler points in the yearling age class decreased from 3.3 to 3.0, in the twoling class from 5.8 to 4.8, and in the mature buck class from 7.1 to 5.9. The percentage of bucks with 2x3 or more points declined from 46 percent to 32 percent.

This lesson from the Oak Creek unit is that deer size can significantly change. Furthermore, similar results of declining deer size were reported for the Vernon, Current Creek and Cache units (Austin et al. 1989). The possible reasons for the observed decrease in deer size included phenotypic changes due to hunter selectivity for larger bucks, increasingly wide buck-to-doe ratios, the lowering of the mean age of the buck population (which possibly results in a delay in the mean breeding and fawning dates), an increase in the density-dependent response of the population due to buck-only hunting, declining range conditions caused by increasing human recreation impacts or detrimental livestock grazing, and climatic changes.

Fortunately, the trend in declining size was reversed by lowering hunter pressure and increasing buck-to-doe ratios. Other factors may also have been involved. Although the decrease in size occurred over a 10 to 30 year period depending on the unit, body size, weight and number of antler points appeared to be recovered on the Oak Creek and other units by 2000, or within an estimated five to ten years or two to three generations of mule deer.

Table 14-2. Changes in hog-dressed weights (lbs) of hunter-harvested mule deer bucks by age classes from selected checking stations and years in Utah.

Checking Station	Buck Age	1951–59	1971–72	1990–92	
Oak Creek	Yearling	90	86	78	
.	Twoling	122	113	105	
	Mature	161	155	125	
		1966	1973	1980	1987
Blacksmith Fork	Yearling	104	110	95	94
	Twoling	141	143	134	120
	Mature	164	180	166	164
		1967–68	1975	1980	1987
Daniel's Canyon	Yearling	99	99	90	91
	Twoling	126	129	112	119
	Mature	187	171	160	152
		1980–82	1987–89		
Vernon	Yearling	84	80		
	Twoling	109	102		
	Mature	125	125		

Table 14-3. Percentage of hunter-harvested bucks by number of antler points within age classes from the Oak Creek Management Unit, 1951-1959 and 1990-1992.

	Buck Age					
	Yearling		Twoling		Mature	
Antler Class	1951–59	1990–92	1951–59	1990–92	1951–59	1990–92
1x1	33	48	00	00	00	00
1x2	10	15	01	04	00	00
2x2	51	30	22	64	06	32
2x3	04	05	16	00	07	18

	Buck Age					
	Yearling		Twoling		Mature	
Antler Class	1951–59	1990–92	1951–59	1990–92	1951–59	1990–92
3x3	02	02	33	14	13	14
3x4	00	00	14	00	13	18
4x4	00	00	12	14	41	11
4x5+	00	00	01	04	07	04
Misc.	01	00	02	00	08	04

Daily Harvest

Deer are extremely susceptible to hunter harvest on small mountain ranges such as the Oak Creek range in the Great Basin. Between 1947 and 1959, 66.5 percent of the bucks harvested by rifle hunters were harvested on opening day, 11.4 percent on the second day, and 4.7 percent on day three. On the second Saturday 3.7 percent were harvested and all other days harvested less than 3 percent. Furthermore, before 1960 very few hunters used scopes, off-road recreational vehicles were decades away, and most hunters used an iron sight lever action 30-30 rifle with an effective range of about 200 yards. With increased transportation capabilities and technology, hunters in the twenty-first century would likely be much more effective in removing available buck deer than hunters in the mid-twentieth century. The lesson is that shortening hunting seasons on these ranges would not significantly increase buck populations through increased buck survival.

Mule Deer Mortality

Fawn mortality from birth to the October hunt was about 33 percent, mostly due to poor nutrition and coyotes. Fawn mortality from coyotes averaged about four fawns per coyote per year between birth and the October hunt. Overwinter mortality from the October hunt to following spring green-up in May or early June was about an additional 15 percent. Total mortality from birth through year one averaged 48 percent.

Generally, on well-managed units, mule deer mortality may be generally defined as roughly one-third lost as fawns from birth to the October hunt, one-third lost from hunting over all years, and one-third lost to all other causes including predation, crippling, accidents, poaching, and malnutrition. Typical mule deer mortality on well-managed units may be broken down by time intervals and causes: summer equals 35 percent, winter equals 15 percent, legal harvest of bucks and does equals 30 percent, accidents, crippling, and illegal losses equal 15 to 20 percent, and unknown causes equal 0 to 5 percent.

Legal hunter harvest accounted for 81 to 84 percent of buck mortality on the Oak Creek range for bucks one year and older. The remainder of mortality for bucks one year and older was due to accidents, crippling losses, illegal poaching, predators, winter weather, and unknown causes. Generally, 80 percent or more of bucks reaching one year and older are legally harvested from most Utah units containing extensive public lands, and about 20 percent are lost to other mortality factors.

Fawning Dates

The mean fawning date for Utah ranges peaks during June 19 and 20, following a mean gestation period of 203 days. The mean birth weight for Utah fawns, including Oak Creek, is between eight and nine pounds. However, for the Oak Creek range, the mean peak fawning date was June 12, and 67 percent of fawns were born during the 20 days between June 9 and 28. The mean fawning dates for the small ranges within the Basin and Range topography were found to be about one week earlier than those ranges along the Wasatch Mountains and other higher mountain ranges. The differences were ecological adaptations probably due to the dryer conditions and earlier spring phenotypic vegetative development within the Basin and Range topography.

Chapter 15

Lessons from the Cache Management Unit

On most of Utah's units, the current and future acreage of browse-covered winter ranges limits mule deer populations and management options.

The Complex Problems of Maintaining Sustainable Populations

For the non-hunter, mule deer management may simply be defined by this heading. Because almost all ranges continue to support sustainable populations, management must be viewed successful by this definition. However, from the view of game management the definition would be extended to read: The complex problems of maintaining sustainable populations and harvest objectives. This second definition and the inherent changes in mule deer populations lead to considerable discussion and consternation.

Mule deer populations have been decreasing throughout their entire range, including Utah and the Cache Wildlife Management Unit, at least since the early 1970s. Not only have numbers significantly declined, but geographic range has greatly decreased. On some ranges where small, scattered populations of mule deer were hunted in the 1950s, 1960s, or 1970s, they have vanished. On many ranges where mule deer were once observed by the thousands, numbers have now decreased to hundreds or fewer. Although sustainable populations have been maintained on most ranges, many units have exhibited drastic reductions in mule deer, and management has often not been successful in maintaining populations at previous numerical or harvest levels.

Trends on the Cache Wildlife Management Unit

On the Cache Unit, the quantity and quality of winter ranges have declined. On 26 long-term trend transects assessed during 1984 and 1996, for example, the mean number of shrubs of big sagebrush *Artemisia tridentata* declined from 3,278 to 2,650 shrubs per acre. On 10 transects containing antelope bitterbrush *Purshia tridentata*, the mean number of shrubs declined from 610 to 550 plants per acre, and on 11 transects containing low rabbit-brush *Chrysothamnus viscidiflorus*, the mean number of shrubs declined from 1,911 to 1,565 plants per acre (Utah DWR 1958–2008). Since 1996 numbers have mostly continued to decline.

On the Cache Unit, the mean buck harvest declined from 3,600 during the period 1951–1983, to almost 3,300 during the period 1984–1992, and to about 1,500 during the period 1993–2008 (Utah DWR 1951–2008). Furthermore, the mean post-season fawns-per-100-does ratios have declined from 87 during the period 1951–1983, to 82 during the period 1984–1992, to 73 during the period 1993–2008. The mean number of buck deer checked at the Blacksmith Fork Checking station has followed this same downward trend with a mean of 244 deer checked between 1951 and 1983, a mean of 178 checked between 1984 and 1992, and about 60 or fewer checked between 1993 and 2008. In 2009 only 18 bucks were checked.

However, the critical spring recruitment ratio of fawns to adults has not been affected by changing buck-to-doe ratios. Although highly variable between years and dependent on the severity of the winter, recruitment continues to average between 50 and 60 fawns per 100 adults. For example, a mean of 52 fawns per 100 adults was recorded between 1994 and 2008. This is a significant finding in view of the declining post-season buck-to-doe ratios. Between 1951 and 1983, the mean post-season classification count found 29 bucks per 100 does; for the 1984–1992 period the mean ratio was 13 bucks per 100 does, and between 1993 and 2008 the mean ratio was also 13 bucks per 100 does. Numerous examples from many herd units are available in which changes in the number of post-season bucks show no effect on recruitment the following year.

Lesson One. Factors Attributed to Causing the Decline of Mule Deer Populations

In 2000, I identified and prioritized six factors contributing to the decline of mule deer on the Cache Wildlife Management Unit. Although designed for the Cache unit, these factors can be applied to any management unit which has shown a significant decline in the numbers of mule deer. However, the order of prioritization may change depending on the unit. An outline of those factors is presented below, followed by a brief discussion of each factor.

Prioritized Factors Contributing to the Decline of Mule Deer on the Cache Wildlife Management Unit.

(1) Reduced carrying capacity on winter ranges:
   (a) Excessive populations of mule deer resulted in overutilization of shrubs and reduced carrying capacity.
   (b) Wildfire destruction of winter-range shrubs.
   (c) Introduction of competitive exotic species.
   (d) Succession of winter ranges toward reduced shrub productivity and species diversity.
(2) Increased human population:
   (a) Urbanization and destruction of foothill winter ranges.
   (b) Highways blocking migration corridors, habitat fragmentation, and increasing vehicle mortality.
   (c) Outdoor recreation vehicles and snowmobiles reducing wildlife habitat use, especially on winter ranges.
   (d) Human and dog harassment on both summer and winter ranges.
(3) Changes in livestock grazing on winter ranges:
   (a) Lack of livestock grazing in spring.
   (b) Reduced rates of livestock grazing in spring.
   (c) Livestock grazing in late summer, autumn, winter, or year-round.
   (d) Shift from sheep to cattle grazing.
(4) Increased effects of predators:
   (a) Decreased control and increased populations of coyotes.
   (b) Increase in the number of cougars.

(c) Reduction in alternative prey species available for coyotes and cougars, especially rabbits and hares.

(d) Increase in red fox and golden eagle populations.

(5) Increased competition with elk:

(a) Elk causing displacement of mule deer.

(b) Elk competition for critical winter forages.

(c) Elk concentrations on winter ranges decreasing shrub viability.

(6) Changing public values:

(a) Decreased public support for traditional management tools, including predator control, livestock grazing and prescribed fire.

(b) Increase of public input into management decisions, which conflicts with optimizing mule deer populations and hunter harvest.

Factor One: Reduced Carrying Capacity on Winter Ranges

Since about the mid-1940s, the four elements of factor one—overutilization of shrubs, wildfire destruction, new competitive plant species, and reduced shrub productivity and plant diversity—have significantly contributed to decreased carrying capacity.

One element rarely recognized is that excessive populations of mule deer cause damage to winter ranges. These build-ups have occurred intermittently at various locations in the state and result in the overutilization of shrubs. Over-utilized shrubs loose vigor, resulting in reduced vegetative productivity, increased shrub mortality, and, importantly, reduced future carrying capacity. The effects of overpopulation on winter ranges are worsened by harsh winters. For example, during the winter of 1983–1984, deer populations throughout Utah exceeded the carrying capacity of the winter ranges. The frigid winter resulted in an estimated winter kill of 50 percent of Utah's total deer population and 70 percent of the Cache unit population. However, even more significantly, massive amounts of winter range shrubs were severely damaged or destroyed. Overutilization of big sagebrush occurs when use exceeds 50 percent of the current annual growth. For most deciduous shrubs, such as antelope bitterbrush, the acceptable utilization level is about 65 percent, and for evergreen species, such as Utah juniper or curlleaf mahogany, the critical level of utilization is only about 30 percent (Austin 2000). Excessive overpopulations of mule deer quickly surpass these forage limitations and therefore damage their winter ranges.

Wildfires also destroy winter ranges. Since 1998 wildfires have played a major role in changing winter range carrying capacities throughout the western United States. For example, it has been estimated that between 1994 and 2003, one-third of the sagebrush-steppe habitat in Nevada burned. On sagebrush-steppe habitat, which comprises the majority of mule deer winter range, fire almost totally removes the big sagebrush. Unlike perennial grasses and forbs, big sagebrush dies in wildfire. Fire also kills some of the other important shrubs on winter ranges, such as antelope bitterbrush and Utah serviceberry, but these plants can re-sprout some of the time. For example, after the 1994 fire on the Richmond Wildlife Management Area on the Cache unit, I observed 30 percent of the antelope bitterbrush to re-sprout and survive. Observed estimated recovery time following a wildfire, including extensive re-seeding efforts, is estimated to take 20 to 30 years. With no efforts in re-seeding, the recovery interval can be 40 years or longer or even never when combined with competition from exotic plants.

Introduced competitive exotic plant species destroy ranges in two ways. First, the presence of these species results in direct competition for soil moisture and nutrients. This competition results in reduced shrub productivity and increased mortality of native shrubs. Second and indirectly, the presence of introduced species blocks or inhibits plant succession from proceeding toward increased species diversity. Mule deer cannot survive with only big sagebrush available for forage on winter ranges. Shrub productivity and species diversity on winter ranges is critical for mule deer to maintain adequate levels of nutrient intake during winter.

The fourth element contributing to reduced carrying capacity on winter ranges is the subtle succession of the ranges toward decreased shrub productivity and species diversity, which can be directly linked to the effects of the first three elements, particularly competition with exotic species. Overpopulations of mule deer lead to decreased shrub productivity and species diversity when their use of these forages exceeds the plants' level of proper utilization, especially when combined with harsh winters. Wildfire decreases productivity and diversity when it kills some shrubs and severely damages others to the point that many years are required for recovery. Exotic plant species reduce productivity and

Urbanization encroaches on winter range near Green Canyon outside
Logan. This aerial view defined the winter range in 1996 prior to
later housing developments.

diversity by taking the soil moisture and nutrients that native shrubs
need to adequately supply the forage needs of mule deer. Shrub productivity and species diversity define winter ranges; when they decrease, the
range's carrying capacity plummets.

Factor Two: Increased Human Population

Major portions of winter ranges are being lost to the changes in urbanization. Urbanization destroys foothill winter ranges in three ways. First, a
portion of the rangeland is removed to build houses and lawns. Second, a
portion of the rangeland around the new houses is lost as an effective winter range simply by the invading presence of people. Third, new trails and
heavier uses, especially during winter, by not only people but also by dogs
and cats greatly curtail mule deer's use of the winter range. I have estimated that for every home built on previously unoccupied winter range,
five acres and one wintering deer are essentially lost due to human usage.

Parallel with the losses from urbanization are the direct and indirect
losses from highways. Enlarged highways directly remove rangeland,

Photo by Dan Miller

As shown in this 2009 aerial photograph, thirteen years
later, urbanization continues to encroach on winter
range near Green Canyon.

block migration corridors, and force deer to winter on more restrictive winter range. Highways also fragment habitat, which often leads to differential degrees of usage on either side of the road. But most importantly, increased highway speeds lead to an increase in vehicle collisions. Recent observations, such as on highway U.S. 89-91 over the Wellsville Mountains, have indicated highway mortality may exceed predator mortality or total hunter harvest. Underpasses and overpasses along fenced highways, again such as in Sardine Canyon between Mantua and Wellsville, have restricted values as usage is generally limited to only a fraction of the previous migration.

The use of outdoor recreation vehicles and snowmobiles has increased at exponential rates. Increased use on winter ranges has led to decreased habitat available for mule deer. Similarly, the increased presence of recreating people, and especially people with non-leashed dogs, has increased harassment on both summer and winter ranges. These human harassments in all likelihood decrease the productivity of mule deer.

Photo by Dan Miller

Deer caution signs may be viewed near highways such as US 89-91.
Increased highway mortality of deer, especially does, has become a
major factor affecting population dynamics.

Factor Three: Changes in Livestock Grazing on Winter Ranges

The number of livestock grazing Utah's rangelands has gradually decreased at least since the 1950s. In many cases this decrease was better for the landscapes due to the previous overgrazing of forage resources. However, the lack of livestock grazing on winter ranges in spring and early summer results in a slow change from shrub lands to grasslands.

On winter ranges where livestock grazing still occurs in spring, often that grazing is very light. Light grazing is marginally effective in reducing the grass component of the range and allowing the shrub component to gain the competitive advantage of being able to utilize the moisture and soil nutrients.

On many winter ranges livestock grazing occurs in late summer, fall, winter, or year-round instead of occurring only during spring. All of these grazing regimes have resulted in reduced winter shrub forage for mule deer on the Cache unit.

Finally, the shift from sheep to cattle grazing has tended to lessen the positive effects of spring grazing. Sheep are normally tended by a herder, which results in more evenly distributed use of the range resource, whereas cattle are normally free ranging and tend to concentrate heavily near water. The differences in body size of the classes of livestock change the levels of soil compaction under damp soil conditions, the effects of which are much lessened by sheep. Also sheep, having a smaller head, tend to be able to graze and remove grasses under and nearer the base of shrubs, thereby improving the shrubs' competitive advantage.

Factor Four: Increased Effects of Predators

Before the 1970s, strychnine was used to control coyote populations. Since the outlawing of the poison in the 1970s, in many areas coyotes have responded with higher populations, leading to increased mule deer mortality, especially of fawns within the first eight weeks following birth and under deep snow conditions in winter.

Cougars have increased throughout the West. Studies have clearly and repeatedly identified mule deer as the primary component of the cougar diet. A good estimate for cougar-caused mortality remains at almost one deer per week per cougar, or about 30 to 50 deer per cougar per year. However, deer mortalities can be lessened depending upon the alternate prey base. For example, I suggest under conditions of a plentiful supply of rabbits, cougar impacts may decrease to a rate of about 25 deer per year per cougar. Also the age and sex of the individual cougar can affect rates of kills. For example, females with kittens, while teaching the skills of stalking and killing, may have a rate exceeding 100 deer per adult female cougar with kittens per year, whereas yearlings, in habitat containing several abundant alternative prey species, may have a rate less than 25 deer per cougar per year.

Population indices of cottontail rabbits and probably hares, as indicated from data collected along survey routes on the Cache unit, have greatly declined since the mid-1960s. These declines have reduced a major alternative prey base, resulting in more predation on mule deer. Long-term potential changes in other small mammal populations are largely undefined; however, it is likely that some populations have experienced similar declines. For example, along Breeding Bird Survey routes, I have observed reduced populations of the Uinta ground squirrel in portions of Rich County, Utah.

Finally, a new major predator was recently added to the list of deer problems. The red fox, which appears questionable as a native species of Utah, invaded the West a few decades ago and its population has some effect in increasing predator mortality of mule deer, particularly fawns less than eight weeks old. On one occasion I observed a red fox chasing, cornering along a fence line, and killing a young fawn. Similarly, increased populations of golden eagles have some minor effects on newly-born fawns, and both golden and bald eagles add minor predatory effects in late winter.

Factor Five: Increased Competition with Elk

Elk are a major competitor with mule deer when resources are not adequate for the combined species on winter ranges. Simply because of their larger size and presence, elk will displace mule deer. Generally elk, like mule deer, seek the best habitats on the winter range. When elk settle into those habitats they often force deer to seek alternative areas, usually of lower quality.

Elk eat the same forages as mule deer but can tolerate a wider range of species and coarser materials. Elk can reach higher and consume a higher proportion of the current annual growth as well as the older second-year growth. Mule deer have more difficulty digesting the larger sized current annual growth twigs, and great difficulty digesting any of the second-year growth.

Usually deer travel in small groups most of the winter and move constantly over a winter range. A shrub plant may receive two or three bites or stem removals from a deer before it moves on. Later a second deer may remove a similar amount of stems. However, elk usually travel in large groups and tend to "camp-out" at particular sites. At those sites two to five elk may key in on a palatable shrub and in one feeding remove nearly 100 percent of the current annual growth. In an extended camp-out, the second or even third year growth may be removed. I have observed that this effect of elk concentrations on winter ranges and heavy use at specific locations and on selected shrubs often leads to greatly decreased shrub viability and productivity, and increased shrub mortality. In essence, elk are much harsher on winter range shrubs than deer, particularly when the forage base is restricted or populations exceed carrying capacity.

Factor Six: Changing Public Values

Societal values and opinions about maintaining wildlife populations have greatly changed. Much of this change has been positive in that many species now receive improved protection and endangered species have a fighting chance to survive. However, the changing public opinion has reduced the availability of traditional management tools, including intensive predator control. In some cases decreased or eliminated livestock grazing has significantly limited the positive management of grazing on winter ranges. The required paperwork for prescribed fires has curtailed the use of this tool on public lands.

Public input into management decisions occasionally conflicts with optimizing mule deer populations. Wintering deer eating landscaped shrubbery is an obvious example. Similarly, hunter preferences for harvest have sometimes affected manager's options in management decisions. Responding to public opinion is gradually consuming more management time, thereby effectively decreasing the time managers can devote to the understanding and management of the resources.

Lesson Two. Costs of Feeding Mule Deer in Winter

Following is a discussion of the costs involved in attempting to improve survival of mule deer during the extremely cold and snowy winter of 2001–2002 on the Cache Wildlife Management Unit. The extent and productivity of winter range for mule deer has been recognized as the primary factor limiting mule deer populations on most units, but is especially true for Utah deer units associated with extensive mountainous habitats. Winter range is broadly defined as the geographic area used by mule deer in winter. The winter period, although often shorter on both ends, extends for a maximum of six months from about November 1 to April 30.

The pertinent data and information associated with the wintering deer on the Cache unit during the winter of 2001–2002 include mule deer population indices of classification counts, mortality estimates, overwinter browse utilization estimates from permanent plots, pellet group densities, costs and effort associated with deer feeding, and costs associated with depredation payments.

Brief History of the 2001–2002 Winter Conditions and the Cache Mule Deer Feeding Effort

After two years of unusually mild winters in northern Utah, and a normal fall in 2001, major snow storms began hitting Cache Valley on November 24, 2001. At some locations 24-hour snow depth accumulation exceeded 20 inches, and temperatures dropped considerably below normal.

These conditions, unusual for the November–December period, forced deer to make a rarely observed rapid migration to lower winter ranges. Under normal winter conditions deer gradually descend to the lower elevation winter ranges, often spending two to three months on transition ranges between summer and lower winter ranges. In winter 2001–2002, the majority of migrating deer were found within a few days on lower winter ranges. Although forage production on most of the Cache's winter ranges was considered adequate for the herd size under normal winter conditions, this early migration caused concerns for carrying capacity potential, even under the condition of the Cache deer herd population being under the management goal.

Deer were in good physical condition going into the winter. The fat depth index measured at the xiphoid process at deer checking stations in Logan and Blacksmith Fork canyons indicated all age classes of buck deer were in good to excellent condition.

Deep snow and colder-than-normal temperatures prevailed through the end of December. The first observations of loss of vitality for many fawns were clearly noted at the end of December. Conditions became critical for fawn survival. According to the Utah Wildlife Review, "A concerned coalition of sportsman's groups, recognizing the stresses deer were beginning to exhibit, began a feeding program in late December. Feeding sites were selected on private property, and DWR biologists provided advice on foods to feed and feeding operations" (*Utah Wildlife Review*, 2002). Three dedicated sportsmen supervised the feeding program at the beginning and throughout the winter in Cache County.

Following a request for feeding from DWR's biologist in Cache Valley, DWR's Salt Lake City and Northern Regional staff conducted a field tour of the valley on January 8, 2002. During that tour, a formal written proposal for feeding Cache Valley big game was handed to the DWR administration by the Cache DWR's biologist. The proposal listed six reasons that necessitated a feeding program on the Cache unit:

(1) Reduction of depredation of agricultural haystacks and land-
     scaped residential properties.
(2) Reduction in competition and shrub utilization pressure on
     big game winter ranges, particularly as shrubs were limited by
     snow cover that year.
(3) Reduction of human safety concerns on US-91 in the
     Richmond area. Warning signs of big game along the highway
     had been installed by Utah Department of Transportation fol-
     lowing the request from the Cache biologist.
(4) Snow depths between November 26 and January 7 greatly
     exceeded normal levels. Temperatures during the same period
     were also much colder than normal.
(5) DWR's license revenue from the Cache unit comprises a com-
     pellingly high percentage of the state's revenue. This revenue is
     primarily due to three factors: large blocks of public land avail-
     able for hunting; location with respect to the human population
     centers; and adequate big and small game populations. Thus the
     argument was that a minimum population of mule deer should
     be maintained to provide broad-based hunter opportunity.
(6) Elk migration from Idaho had increased depredation difficul-
     ties in the towns of Cornish, Cove, and Richmond.

On January 21, 2002, DWR granted formal approval for feeding
big game at six sites, each north of Logan Canyon. DWR immediately
began purchasing alfalfa hay, deer pellets, and whole corn to be fed at the
approved sites. This program continued until green-up, about April 1,
when deer diet switched from winter browse and prepared feeds to new
growth of spring grasses. During the remainder of the winter, volunteer
sportsmen conducted the feeding with the DWR overseeing the operations and purchasing.

From January 5 to 27, 2002, the weather moderated and some traditional winter ranges began to 'bare-off' providing some native forage
for mule deer. However, on January 28, an extremely heavy, all-time
record snowfall was recorded. More than two feet of snow fell, covering the valley and winter ranges and creating critical conditions for
deer survival.

On January 28, a request was again made by the Cache biologist
to expand the feeding operation from 6 to 15 feeding sites located

throughout Cache Valley. On the same day, approval was granted by the DWR administration to feed as needed and as limited by sportsman volunteers in the Valley, but excluded the Cornish area. Fourteen stations were established in Cache County. On the same day and at the same time, the request was also made by the Cache biologist to begin limited feeding of deer in Bear Lake Valley of Rich County. Approval was immediate and feeding of deer commenced within a few days thereafter at four designated sites. Two individuals coordinated the feeding in Bear Lake Valley.

In addition to feeding deer, the volunteers were asked to assist the DWR in trapping and marking deer with radio collars. Seventeen does, nine from feeding areas and eight from non-feeding areas, were captured and marked. The study was designed to determine the effects of feeding on doe survival. DWR made a doctoral research assistantship available and began a detailed study of the effects of feeding.

Feeds and Feeding Costs

The Cache biologist recommended two pounds of feed per deer per day at the feeding sites. It was also recommended that alfalfa hay and deer pellets constitute the majority of the feed, with rolled barley fed in much lesser amounts. Although various combinations of rations were used at the daily feed stations, all feed was consumed by the next day.

At approximately $100 per ton for alfalfa hay, $180 per ton for deer pellets, and $130 per ton for whole corn, the DWR expenses for feed are shown in Table 15-1. Rolled barley was not fed, and therefore is not included in the table.

Table 15-1. DWR expenses for 2001–2002 feeding program, Cache and Rich counties.

Feed	Cache County	Rich County	Total
Alfalfa Hay	$5,094.56	$650.00	$5,744.56
Deer Pellets	4,600.00	1,502.60	6,102.50
Whole Corn	864.00	634.00	1,498.00
Sub Total	$10,558.56	$2,786.60	$13,345.06

In addition to DWR costs, the donations made for Cache County are shown in Table 15-2.

Table 15-2. Donations to Cache County for
2001–2002 feeding program.

Monetary donations from individuals:	$1,660.00
Alfalfa hay donations from individuals:	1,100.00
Feed purchases by the Mule Deer foundation:	840.00
Feed purchases by Sportsmen for Fish and Wildlife	2,971.93
Feed barrels donated by Tyco	500.00
Total donations:	$7,071.93

Total costs of the feeding program were $17,630.49 for Cache County and $2,786.60 for Rich County, or a total cost of $20,417.09.

Two formulations of deer pellets were fed. Although the Trenton Feed pellet at 15 percent protein was more readily eaten than the Walton Feed pellet at 14.5 percent protein, both formulations were totally consumed. The two mixes are shown in Table 15-3.

Table 15-3. Trenton and Walton pellet compositions compared.

Ingredient	Trenton Pounds/ton	Walton Pounds/ton
Alfalfa meal	596	460
Corn, ground	425	400
Barley, ground	385	220
Wheat bran	325	280
Soybean meal	175	170
Molasses	050	140
DiCalcium	20	20
Salt	20	20
Maxi bond	4	0
Beet pulp	0	270
Calcite	0	20
Total	2,000	2,000

A lamb grower pellet and a high-energy deer pellet were also available from feed stores and fed by some individuals. The lamb grower pellet with second or third crop alfalfa hay and occasional rolled barley was used for many years in maintaining tame deer at the Utah State

University research facility. The approximate composition of these feeds is shown in Table 15-4.

Table 15-4. Lamb grower and deer pellet compositions compared.

Nutrient	Lamb Grower	Deer Pellet
Crude protein	12%	14%
Crude fat	02%	04%
Crude fiber	12%	10%
Salt	01%	00%
Calcium	01%	01%
Potassium	00%	01%
Phosphorus	>1%	>1%
Selenium	>1%	>1%
Zinc	>1%	00%
Magnesium	00%	>1%
Vitamin A	>1%	>1%
Vitamin D	00%	>1%
Vitamin E	>1%	>1%

The lamb grower pellet is generally recommended for backyard feeding for a limited number of deer because of its common availability at most feed stores, whereas the various deer pellets are often unavailable at feed stores or available only under special order. Nonetheless, all four pellets are considered to be excellent deer foods for emergency feeding.

Table 15-5. Volunteer work hours, Cache and Rich counties.

Category	Cache County		Rich County	
	Hours Donated	Value at $10.00/hour	Hours Donated	Value at $10.00/hour
Feeding	2,088	20,880	200	2,000
Deer Trapping	204	2,040	0	0
Hay Hauling	198	1,980	10	100
Administration	87	870	10	100
Total	2,577	$25,700	220	$2,200

Volunteer Hours

The work-hours contributed by sportsmen are shown in Table 15-5.

The total costs of the feeding operation on the Cache unit during the winter of 2001–2002, including volunteer hours valued at $10 per hour, was $48,317.09. I selected the rate of $10 per hour as a minimum rate for volunteers and for simplicity of comparisons.

Landowner Depredation Payments

Numerous landowners in both Cache and Rich Counties received depredation damage primarily from mule deer and elk, although some damage was also reported for pronghorn and moose. Many homeowners received damage to landscaped plants, but complaints were relatively few compared to the number of homeowners receiving landscape damage. Most agricultural damage was limited to small, dollar amounts due to preventative actions involving feeding locations and haystack fencing, both permanent and temporary, and damage payments were mostly not necessary. In several cases free and fee landowner mitigation permits for mule deer and elk covered the compensation costs. Despite these efforts, several agricultural landowners received significant crop loss due to depredation by mule deer and elk. In Cache County, 18 processed damage claims totaled $17,416. Claims ranged from $200 to $2,000. In Rich County, 13 processed damage claims totaled $16,900. Claims ranged from $250 to $4,000. In total, 31 damage claims were processed with a total of $34,316.00. Landowners with damage under $200 did not choose to process a claim, usually replying, some big game use of crops is just part of the farming and ranching lifestyle.

Final costs for maintaining mule deer during the winter, including feeds, estimated labor costs, and depredation payments totaled $82,633.09.

Lesson Three. Deer Survival under a Feeding Regime

Comparing Post-Season and Spring Classification Counts

Post-season classification on the Cache unit collected between November 15 and December 31 showed 1,522 deer were counted with 101 bucks, 831 does, and 590 fawns. These numbers indicated that the fawn-to-adult ratio at the beginning of the winter was 63.3 fawns per 100 adults. This ratio was near the average of 66.5 fawns per 100 adults for the preceding eight years. The ratio of 63.3 fawns per 100 adults was consistent over all subunits on the entire Cache unit.

Spring classification counts, primarily collected after March 15, showed significant change in the fawn-to-adult ratios from the post-season count. These data are summarized by subunits in Table 15-6.

Table 15-6. Spring classification counts comparing feeding and non-feeding sites.

Area	Adults	Fawns	Fawns to 100 Adults
Blacksmith Fork Drainage			
Feeding sites	062	042	67.7
Non-feeding sites	156	013	08.3
East Face (Cache County)			
Feeding sites	290	158	54.5
Non-feeding sites	056	002	03.6
Logan Canyon			
Non-feeding sites	069	007	10.1
South Cache County			
Non-feeding sites	137	042	30.7
Wellsville Mountains			
Non-feeding sites	028	001	03.6
Clarkston Mountains (Box Elder County)			
Non-feeding sites	050	030	60.0
Laketown (Rich County)			
Feeding sites	121	047	38.8
Non-feeding sites	023	002	08.7
East Bear Lake (Rich County)			
Non-feeding sites	217	025	11.5
Randolph-Woodruff			
Non-feeding sites	091	026	28.6

Crawford Mountains

Non-feeding sites	<u>096</u>	<u>017</u>	<u>17.7</u>
Totals	1,396	412	29.5

The number of deer fed in Cache County was estimated to be a minimum of 1,500, and the number fed in Rich County was estimated at 600. From these classification counts, comparing feeding sites to non-feeding sites, feeding increased fawn-to-adult ratios by a factor eight, fifteen and four in Blacksmith Fork, East Face along the foothills in Cache County, and Bear Lake Valley, respectively. These figures mirror the observed weather severity with the East Face receiving the harshest winter conditions, Blacksmith Fork drainage not quite as severe, and Bear Lake Valley the least severe of the three.

Using the figure of estimated total costs, $82,633, and the estimated number of deer fed, 2,100, the cost per deer fed was estimated to be about $39 per deer. If the costs of volunteer labor, $48,317, are deducted, that estimate reduces to just over $16 per deer.

Although the positive effects of feeding on survival may have been much higher, I conservatively estimated that roughly 400 deer (200 adults and 200 fawns) that would have died without feeding survived. Using these same estimated figures, the cost per deer saved was estimated at $207 with labor included and about $86 with no labor costs. Assuming that 90 buck fawns and 10 adult bucks were in the following years harvested by hunters, the feeding costs per harvested buck were estimated at $826 and $483 including volunteer labor and without labor, respectively. The population of deer, including male and female fawns and their offspring, produced from surviving does that would have died without the feeding effort cannot be estimated.

In 2005, emergency feeding of mule deer was again conducted on the Cache unit. Results were similar. An estimated 2,800 deer were fed, compared to 2,100 deer in the winter of 2001–2002. DWR costs were estimated at about $39,000, compared to $34,000 in 2001–2002, and volunteer labor costs at about $31,000, compared to $48,000 in 2001–2002. Total costs per deer fed were about $25 including labor, compared to $39 in 2001–2002, and with the costs of volunteer labor deducted they were $14, compared to $16 in 2001–2002 (Dolling 2005). The number of deer saved was not estimated.

As other studies have shown, despite the successes of supplemental feeding the costs are often prohibiting (Doman and Rasmussen 1944; Urness 1980). Furthermore, the labor costs of feeding are significant, and unless the labor is volunteered, feeding deer in winter may be economically difficult to justify.

During winter of 2001-2002, in areas where winter weather was most severe and no feeding was provided, fawn-to-adult ratios in spring ranged from only 3.6 to 11.5 fawns per 100 adults. On less severe areas these ratios ranged from 17.7 to 30.7 fawns per 100 adults. On feeding sites the ratios were significantly improved and ranged from 38.8 to 67.7 fawns per 100 adults. By comparison, on the east slopes of the Wellsville and Clarkston Mountains, where winter conditions were near normal, the fawn-per-100-adult ratio was about 60 and showed almost no change from the earlier post-season classification.

Comparing Classification Counts between Winter Periods at Feeding Sites

Four sets of classification data are available from the same feeding sites. Classification counts were conducted during two or three time periods separated by an interval of at least two weeks. These data indicate the change in fawn-to-adult ratios during the time periods between counts. Mean data from these counts is presented in Table 15-7.

Table 15-7. Classification counts between winter periods at feeding sites.

Location	Date	Fawns	Adults	Fawns per 100 Adults
Hyde Park	Jan 25	31	48	64.6
	Feb 28	45	107	42.0
Meadowville	Feb 21	54	118	45.8
	Mar 28	47	121	38.8
Smithfield	Jan 25	49	98	50.0
	Feb 22	63	125	50.4
Green Canyon	Jan 12	62	98	63.3
	Feb 15	32	66	48.5
	Mar 4	51	94	54.3

In three of the four comparisons, the fawn-to-adult ratio declined significantly. The Hyde Park data are considered excellent. These data were recorded by the same individual during both counts. The Meadowville data were collected by the Cache biologist and are also considered an excellent comparison. In these two areas, the deer observed were considered to be the same population. Counts at Smithfield and Green Canyon may not be as consistent because the deer observed between counts were more likely to be from different populations due to changes in groups of deer using these feeding stations.

At non-feeding locations fawn mortality in Cache County from winter weather was first observed beginning about January 1. Mortality from buck deer was first observed about February 1, and for does about March 1.

At the end of the winter, the Utah deer population on the Cache Wildlife Management Unit was estimated by the DWR biologist at about 7,000 deer, as shown in Table 15-8. This estimate did not include about 500 Idaho and 500 Wyoming deer, which had migrated from their respective summer ranges in the adjacent states.

Table 15-8. Estimate of the Cache deer population in spring 2002 by subunits.

Bear Lake Valley	1,100
Randolph-Woodruff	800
Wellsville-Clarkston Mountains	800
Blacksmith Fork Drainage	1,800
Logan Canyon Drainage	500
Cache Valley East Face	2,000
Total	7,000

Lesson Four. Maintaining Balance between Big Game Numbers and Winter Range

Annual Big Game Browse Utilization, Overwinter Mortality, and Pellet-Group Count Data

Between 1997 and 2002, sixteen transects 500 meters in length and 24 plots measuring 10 by 10 meters were used to evaluate overwinter utilization on the Cache unit. These data are summarized are summarized in Table 15-9.

Table 15-9. Overwinter transect data from the Cache unit, 1997–2002.

Year	Deer Days/ha	Elk Days/ha	Deer Mortality	% Browse Utilization			% Carrying Capacity
				Artr	Putr	Other	
1997	66	18	43	45	62	45	75
1998	27	10	75	30	56	24	50
1999	27	4	26	17	29	22	26
2000	19	5	6	6	20	13	13
2001	47	4	7	17	37	23	29
2002	53	3	55	36	56	36	71

Note: In my opinion, the relationship between numbers of big game animals and the annual utilization of the available winter range forages should be determined on a yearly basis in spring. In order to properly balance big game populations with the forage resources available, these data are an essential component of big game management, management plans, and recommendations. Management plans consistently describe and require this animal-forage balance, but data are rarely collected to facilitate the necessary understanding and documentation. The range data collected on the Cache unit beginning in 1997 fulfilled this requirement. Most management systems collect intensive data on the populations dynamics, including sex ratios, fawn-to-adult ratios, age structure and antler characteristics of the harvested buck population, and physical condition indices, but most data collection systems simply forget or ignore the first half of the management prescription—the animal relationship with the forage resource. For example, in recommending hunting seasons and number of permits, knowing the number of big game animals available on a range is only important if the browsing impacts on the range are also known. When the range relationships are unknown, unsupported recommendations are submitted, which often lead to expanding populations in excess of range resources. Although the Utah big game range trend studies provide excellent data on a periodic, five-year cycle, these studies do not consider utilization on an annual basis, and therefore, do not address the causes of the trends. Both sets of data are essential.

Mule deer and big game in general have the unusual ability to destroy their habitat in a few short years of overpopulation. The first result of overpopulation is severe die-offs during a harsh or even moderate winter. The second result of overpopulation is excessive use of critical shrub species, especially during years of harsh winter weather. The consequence of excessive utilization of shrubs leads to the third result of reduced shrub productivity, increased shrub mortality, and decreased ability of the habitat to support mule deer. The fourth result is the logical and unfortunate decrease in the future carrying capacity of mule deer. Since about 1930 various units have experienced years of significant overpopulations and overused ranges, followed by severely decreased deer populations. Many of these significant die-offs and losses of range resources, due to the effects of deer populations in excess of carrying capacities on many or most of Utah's ranges, occurred during the winters of 1983–1984, 1988–1989, and 1992–1993.

The winter of 2001–2002 showed a significant increase in utilization of winter shrub forages compared to the three previous mild winters. Deer pellet group density increased while elk pellet group density slightly decreased. Temperatures were extremely cold, and snow depths on winter range were above average. Overwinter mortality was major. An estimated 50 percent of the Cache deer herd died during this harsh winter, including 80 to 90 percent of the fawns, 40 to 60 percent of the bucks, and 20 to 30 percent of the does. Minor losses were also observed for calf elk and moose.

The wintering period was long, fall regrowth was slight, snow cover was constant, and deer were forced onto critical winter ranges early into the winter. These factors caused deer to utilize winter range shrubs at an earlier and higher rate than under average winter conditions, despite the fact that deer numbers were considerably under the management goal of 25,000. In the spring, shrub utilization by subunit indicated that the Clarkston Mountains were under carrying capacity; the East Face, Garden City-Laketown, and Crawford Mountains were slightly under carrying capacity; the Blacksmith Fork drainage, Logan River drainage, East Bear Lake, and Woodruff Creek were about at carrying capacity; and the Wellsville Mountains in the Box Elder Canyon exceeded carrying capacity. Over the entire Cache unit the percent carrying capacity, determined by the utilization means of big sagebrush, antelope bitter-brush, and other palatable shrubs on deer winter ranges, was measured at 71 percent. These data indicated that big game populations on the Cache unit remained below carrying capacity.

Lesson Five. Redefining the Concept of Necessary Mule Deer Winter Range

All winter range is not equal in importance for sustaining mule deer populations. Also the importance of any habitat or subunit may change between years depending on the winter weather conditions of those years. Numerous titles describe various aspects of winter range and include transition range, upper, middle and lower winter ranges, critical winter range and important winter range. From my observations on the Cache unit during the extreme, and challenging for deer survival, winter of 2001–2002, I recommend using the term "vital mule deer winter range."

"Vital mule deer winter ranges" are those areas where mule deer are found in significant numbers when weather conditions exceed the following parameters: nighttime temperatures are colder than zero degrees Fahrenheit and snow depth on winter ranges exceeds eight inches.

Under these conditions, deer seek the vital locations of winter range where plant cover, slope, and aspect maximize thermal cover and temperatures, and thereby maximize the opportunity for survival. Additional criteria for vital mule deer winter ranges include the area's size and its ability to support mule deer through very cold and difficult winters. The area must first act as a gathering place for mule deer when the above two conditions are reached. Vital ranges always contain thermal cover, such as Utah juniper, or have steep south-southwest–facing slopes. The area must contain at least 500 acres and be capable of supporting at least 100 deer.

Numerous small areas of survival habitat are available, such as small protected draws of a few acres; well-landscaped backyards; small hillsides above roads, canals, or homes; and unimproved land within urbanized developments. Although deer may survive in such areas under severe weather, because of the limited numbers of deer that can be supported and the usually short-term or temporary availability of these habitats before development, they are not considered vital winter range.

On the Cache unit during the winter 2001–2002, the vital deer winter range was clearly defined by the locations of mule deer during the late

January to February period. The portion of the total winter range occupied by mule deer during this period was less than five percent of the defined winter range.

Vital mule deer winter range is simply restricted to only those areas where significant numbers of deer can survive during the harshest of winter conditions. These vital winter ranges must be defined and preserved to maintain deer populations on each of Utah's 30 deer units. Vital deer winter ranges have been identified and mapped on the Cache unit. On ranges where winter range is the bottleneck, loss of these vital winter ranges, due to development, highways, or wildfires, will clearly lead to the demise of the deer herd during severe winters.

Lesson Six. Triggers for Emergency Feeding of Mule Deer in Utah

Generally, deer should not be fed due to numerous economic, disease, and range deterioration reasons. Feeding should only proceed under emergency winter conditions to control big game damage to agricultural crops, to promote public safety by attracting big game away from highways and urban areas, to maintain minimal big game populations, and to relieve stress on populations during severe winter weather. DWR feeding programs must be approved by the division's director.

I believe that the experience gained during the winter of 2001–2002 on the Cache unit indicated certain considerations that should be evaluated before initiating a winter feeding program for mule deer. These criteria are similar to the DWR feeding policy, but were determined before that policy was approved. Feeding should only be initiated if all four of the following criteria are present:

(1)   Temperatures at night have decreased to zero degrees Fahrenheit or colder. Nighttime temperatures are forecasted to be subzero for one or more weeks.

(2)   Snow depth on the winter ranges generally exceeds eight inches. Snow depth in the adjacent valleys exceeds eight inches and is generally continuous.

(3)   Deer or elk have concentrated on vital deer winter ranges.

(4)   Native browse forages are expected to be insufficient to maintain big game throughout the winter.

If any of the above four conditions are marginal and the feeding decision remains debatable, the following criteria should be considered:

(1) Range forage conditions are poorer than normal due to reduced summer production. Fall regrowth of grasses is minor.

(2) Physical condition of deer at the beginning of winter, as determined by the xiphoid fat index, is rated in the poor to fair condition classes.

(3) Migration onto winter ranges occurred earlier in the winter compared to most years.

(4) Commercial feeds, including second and third-crop alfalfa hay, deer pellets, lamb grower pellets, rolled barley, and cracked corn, are readily available.

(5) Monies are available and have been designated for emergency feeding.

(6) Feeding sites have been previously selected and landowner permission obtained, and an emergency feeding plan has been written for the unit.

(7) To maintain deer numbers within carrying capacity of the winter range, sport harvest of antlerless and antlered deer can be accomplished.

(8) A reduction in mule deer–vehicle accidents is likely, resulting in a reduction of human safety concerns.

(9) Reduction of agricultural crop loss is probable, and a reduction of damage to landscaped residential properties is likely.

(10) Public opinion favors feeding of deer.

(11) Sportsman's groups and other volunteers are organized to conduct the feeding. Leaders have volunteered to coordinate the program.

Feeding should be initiated between December 15 and January 31. Generally the most appropriate time to initiate feeding appears to be about January 1. Upon program initiation, feeding should continue through about the end of March, or until green-up. At this time, deer diets rapidly change in only a few days from the provided commercial feeds and available browse to the new spring growth of grasses, followed in a few more days by the availability of spring forbs.

Chapter 16

Defining Management Techniques

Every management question must deal not only with the question of how many deer, but what sex and age . . . .At present we do not even know how to tell the age of a deer!

Aldo Leopold, 1931
Game Survey of the North Central States

Age Determination

The age of mule deer cannot be determined by the number of antler tines or any other antler measurement. For example, although a high proportion, often 50 percent or more, of yearling bucks have 2x2 point antlers, yearling antlers can vary from 1x1 to an occasional 3x3 or even 4x4. Accurate age determination can only be made from dental examination or cementum annuli analysis (Severinghaus 1949; Robinette et al. 1957). Dental examination involves evaluating the teeth in the field, whereas in cementum annuli analysis the two front incisors are cut and removed from the jaw for laboratory inspection. In a laboratory, teeth are decalcified, thinly sliced, and stained, and the annual depository rings, similar to tree rings, are counted under a microscope for accurate age determination (Erickson et al. 1970).

Using tooth eruption, replacement, and wear criteria, most deer can be accurately aged in the field. Once the technique is learned, nearly 100 percent of yearlings, aged one-and-a-half years, 80 to 90 percent of twolings, aged two-and-a-half years, and 70 to 80 percent of mature deer aged three-and-a-half and four-and-a-half years can be aged accurately. Accuracy greatly declines for field determination of deer aged five-and-a-half years and older.

Using cementum annuli analysis, accuracy is often determined by the precision of the laboratory work. If done exactly correctly, cementum annuli analysis is nearly 100 percent accurate. However, because of the difficult techniques involved with the laboratory work, this analysis typically yields levels of accuracy between 80 and 95 percent. Generally, when deer age structure of a herd is important to determine, yearling and twoling deer should be aged in the field, and with much higher costs, cementum annuli analysis should be used only for older deer. Buck and doe deer have identical dental patterns.

Fawns are easily identified by their small body size, with a hog-dressed weight usually between 35 and 55 pounds, and small deciduous milk teeth. Yearling and older deer rarely have hog-dressed weights of less than 70 pounds.

To determine the field age of yearling and older deer, first cut the cheek between the upper and lower jaws and spread the jaws. In October, yearling deer are about 16 months of age and usually have new, large white incisor teeth at the center and front of the lower jaw. Often next to the incisor teeth are very small deciduous milk teeth. Sometimes next to the incisor teeth are empty spaces where the deciduous milk teeth have recently fallen out. The presence of milk teeth or empty spaces is an absolute indicator of a yearling. However, many yearlings have replaced all deciduous teeth with permanent incisors, and age must be determined using the third pre-molar. The third pre-molar is the third molar tooth counting back from the incisor teeth. The third pre-molar on all yearling deer in the fall is a deciduous tooth showing heavy wear and is tri-cuspid, or having three peaks. The tri-cuspid tooth always defines the deer as a yearling. The third premolar is replaced early the next summer when the deer is about 24 months of age. By the following fall at the age of about 28 months, all deciduous teeth have been replaced by the permanent teeth.

Twolings, or deer aged two-and-a-half years are identified by three dental examination criteria: the difference in staining between the lightly stained, new pre-molars toward the front of the jaw and the more darkly stained older molars toward the back of the jaw; sharp lingual crests, distinct lines along the outside upper teeth edges, of the first and second molars; and slight wear, if any, on the white-tipped posterior cups on the third molar, the tooth farthest from the incisors and often still emerging. Although sometimes difficult to deeply cut the jaw back and examine the third molar, the condition of that tooth will almost always accurately age a twoling deer.

Prime deer aged three-and-a-half years and older are separated by evaluating the increasing wear on first and second molars. Most data collection and studies do not split prime age classes into years. However, experienced biologists can readily separate the three- and four-year age classes from older deer. The age classes five, six, seven, and eight become increasingly difficult to age accurately in the field due to the differences in dietary habits by individual deer over their lives. At about seven-and-a-half years deer begin to loose teeth and by nine-and-a-half years many or most teeth are missing from the jaw. Only rarely do mule deer live beyond 12 years.

Classification Counts

Determination of buck-to-doe-to-fawn and adult-to-fawn ratios are an essential part of big game management data collection. Classification counts are collected during three periods.

Pre-season counts are taken from about September 15 to October 15 when fawns and does stay mostly together in small groups. During this count bucks are more isolated and often fewer bucks are counted than are actually represented in the herd composition. The pre-season count yields data on the summer fawn rearing success and the expected number of deer available for the October general hunt. The pre-season count is most useful on units where the later counts are difficult to accomplish and cannot obtain adequate sample sizes. As expected, usually the pre-season fawn-to-doe ratio is extremely close to the fawn-to-doe ratio obtained during the post-season count, especially when the unit is closed to antlerless harvest. The pre-season count is not critical to deer management, especially when the other two classification counts are conducted. Furthermore, significant migration from a unit before the October hunt is rarely a concern, and harvest forecasts are not essential.

However, pre-season counts on private lands, especially Cooperative Wildlife Management Units, are highly recommended and contain several advantages for the landowner. First, because ranches are considerably smaller than wildlife management units, data on the herd composition on private lands may be considerably different than whole units. These data become extremely important on a year-to-year basis in establishing number of hunting permits. A reasonably limited number of hunting permits leads to the second reason why pre-season count data are important. Pre-season count data allow the private landowner to maintain the desired quality of the harvest over time, such as buck size and antler spread, since fewer hunters means more bucks can live longer and grow bigger. Third, due to the interests of hunting clientele, the landowner often needs to be able to present data from the current year. This provides the clientele hunter with information that may help refine selectivity in the harvest of a buck. Fourth, if deer tend to move off the private land before the post-season counts are conducted over entire units, the post-season data may not be reflective of the herd composition on the private land.

The post-season classification count is conducted from about mid-November through the end of December after most deer hunts have ended. The classification count should begin at least seven to ten days after most hunts have finished and bucks have settled into less hunter-wary breeding behaviors. When most big game hunts end about October 31, a good starting date for classification is November 10. Classification counts can continue until almost the end of December when buck deer begin to shed antlers. Although antlers are occasionally shed as early as December 15, a good ending date for the post-season classification count is December 23. The important ratios of bucks per 100 does, fawns per 100 does, and fawns per 100 adults are determined in the post-season counts.

The post-winter classification counts are conducted in late March, April, and sometimes into early May. During this count only the fawns-per-100-adults ratio is determined. However, this is the most important of the classification counts because it indicates the annual recruitment to the deer herd. The count is also compared to the post-season fawns-per-100-adults ratio for an estimate of potential overwinter losses. Spring counts must not begin until the earliest signs of spring green-up are evident. New growth of grasses must be visible on the winter ranges. At the end of winter mortality losses are accelerating, and counts taken before green-up often overestimate actual recruitment. However, within a week following initial green-up, and the consumption of highly palatable and nutritious forages, overwinter mortality has declined to almost zero, and deer begin recovering from winter stresses.

Interestingly, the post-winter count was not conducted for many years because it was thought that by spring fawns could not be accurately separated from adults using visual field observations. However, my unpublished observations conducted in the Uinta Basin on Blue Mountain in the early to mid-1970s, using trapped deer marked with visible numbers, clearly showed that accurate separation of fawns and adults was very feasible. It is highly probable that reports by other Utah biologists reached the same conclusion. Post-winter classification counts were adopted in Utah as a regular management tool beginning statewide about 1980.

Because deer are crepuscular, that is, most active during twilight, classification data are collected using binoculars and spotting scopes only during early morning or late afternoon into evening. Good criteria for count times are to end two hours after sunrise and to begin two hours before sunset. Spotlight counts are inaccurate. Counts should be taken throughout the geographic range and elevation extent, and not just the "better areas" on each deer unit. For example, on the Cache unit, for an in-depth analysis, all counts were separated into 10 geographic areas during the 10-year period from 1994 to 2003. Consistent differences between some of the 10 areas became evident and management recommendations were made accordingly.

In my experience, on good deer ranges a wildlife biologist can usually classify between 25 and 100 deer per observation period. A classification of 50 deer per observation period is about average, and 50 is a good sample size per observation period to maximize and maintain the accuracy and precision of counts.

Some variation exists in the ability of biologists to separate fawns and adults during both post-season and post-winter classification counts. Especially difficult is the split between large male fawns and small yearling does during the post-winter count. However, most paired trials show a variation in ratios of less than 10 percent between experienced biologists classifying the same areas. Some, perhaps most, of that variation can be attributed to differences in the individual deer observed by each biologist.

The higher the number of deer classified on a unit, the greater the accuracy and reliability of the resulting ratios. Highly accurate ratios are obtained when 1,000 or more deer, or 400 or more does, are classified on a unit. A minimum count to retain reasonable accuracy is about 200 does per management unit.

Checking Stations

Utah operates about 12 deer checking stations on the opening weekend of the general deer hunt. One of those stations, Blacksmith Fork, has been run almost continually since 1945. Checking stations are primarily run to collect biological data, although they also serve many other functions. They give the wildlife manager and the sportsman the first indication of the hunt's probable degree of success. They provide an opportunity to share ideas and concerns with hunters and distribute information to the media, aid in law enforcement, and act as a training and education site for students and occasionally sportsmen. Since about 2000, checking stations in Utah have become voluntary stops for hunters transporting deer. However, informal observations indicate that more than 95 percent of hunters who have harvested deer stop at the stations to have their deer examined. Law enforcement has a minor role at checking stations.

Data collected at checking stations usually includes: hunter success on a daily and trip basis by hunting unit and often by location of kill; composition of the harvest, that is the percentage of bucks, does and fawns in the harvest; data from individual deer including age, carcass or hog-dressed weight, fat depth at the xiphoid process as an index to pre-winter physical condition, antler spread and height, number of tines as related to age, parasite load, and often, samples for chronic wasting disease; and miscellaneous information meeting the specific needs of the unit or manager including blood and tissue samples, number of unretrieved deer observed, wildlife violations observed, hunter opinion questionnaires, other species of wildlife observed such as the number of bull, cow, and calf moose, and hunter recommendations.

Three essential pieces of data are collected at checking stations. The first is age composition of harvested bucks, which is used to determine the age structure of the buck population. Combined with the buck harvest and several other pieces of data collected in the field, and through simple computer models, the population size of the herd can be estimated. The second is the physical condition index of fat depth, which is used for later evaluation with winter severity, particularly in regard to supplemental feeding. The third essential data are disease testing. A recent example is the tissue samples collected to test for chronic wasting disease, which are very important for hunter safety and management concerns.

Trapping and Marking

Generally deer are trapped in late fall and early winter. Trapping efforts begin immediately following the end of the deer hunts. At that time of year physical condition of deer is near optimum. Bait is placed on winter ranges to attract deer to the trapping sites for usually five to ten days prior to setting of the traps. However, with good technique, the traps are in place at the beginning of the baiting period to allow deer to become accustomed to the presence of the traps. Invariably, the most successful trapping occurs immediately after the first major snowstorm when deer are adjusting their diet from fall grass regrowth, leaves, and dry forbs to winter browse. At this time tasty alfalfa hay is a strong food attraction to a deer. Because of declining deer physical condition, all trapping efforts should usually end by mid-January and extend no later than the first of February.

The box trap commonly used to trap individual deer, but may trap two or even three deer, consists of a collapsible half-inch diameter pipe frame, measuring about four by four by eight feet, and covered with nylon netting on all four sides and top. The trap, weighing 70 to 80 pounds, is secured to the ground by ropes tied to the bottoms of steel posts that are driven into the ground about four feet away from the midpoint of the long sides of the trap. Juniper trees are often used instead of steel posts where available. The single gate is string-tripped by deer entering the trap to feed on bait. Bait usually consists of second or third-crop dry alfalfa hay, but sometimes apples, apple mesh, rolled barley, or other feeds are used when available. Once deer are in the trap, biologists can either enter the trap directly and wrestle the deer to the ground, or collapse the trap by releasing the ropes tied to the posts. To reduce stress, trapped deer are handled as quickly as possible. Traps are checked at least daily by one or two biologists.

Few deer, only one or two percent, are killed from trapping efforts using box traps. Although biologists may receive many nicks and bruises, injuries are almost never serious. When a biologist enters the trap, the deer, in a frantic effort to escape, usually slam into the far end of the trap. The biologist rapidly crosses the trap, corners the deer, lifts and pulls the legs out from under of the deer, and both fall to the ground with the biologist on top. The take-down is similar to that in wrestling. Once on the ground, the biologist covers the deer's head, particularly its eyes, with a jacket or small blanket to keep it calm while the biologist attaches tags and collars and performs any other work.

Tangle-net traps are used to trap groups of deer and consist of a large net, suspended six to eight feet off the ground and secured by ropes and poles over a baited area. When the net is tripped, up to 20 deer may become tangled and trapped. Trapped deer are usually tranquilized with mild drugs to avoid injury to deer and biologists during untangling, marking, and release. Several biologists are needed to set up and operate large tangle-net traps.

The helicopter rocket tangle net is a relatively new application of the tangle net. Mounted at the base of a helicopter, four small rockets arranged in a square with the net between are fired from close range at selected big game individuals. This technique is very effective and highly selective, and big game injuries are few, but the technique is very costly.

In addition to trapping during winter, small fawns are simply captured by hand or by using long-handled nets when they are only a few days old. By attaching radio collars to captured fawns, this method is often utilized to determine causes of fawn mortality from birth to about six months.

The use of tranquilizing drugs, injected from darts shot from wildlife capture guns, is occasionally used in deer capture. This technique is usually employed in depredation situations when the deer would be translocated to a distant range.

Most captured deer are marked with numbered ear tags and radio telemetry collars. The radios emit signals for up to five years, while the location and movements are monitored. Radio signals can be monitored by fixed-wing aircraft and precisely located using GIS technology, or from ground crews using the same technology. With advances in radio telemetry not only are individual deer movements and locations monitored, but also mortality events, body temperatures, and even birthing dates and locations of fawns.

Previous to the technological development of radio telemetry, biologists relied on visual observations of ear streamers and colored neck collars. Since ear streamers, and color codes or numbers on neck collars were only discernible at distances of usually less than 200 yards, identifying and monitoring individual deer was very difficult and time consuming. Using this methodology, generally only annual migrations routes and major herd movements could be determined.

A Clover deer trap is used in winter to capture deer for research
and migration studies.

Spring Range Rides, Pellet Group, Browse Utilization and Overwinter Mortality Transects

Overall impacts on the winter range are measured and determined in spring shortly following green-up. The relationship between numbers of big game animals and the annual utilization of available winter range forages should be determined on a yearly basis.

Annual range rides are an opportunity for biologists and sportsmen to look at the range in the western "cowboy" tradition. Although the popularity and number of range rides have greatly decreased in recent years, participants continue to look forward to the often first horseback ride of the year. Most spring range rides begin in early morning on saddle horses and cover many miles of winter range during the day. Range rides are an opportunity for riders to observe general range conditions, overwinter browse use by deer, and overwinter mortality. When used in conjunction with the recorded objective data, the range ride impressions and descriptive write-ups are an important input into management decisions.

Pellet group transects show deer population trends on winter ranges (Neff 1968). A transect usually consists of a minimum of 100 plots along a line and spaced at about 30 to 50-foot intervals. Plots are usually circular, contain 100 square feet, and are permanently marked at the center with an iron stake. Pellets are counted in the spring after deer have left winter ranges. All pellets are removed or swept from each plot to avoid counting pellets deposited from previous years. Pellet group transects are almost exclusively used on winter ranges because summer ranges usually contain large acreage, require numerous transects for accuracy, and have heavy vegetative growth that makes accurate counts very difficult. Because about 20 percent of pellet groups are not in a pile and are "strewn-out" or dropped while the deer is walking, usually a minimum of 25 pellets needs to be present on the plot for the group to be counted.

Browse utilization transects show the percentage of the current annual growth of key browse species that were eaten by deer during winter. The data are used as an index to deer herd numbers as well as range utilization. Browse utilization transects are usually located on important winter ranges or deer concentration areas. Randomly selected branches of shrubs, usually one branch per shrub, are marked with colored wires or numbered metal tags. Usually transects are run in a particular direction with each shrub along the direction sampled. At least 100 shrubs must be marked and sampled for browse utilization transects to begin to show accuracy. In fall before deer migrate to winter ranges, and in spring after they have left, browse transects are read by measuring the twig lengths of all annual growth above the tag on the branch. The differences in total twig lengths between the two measurements are used to calculate the percentage of overwinter utilization.

Browse transects can be an effective measure of range use by deer, however, they come with several problems. To be useful, many transects are needed within an area to yield an accurate data set. Separate transects must be established for each species and at several elevations. Big sagebrush, the key winter forage species in most areas, is very difficult to measure accurately. All transects require two readings each year and are very time consuming. Tagged branches are at times difficult to locate, and the need to periodically change branches within a shrub, due to branch mortality, reduces the accuracy of the technique. Consequently, except for special study areas, few browse transects are read.

Mortality transects are almost always completed along the same routes as pellet group and browse transects. Mortality transects simply record all deer by sex and age classes observed.

> *Note:* I recommend the following method for appraising over-winter range use by mule deer. It combines and improves upon all of the above methods. I successfully used this method on the Cache management unit between 1994 and 2003.

I recommend that 15 transects be established on each deer management unit. It is estimated that the 15 transects would require an annual field time of 40 hours in the spring to collect data. Additional hours may be required in the fall to sweep the plots from any transect used by sheep in summer or fall. All transects should be placed in the vicinity of five-year permanent trend transects on critical winter range.

Each of the 15 transects are comprised of 50 plots. Plot numbers 1 and 50 are marked with six-foot T-steel posts driven into the ground as deep as possible. Plot numbers 2 through 49 are marked with 24 to 36-inch long, three-quarter-inch wide angled iron, with 6 to 12 inches remaining above the ground. All plots are spaced at 10-meter intervals in a line. Directions are given with respect to magnetic north. At each plot, a one-meter-squared circular area (radius equaling 0.56 meters) is used to count rabbit pellets, and a 10-meters-squared circular area (radius equaling 1.78 meters) is used to count big game pellet groups. All pellets are annually removed from the plots. In each plot the individual shrub nearest to the plot center, but within a maximum distance of five meters from the plot center, is located. An ocular estimate for percent overwinter utilization of the current annual growth at five percent intervals is made for each available shrub species.

Overwinter mortality is recorded from the time the investigator leaves the vehicle. Following completion of the data collection for that transect, the investigator returns to the vehicle via a different route. Using the length of the route, including the 490 meters along the transect, and the average hiking distance to the first plot plus the return distance to the starting point, and an estimated 100 meter mortality sampling width, I estimated each transect represents a mortality assessment on about a mean of 15 hectares of winter range.

Range Trend Surveys

Determining long-term changes in vegetative production, cover, and composition on winter ranges is important because the amount and types of vegetation determine the carrying capacity of the range. In cooperation with other state and federal agencies, the Utah Division of Wildlife Resources has monitored range trend throughout Utah on state and federal lands since 1957, and has been using permanently marked plots since the mid-1980s (Utah DWR 1958–2008). Permanently marked plots have the advantage of evaluating range conditions from the exact same locations. Range trend surveys are conducted on each unit on a five-year rotating basis.

Range trend is monitored during summer using between 20 and 40 transects on each of Utah's 30 deer management units. Selected "key" areas where mule deer traditionally have established a pattern of winter use during normal weather conditions over a long period of time are normally selected as study areas by the biologist or conservation officer with the most experience on the unit. Each transect consists of five 100-foot sampling belts, with the ends permanently marked with steel rods to insure precise area sampling. Data collected at plots along the sampling belt include vegetative cover and density, species composition, ground cover, and shrub age, form, and vigor classes (Daubenmire 1959).

From these data, the trend of range conditions can be determined. Range trend data answer several questions: Is the general range condition improving, declining, or remaining the same for mule deer in winter? Are weedy species invading the range? Is shrub productivity changing? Is vegetative composition changing? Is ground cover changing, leading to possible changes in surface erosion? In general, what has been the degree of deer utilization of shrubs in winter? Does the current management plan for the area need to be altered to meet the changing range conditions?

Field Notes

Wildlife biologists, who spend considerable time in the field observing wildlife and habitat, acquire a "feel" for the ecology of the deer herd. They can detect when a herd is doing well and when it is struggling, and then use the hard data to back up their understanding. Before the methodologies of data collection were developed, biologists relied very heavily on the "feel of the system." Simple field notes can be used to clarify and strengthen points for which collected data may be somewhat inadequate or even fail to clearly answer the question.

Field notes are recorded throughout the year. Records made during hiking or horseback trips or while traveling by vehicle are often used in reference to evaluate populations and are sometimes heavily relied upon for making hunting recommendations. A few examples from my field notes follow:

- June 15, 1982. Several photos of the Little Valley area on the Vernon deer unit were taken from the ridge top immediately north of the major spring and above the campground.
- February 21, 1984. In Blacksmith Fork Canyon near Left Hand Fork, several fawns were heard moaning. One fawn I approached was unable to stand. Winter mortality is high, most fawns and many adults will die before spring.
- May 23, 1990. On the large alfalfa field in Lost Creek, 13 deer and 4 elk were observed using a spotlight count about 1 hour after sunset.
- September 25, 1991. 10:30 pm. An anonymous caller left a message of spotlighting activity and probable poaching on the Bunch Grass road of Logan Canyon. Blue and white Ford pickup. No further information.
- April 18, 2003. 6:10 am. Arrived at six-mile lek (sage grouse) in the dark, wind at 2 (Beaufort scale), overcast, 35 degrees F. About 8-10 birds flew off lek at first light before a good count could be taken. Weather prevented counts on other leks and spring classification deer counts.

In the first example, a visual comparison to vegetative change was obtained in an area that was later burned by wildfire. In the second example, the field observations in February supported the recruitment classification counts collected later in the spring. In the third example, all observations regarding depredation of private crops become important if the landowner feels justified in submitting a crop loss claim. The fourth example is the kind of information which often leads to the apprehension of wildlife violators. In the final example, where hard data could not be collected, field notes may be the only reliable source of information, especially if no other counts were subsequently obtained from that particular lek. Also, the lack of deer classification data collected on that date could be back-checked and attributed to weather.

Questionnaire Surveys

Most statewide information on yearly deer harvest and hunter success, as well as hunter attitudes, is obtained through questionnaires. Postal service mail questionnaires are sent to randomly selected hunters immediately after the end of the specific hunts to obtain hunter success and harvest. Unfortunately, return rates of mailed questionnaires are low, usually less than 50 percent, even with repeated mailings. Harvest is calculated using only those cards returned. Non-response bias from questionnaires not returned can inflate calculated harvest figures. Mailed questionnaires are most effective for smaller hunts and hunting areas when all participating hunters are sent questionnaires. Examples of uses of mailed questionnaires, which are now rarely used, include pre-season antlerless control hunts and limited-entry hunts.

Telephone surveys virtually eliminate non-response bias and are used to assess the general deer hunts. Telephone surveys are more accurate than mailed questionnaires, especially for statewide hunts. After hunters are randomly selected, they are called on the telephone by trained operators. Generally the same hunter success and harvest data that were collected with the mailed questionnaire are obtained using a telephone survey.

Longer surveys, addressing hunter attitudes and opinions, can be obtained by both methods. However, because of the extremely low response rate to written questionnaires, telephone surveys are currently used almost exclusively.

Applied Research

Often the most important branch of any organization for maintaining long-term viability is its research division. In most cases, investments made into research yield benefits far exceeding the costs associated with the research. Applied research, which can be directly related to management decisions, invariably results in economic as well as long-term benefits to the resource and the resource user.

Applied research addresses problems or questions identified by management. Once a problem has been identified, the researcher writes a proposal critically defining the issues to be addressed and the scientific methods used to address the problem. Proposals often are rewritten several times until the manager and the researcher are both satisfied that the proposal will address the problem, and that the approach will answer the questions. The research is then conducted using the defined scientific methods and for the period of time specified in the proposal, with periodic progress reports submitted to the manager. In most deer management applied research, project length is usually between one and five years. At the completion of the project a final report is written, often in the form of a publication, and submitted to a technical journal.

> *Note:* Publication of results is extremely important to maintain the results for future reference and management decisions not only within the state, but also to share research efforts, costs, and results with all other interested states and parties. For example, one of my research publications on rangeland management was referred to by a guide explaining range management methods during a Kellogg Foundation tour on the Serengeti grasslands near the borders of Tanzania and Kenya, East Africa.

Chapter 17

How to Manage a Mule Deer Herd—Essentials in Data Collections and Management Decisions

Management Limitations

During the non-hunting season, which is unfortunately most of the year, many hunters reminisce of past experiences but, probably even more often, daydream of the forthcoming hunts. Similarly, wildlife biologists in charge of managing Utah's deer herds dream, consider, and analyze various alternatives to improve the management within their geographical areas. Certainly all managers could do a better job of understanding the wildlife resources within their areas if they were not constrained by time and money.

Consequently any discussion on "how to manage a deer herd" must be defined in terms of resources available to a herd's management. As a practical estimate for this chapter, it is assumed the deer unit is of medium size for Utah or about 650,000 acres, and an experienced biologist can devote about one-sixth of his or her time, two months per year or 40 days, in collecting data, observing, and managing the deer herd. In reality, few if any of Utah's 30 or so in-the-field wildlife biologists have that much time available to focus on a single species on an individual management unit.

The Blue Mountain Mule Deer Herd

The first necessary piece of information the biologist must have is the delineation of the herd boundary and unit. That is, the home ranges of deer, both summer and winter, must be defined for each individual herd

238

unit. In many cases, distinct deer populations occupy different ranges on the same management unit, and these sub-populations along with their ranges should be further defined (Pac et al. 1991). Also, in some cases deer populations may occupy a common summer range but separate onto distinctly different winter ranges.

For example, the Blue Mountain summer range plateau, in northeastern Utah, lies at the eastern end of the South Slope Wildlife Management Unit, and borders the Utah-Colorado state line and Dinosaur National Monument. During the period between 1972 and 1976, mule deer were trapped and tagged on the two major winter ranges on the Utah side of the plateau: in Miners Gulch, which is on the south side of the summer range plateau, and in the Cub Creek area which is on the west side of the summer range. These two winter ranges were separated by minor geographical barriers with few if any deer found in the intermediate area. During five years of observation with over 100 marked deer, deer from both winter ranges mixed and utilized the same summer range plateau. The dispersal of both groups was random over the summer plateau, including some dispersal into Colorado and onto the Monument. However, after migration to winter ranges in late fall, the two groups remained distinct. No observations were made of deer being marked on one winter range and later being observed on the opposite winter range.

The two groups of deer on winter ranges showed different population dynamics over winter (Austin et al. 1977). As expected, because of the occupation of same summer range, both subpopulations migrated onto the separate winter ranges with similar fawn-to-adult ratios, averaging 60 for Cub Creek and 53 for Miners Gulch. However, after winter the ratios were widely different. The Cub Creek area remained essentially unchanged and averaged 59 fawns per 100 adults, but the Miners Gulch population declined to 29 fawns per 100 adults. I further postulated that the initially slightly lower fall ratio in Miners Gulch may have been due to fawn losses before classification counts were completed. Clearly, the population dynamics on the winter ranges were different between the two subpopulations.

These kinds of information are important to managers in maintaining healthy populations. If, for example the total population increased dramatically and needed to be substantially reduced to bring the herd back into balance with the winter range resources through issuing of antlerless control permits, both populations should not be equally hunted. If the hunts were conducted in the early fall when the subpopulations occupied the common summer range, both subpopulations would be hunted equally and the manager may not achieve the harvest and total population goals for each subpopulation. Because the Miners Gulch subpopulation is much more susceptible to hunting losses, hunting on the summer range may remove an excessive number of deer from the Miners Gulch subpopulation. Furthermore, as a second management option, if the subpopulations were hunted late in the fall on winter ranges and permits were issued over the entire area, which is often the case, that part of the area with the better access would receive the majority of the hunters and hunting pressure, particularly if weather limited the access to the second area. The subpopulation with better access and more public land was the Miners Gulch, and again this option would leave the Miners Gulch subpopulation susceptible to over-harvest. The obvious solution to address an excessive number of deer in this real example would be to issue permits for each subpopulation separately, with the Miners Gulch population receiving a much more conservative number of permits issued.

This example demonstrates how excessive harvest could easily occur on a subpopulation through a management decision if the population dynamics for the separate subpopulations were unknown. Critical points to this example include the concept that subpopulations are restricted to certain ranges during only parts of the year, and consequently, are more susceptible during that period and importantly, can be over-harvested. Subpopulations and subunits, especially on winter ranges, often need to be evaluated separately. Finally, emigration, movement and reestablishment of deer populations onto winter ranges where deer numbers have been greatly reduced is extremely slow, usually taking several years, even when adjacent populations are high.

Although this example used the analysis of how a manager might use various options to address an overpopulation of deer using subunit winter ranges, the same evaluation could be considered for a low deer population. With respect to several management factors, including differences in predation, winter range forages, winter range condition, development, access, migration corridors, human harassment, and many others, the management strategy would often be different between subunits.

Most units require similar evaluations of subpopulations. On the Cache unit, for example, the deer use of winter ranges is further complicated by deer migrating from both Idaho and Wyoming onto Utah's

Photo by Dennis Austin

Jared Austin feeds deer at a Hardware Ranch enclosure. The research determined dietary choices, activity patterns, and consumption rates of alfalfa hay.

winter ranges. To address the problem, the Cache unit has been subdivided into 10 distinct subpopulations for assessment of dynamics on the winter range. Three of those subpopulations contain a mixture of Utah-Idaho or Utah-Wyoming deer, and seven subpopulations are composed of almost all Utah deer.

Essential Data

Seven sets of data are usually considered essential by wildlife professionals. These data are necessary for understanding deer population dynamics and for efficient and knowledgeable management of the deer herd. These seven sets of data are:

(1) Hunter harvest
(2) Age and sex determination of harvested deer
(3) Reproduction and sex ratio classification
(4) Recruitment classification

(5)   Annual winter range condition and utilization assessment
(6)   Long-term winter range condition trend assessment
(7)   Hunter opinion assessment

Hunter Harvest

The administrative segment of most wildlife agencies, including Utah, collects total harvest by management unit through the use of hunter surveys. These surveys are usually in the form of telephone interviews conducted following the hunts. These data are extremely important in assessing yearly changes in the harvest and long-term trends in harvest. These surveys determine the total number of buck and antlerless deer harvested statewide and within management units.

The accuracy of harvest data, especially the buck harvest, is essential in making population estimates and understanding the dynamics of each unit. Sometimes the accuracy of harvest data is questioned due to the inherent difficulties of data collection from a sample of hunters. Those potential inaccuracies primarily occur from non-response bias and inaccurate hunter response. Non-response bias occurs when selected hunters cannot be contacted by phone. Inaccurate hunter response sometimes occurs when hunters report harvesting a buck when they did not. Two examples of this factor lead to relatively common inaccuracies. In one scenario, two hunters in a party shoot at the same buck and they both claim the harvest even though only one tags the deer. In the second, a hunter wounds a buck and is unable to locate the animal, but reports a harvested buck. Both of these factors—non-response bias and inaccurate hunter response—generally lead to inflated harvest figures. Furthermore, regression analysis, which compares checking station data with harvest data, usually supports the probability of somewhat inflated harvest figures.

Age and Sex Determination of the Harvest

To obtain age and sex composition of the harvest requires observation of hunter-harvested deer during the hunts. This is usually accomplished either through randomly obtained field checks or checking stations. Checking stations are usually more effective because a larger sample can be obtained and more detailed information can be collected. As a minimum data set, all deer checked by either method should be recorded as male or female and aged as fawn, yearling, two-and-a-half years, or three-and-a-half years and older. Ages must be determined by cutting the cheek, splitting apart the jaw, and examining the teeth for replacement and wear.

Age classification of the female population is very important in the use of modeling populations and general management of the herd. For example, a herd containing more than 20 percent does over the age of eight years would have lower reproductive rates than the same herd with less than five percent of the does exceeding eight years in age.

Whenever possible, I suggest information on carcass weight, antler parameters, physical condition and a more detailed age classification should be obtained at checking stations. These more detailed data should be collected at least once every three to five years. Although often very difficult to achieve, a minimum sample size of 15 deer should be obtained in each age and sex class. Thus, excluding fawns and using four age classes, the two sex classes, and 15 deer within each class, a minimum of 90 deer are needed for each herd unit. On buck-only units a minimum of 45 bucks are needed. On some units two or three years of combined data may be needed to obtain an adequate sample size. A practical goal for most herd units would be to check 50 bucks yearly, 100 bucks during the years of higher intensity data collection, and annually as many does as possible.

Carcass weight, or hog-dressed weight, is obtained by weighing the entire dressed carcass with viscera removed, but legs intact on a platform or hanging scale. The scale should be sensitive to half of a pound and the weight recorded to the nearest whole pound. Carcasses that have legs removed or have significant portions of the carcass removed either from bullets or knife trimming should not be used to obtain weight data.

Two measurements should be taken on antlers: the number of tines exceeding one inch excluding brow tines, and the maximum spread of the antlers. Small tines must be one inch or longer as measured from the intersecting edge of the larger beam. Maximum spread is measured from the outside edges of the rack and includes all tines.

Physical condition is usually measured by the depth of subcutaneous fat. Fat depth measured in millimeters at the xiphoid process and perpendicular to the body cavity provides an easily-obtained index that can be compared between years and units (Austin 1984).

Reproduction and Sex Ratio Classification

Post-season classification counts are obtained following the end of the big game hunts in November and are usually completed before

Christmas. The purposes of the counts are to determine the adult sex ratio after the hunt and to obtain the reproductive rate for the previous breeding period.

Adult sex ratios vary from less than two bucks per 100 does to more than 30 bucks per 100 does. In general terms, ratios containing less than five bucks per 100 does indicate almost all bucks are being harvested during the hunts, and the buck portion of the herd is likely being overly exploited. Counts between five and ten indicate the bucks are being heavily hunted and that few mature bucks are surviving the hunt. Counts consistently in the five-to-ten range suggest that hunters may prefer some reduction in the number of bucks being harvested. Post-season counts, recording between 10 and 20 bucks per 100 does, indicate reasonable and adequate hunter pressure. At this level of hunter intensity, many mature bucks are being harvested from the management unit, but many and adequate numbers are also surviving. Most herds should be managed between 10 and 20 bucks per 100 does. At counts exceeding 20 bucks per 100 does, herd management is leaning toward trophy management and the buck segment of the herd may be under-harvested and under-utilized.

Most management units should have the goal of maintaining 10 or more bucks per 100 does during post-season classification counts. In Utah, the minimum goal of 15 bucks per 100 does has been set for most units. The difference between 10 and 15 bucks per 100 does results in fewer bucks being harvested, but with a slightly increased age and size of the harvested bucks. On a unit where the goal is 15 bucks per 100 does, if the buck-to-doe ratio decreases to between 10 and 14 bucks per 100 does for one or even two years, changes in population dynamics and harvest will probably not be discernible and alterations in management strategy are not necessary. In many cases the assumed declines may simply be due to sampling variability in the post-season classification count.

Only when the buck-to-doe ratio remains somewhat below the management goal for three or more years, or it decreases by 50 percent or more, should changes in the management strategy be considered. When the buck-to-doe ratio consistently exceeds 20 bucks per 100 does, hunter pressure is too light and the buck deer resource is being under-utilized. Only where trophy bucks are the primary goal of the manager or landowner should the post-hunt buck-to-doe ratio consistently exceed 20 bucks per 100 does. In this special case, spike bucks and bucks with 1x2 antler points should be annually culled to improve the potential for trophy bucks, and the deer herd should also be kept considerably under carrying capacity to optimize available forage resources to promote maximum body size and antler development.

Natural mortality of adult does is very low between the fawning period and the post-season classification count, almost always measured at less than five percent and often close to zero. Typically, only hunting mortality is considered during this period. Consequently, classification ratios of fawns-to-does in the late fall represent the success of the does in bearing and rearing fawns. Conversely, fawn mortality is usually significant during this period and can be strongly influenced by several factors, including poor range conditions and excessive numbers of predators.

Early estimates for harvest and hunter success for the forthcoming year can be obtained a year in advance using the fall reproductive rate obtained from post-season classification counts. These estimates assume mild to normal overwinter losses. Classification counts in excess of 80 fawns per 100 does are considered good and an increase in harvest may be expected. Ratios less than 50 fawns per 100 does are poor and a decrease in harvest may be expected, especially if the low ratio has continued for two or more years. When only a single year of poor reproduction is realized, often enough bucks survive from the previous year such that the harvest results show very little, if any, reduction. However, because a higher portion of the available bucks are necessarily harvested to prevent a decrease in harvest, the case becomes similar to borrowing from the principle in a savings account rather than just using the interest. Therefore, unless the recruitment rate significantly exceeds mortality during the second year, the buck harvest may decline in the second year following a poor year of reproduction. Ratios of 50 to 80 fawns per 100 does can result in either an increase or a decrease in harvest from the previous year. Minimum reproductive rates of about 30 fawns per 100 adults are necessary to sustain mule deer populations.

Recruitment Classification

Population recruitment classification counts are determined in early spring, beginning about the time green-up occurs. Once green-up begins, with the observable new growth of rangeland grasses shortly followed by the emergence of forbs, overwinter mortality is ended by the availability of nutritious forage and warmer temperatures. Spring counts provide the manager with a major piece of information, especially for making hunting recommendations for the harvest of antlerless deer. When over-winter mortality is high, fawn-to-adult ratios significantly decrease between fall and spring counts, recruitment ratios are lower, and fewer, if any, antlerless deer should be harvested. Because of the increased suscep-tibility of fawns, a small overwinter decrease in the fawn-to-adult ratio is expected. A decrease of five fawns per 100 adults is normal and about average during average or mild winters. On management units where the population size is in balance with the range resources, significantly decreased fawn-to-adult ratios from post-season counts and occasional low recruitment rates are usually the result of winter severity coupled with predation.

Importantly, low recruitment rates can also result from an imbal-ance between population size and range resources. Where population size has increased to exceed the available winter range resources, con-sistently low recruitment rates (determined from post-winter counts) may be a chronic indicator of excessive deer numbers on limited winter ranges. Similarly on units where summer range is limiting, consistently low reproductive rates (determined from post-season counts) may be a chronic indicator of excessive deer numbers on limited summer ranges. The simple solution in both cases, almost always unpopular with hunters, is to significantly increase the harvest of antlerless deer and decrease the size of the population.

Annual Winter Range Condition and Utilization Assessment

Following spring green-up, overwinter utilization of the winter ranges must be annually evaluated. Minimum data to be collected on each herd unit must include the percentage browse utilization by each available shrub species, pellet group density, and overwinter mortality observed and recorded by age and sex classes. Plots to determine browse utiliza-tion and pellet group density must be permanently marked with steel stakes. A minimum of 50 plots per transect and 15 transects per unit are required to assess overwinter utilization. Transects should be located in the vicinities of the long-term, five-year trend transects.

> *Note:* In addition to the transects, at one or two locations per unit, I recommended constructing a small "exclosure" to prevent livestock grazing and deer browsing. These "exclosures" are to be used as annual training sites for browse utilization estimation, to

supply an accurate evaluation of overwinter utilization obtained by comparing browsed and non-browsed plots, and to provide a demonstration site where the range conditions and utilization estimates can be explained to the public. It is recommended that each "exclosure" be located on productive winter range with at least two browse species of good density. Each "exclosure" should measure 24x24 feet with heavy posts at the corners and mid-way between the corners, and a single post in the center, for a total of nine posts. Annually one-fourth of the "exclosure" would be removed from use by installing four 12-foot-long livestock gates. The gates would simply be moved in a clockwise direction annually after range evaluation in the spring. This moveable "exclosure" would replace permanent basketed plots.

Long-term Winter Range Condition Trend Assessment

Changes in vegetative resources on winter ranges over many years are best determined by permanently marked plots, with data supported by exact location photo plots. The DWR has established permanent vegetative transects on critical winter range habitats for each deer unit in Utah. About 20 to 40 transects have been established on each herd unit. These plots, strategically and carefully located on important winter range sites, are read every five years by a range crew specifically trained in the methodology. Range trend data include vegetative composition, canopy cover, browse condition classes, vegetative species density, and ground cover of bare ground, litter, and rock. Data determine the long-term changes and basic health of the winter range. Data are published by DWR by herd unit as part of the Range Trend Surveys series.

The annual and long-term assessments of winter range, and summer range in areas where it is lacking, are the key data to evaluate the carrying capacity of the range and therefore to set hunting rules and regulations (Clements and Young 1997). In Utah over the last 30 years, range trend data are generally downward for most units, suggesting environmental factors are causing a negative trend, or the deer populations during some years exceeded range carrying capacity. The trend of declining condition of winter ranges is especially true for units along the Wasatch Front where winter range is limiting and spring livestock utilization is minimal.

It is critical for the reader to realize that data from both the long-term range trends and the annual assessment of utilization must be available to managers to understand the dynamics of changes in winter range resources. Having available only the long-term data, the manager knows only the changes in range resources, but not the impacts which caused the changes. Having available only the annual utilization data, the manager knows only the annual impacts on range resources, but not the long-term trends. However, with both sets of these data, managers are able to adjust deer herd numbers to protect the range and prevent further declines in productivity, and with the same effort, ensure and maintain long-term sustainability of hunter harvest.

Hunter Opinion Assessment

The preferences, opinions, and satisfaction levels of hunters should be evaluated on a regular basis. Individual conversations, local public meetings, formal RAC meetings, management unit and statewide written or telephone surveys must all be utilized. In all cases the opinion of the average hunter must be the primary target of the opinion survey. Too often only a vocal minority, usually representing special interest groups, are heard in public and even private meetings. Where possible, and when the majority of deer hunters are clearly in favor of changes, management alternatives should be adapted to meet hunter preferences, but only when changes can be made within the biological, economic, and land stewardship constraints of technical, proper, and conscientious mule deer management.

Livestock Grazing Management

Livestock grazing is an important and essential ingredient to perpetuating or improving winter ranges (Belsky 1986). On mule deer winter ranges, livestock grazing in spring provides a growth advantage to the browse species and greatly reduces the potential for wildfire, which can destroy browse productivity. Grazing by livestock, horses, sheep, goats, or cows must be a critical part of the management plan for these ranges.

Grazing of winter ranges by livestock at moderate levels should be accomplished only for six to eight weeks in spring, on about two-thirds of the area used by deer in winter (Austin 2000). Areas rested one year should be grazed the following year. This grazing regime avoids the build-up of plants and materials that may fuel a fire. Flexibility of grazing management is important. During wet years, grazing by live-stock in spring over the entire winter range may be desirable to pro-mote shrub growth and prevent possible wildfires. During dry years, livestock grazing may need to be reduced to prevent overutilization of understory vegetation and to prevent utilization of browse needed by deer in winter.

On summer range, if possible, livestock grazing of fawning areas, especially when fawning areas are restricted in size, should be eliminated until mid-July, or preferably until after the first of August when fawns are approaching two months of age and capable of traveling continuously with the doe. Other than fawning areas, livestock grazing of summer ranges has little negative effect on deer, but only if that grazing is main-tained at a moderate level and summer range conditions are not depleted through overgrazing (Austin and Urness 1986).

On most areas within wildlife management units, deer use of pri-vate lands occurs during some portion of the year. It is often impera-tive for the health of the herd that wildlife managers and sportsmen, whenever possible, support and cooperate with the ranching industry. Cooperative agreements between ranchers and agencies to graze state and federal lands often lead to improved winter range conditions on private lands, decreased depredation complaints, increased accessibil-ity to public lands, range improvements, and benefits to wildlife, ranch-ers, and hunters.

In my experience, ranchers, wildlife managers, and sportsmen should always be friends. Most wildlife managers and biologists, ranchers, and sportsmen recognize the beneficial effects of controlled livestock grazing, and should support grazing in all cases where it is properly regulated and controlled and not harmful to soils or habitat.

Range Improvement

Few, if any, of Utah's deer units do not have areas of needed range improvements. A partial list of possible improvements includes the fol-lowing 11 suggestions.

(1)   Old-aged stands of pinyon-juniper should be chained in a patchy pattern to increase quality and quantity of available win-ter range forage, but retain adequate cover.

(2)   Areas of recent fires, usually less than three years old, where winter browse was destroyed should be reseeded as soon after the fire as possible during late fall or early spring.

(3)   Areas strongly dominated by annual grasses and weeds should be plowed and furrowed just prior to the grass reaching seed viability in spring or summer, and reseeded during late fall.

(4)   Pinyon-juniper areas that were previously chained but now contain numerous small invading trees should have those trees thinned.

(5)   Summer ranges containing dense stands of lodgepole pine should be thinned or clear-cut in strips to improve the forage base and timber production.

(6)   Decadent aspen stands should be clear-cut and livestock grazing eliminated for two to three years while aspen suckers regenerate stands.

(7)   Riparian areas that are overused by excessive livestock grazing may need to be fenced.

(8)   Riparian areas that are overused by dispersed camping may need to be excluded from public use.

(9)   Small springs and seeps may need to be protected from all grazers and, where needed, water piped to a nearby water trough.

(10) Lands owned by the DWR, and other lands managed primarily for wildlife, may need to be surveyed, marked at the corners, and fenced.

(11) Extensive, dense stands of maple, Gambel oak, and big sagebrush should be thinned or clear-cut in small patches to improve upland habitat, especially on fawn-rearing areas.

Each manager should make a prioritized list of needed range improvements on specific geographical areas. A reasonable goal for range improvements is to attempt to annually improve about two to five percent of the acreage in need and available for rehabilitation. Treated lands must be available for wildlife utilization for at least an anticipated 20-year period. With this goal, range depreciation will likely be balanced by improvements.

Predator Management

The four major predators of mule deer—coyote, cougar, bobcat, and black bear—either as a single species, or in the common case as a combined influence, can have a significant effect on reducing hunter harvest and curtailing population growth. The influence of predators becomes increasingly evident as deer populations decline. Indeed, at very low deer populations, a "predator pit" may develop in which the deer recruitment rate may not exceed the mortality rate and the deer population indefinitely stagnates at the low population level. In these situations, significant predator removal should be accomplished at least until the herd rebuilds to the inflection point on the population growth curve, or the point of rapid population growth. Continued predator control beyond the inflection point up to the plateau of the bell-shaped curve, when the population reaches maximum sustained yield, would give greater assurance that the deer population would not sharply decline as the predator populations recovered.

Predator management is a thorny issue in most locations of the state because of the strong emotions people develop on both sides of the predator control issue. To some, predators have very high intangible values even through they are only very rarely observed. To others, predators are considered a nuisance with only negative values. However, few people and fewer managers would prefer all predators to be extirpated from a particular unit, and conversely few people would promote unlimited predator numbers without any control.

Generally from the standpoint of mule deer management, liberal hunting and trapping regulations of predators should be the usual situation, but with the necessity of the manager knowing that at least minor populations of each of these four predators are maintained on each deer unit. Furthermore, predators should only receive protected status under very low predator populations, or when predators are involved with research studies.

Elk Management

If a manager's most important hunting species is the mule deer, and the primary management goal is to maintain healthy deer herds, elk numbers should be allowed to increase only to the point of being complimentary with the resource needs of the deer herd. When elk herds begin to

Photo by Philip J. Urness

The author is shown in Utah's Sheeprock Mountains studying the
effects of cattle grazing on summer range, deer
habitat, and diet selection.

compete with deer for limited range resources, elk numbers should be
reduced, or the management goals must be redefined.

Elk have a much wider range of usable forages than deer, and under
limited available range will out-compete deer for forage resources. Under
winter stress conditions, elk will always have higher survival rates, particularly when forage resources become over-utilized.

When elk numbers increase and begin to compete with deer, management should usually favor deer over elk in most situations for several reasons. First, many more deer can be maintained on the same winter ranges. The trade-off, in my opinion, is about five to eight deer for one elk. This trade-off favoring deer provides for much more hunter opportunity and harvest success. Also, because of the carcass size, deer can be handled by a single individual, whereas elk normally require a horse or several hunters. Second, elk create considerably greater impacts and problems than deer when associated with depredation situations. Third, because elk and cattle diets have high dietary overlap compared with deer and cattle diets, livestock operators and private landowners usually prefer to maintain larger deer herds and smaller elk herds. Fourth, because of the larger size of elk and the behavior of elk to spend the winter in large groups, damage to winter range browse forages can occur on small areas, especially if elk herds become camped for more than a few days at the same location.

Balancing deer and elk numbers on limited range resources can be perplexing. Hunters generally want more deer and more elk. Managers can only assess each situation, evaluate all important factors, and make informed judgments.

White-tailed Deer Management

The white-tailed deer was first verified in Cache County, Utah in 1996. In the subsequent years the white-tailed deer has rapidly expanded its range to all of northern Utah and has been observed in the Uinta Basin. At least three white-tailed bucks were harvested on the Cache Unit in 2006. Similar to elk, white-tailed deer out-compete and replace mule deer through more efficient resource use, adaptability to human activities, and one-way hybridization. Furthermore, the potential problems of diseases that are more easily carried and tolerated by white-tailed deer, but which may have much higher mortality effects for mule deer, present a possible major concern for perpetual maintenance of mule deer populations. The replacement of mule deer by white-tailed deer is obviously occurring throughout the western United States. I have observed that less than 20 years ago on some ranges outside of Utah where only mule deer were found, white-tailed deer now outnumber mule deer.

Because of direct competition, one-way hybridization, and the potential disease factors, managing for mule deer simply may require managing to reduce or even eliminate white-tailed deer from some mule deer ranges.

Access Management

Land management agencies and private landowners control hunter access. Wildlife managers are usually in the middle role of making hunting recommendations. Nonetheless, every management unit should maintain areas where vehicles are restricted either by road closures or natural geographic barriers, as well as other areas where vehicle access is high via numerous roads. On units or subunits with extensive vehicle access and especially where dense cover is limited, roads and areas may need to be closed or other hunter-restrictive measures instigated to maintain an adequate number of bucks in the post-season counts. I generally consider areas within one mile of a road to be accessible to vehicles, as opposed to areas further than one mile as vehicle non-access areas. For examples, if two roads are two miles apart and run parallel, all the area between the roads would be considered accessible to vehicles. If the same two roads were three miles apart, two of the miles between the roads would be considered as accessible to vehicles and one mile as not accessible.

I suggest a ratio of 60 to 40 as a general guideline for hunter access to deer habitat, with 60 percent of the unit available to vehicle access, and 40 percent requiring a hike of at least one mile. Using this ratio as an approximation, hunter access is not overly restricted, survival of sufficient bucks is assured, and the variable preferences of hunters for remote to close-to-vehicle hunting are met.

Hunter Management

Probably the most important and certainly the most controversial aspect of managing a deer herd is hunter management. Since total harvest and percent hunter success are the most commonly used criteria for hunt success, hunter management schemes must produce a desired harvest and reasonably high hunter satisfaction. A point of commonality among hunter management schemes, except in the specific cases of limited-entry and CWMU hunts, is the need to provide hunting opportunity for numerous hunters, far in excess of the anticipated harvest.

These constraints are mandated by the economical need to maintain the wildlife program as well as the responsibility to provide public hunting opportunity to as many hunters as is reasonable.

One central, reoccurring question for management is: What is the minimal hunter success needed to provide a satisfactory hunt and sustain hunter participation? The concept of minimum hunter success to provide a satisfactory hunt has been constantly changing since at least the 1950s. In the 1940s, under buck-only hunting, the answer was probably around 66 percent or two-thirds of hunters being successful. Hunters were relatively few and deer were plentiful. In the 1950s and 1960s under either-sex hunting but with increasing numbers of hunters, that percentage dropped to about 50 percent. Considerable discussions among managers ensued during the early 1970s about retaining a 50 percent hunter success goal, regardless of declining harvest and revenue. However, in the 1970s and 1980s the figure dropped to about 40 percent as hunters increased and deer decreased. During the 1990s the minimum hunter success perceived as needed to provide a satisfactory hunt dropped to about 30 percent, and again with considerable discussion, most managers felt that minimum success had to be held to at least 25 percent. Nonetheless, during the early years of the twenty-first century that minimum percentage has continued to drop, at least on some units during some years, to the 20-percent range.

The first significant point from declining hunter success is that, regardless of hunter success, more than enough hunters will want to participate in the hunt to harvest the surplus bucks. Even if hunter success drops below 10 percent or even five percent and hunters continually complain, they will still participate in the forthcoming hunts, if tags are available. A second point is the "grandfather" effect. That is, because of the high success our grandfathers knew in the 1940s and 1950s, the low success, along with the extensive regulations, of the 2000s would be unacceptable to them and, probably, they simply would not participate in hunting. However, youthful hunters beginning to participate in the 1990s would probably find the lower success rates quite acceptable, simply because they have never experienced the much higher success rates. The third point along the continuum of hunters gradually accepting lower success rates is the need to harvest an animal to feed a family. As the economic conditions of most families have improved over the decades, and the possibility of harvesting a deer near home with a common and inexpensive rifle has greatly declined, the need to provide meat to feed a family has faded almost to memories. Not to mention that the costs of harvesting a deer, including high-powered rifles, variable scopes, four-wheelers, SUVs, big trucks, special clothing, and more gear than a 1950s hunter could even recognize, have skyrocketed.

> *Note:* It is unfortunate that antlers have become much more valuable than venison. In the twenty-first century, shed antlers are gathered and marketed for profit, an activity not even considered in the 1950s.

As hunter success has declined, state regulations to provide increased hunter success for special interests groups, such as dedicated hunters, CWMU hunters, and limited-entry hunters, have evolved. Usually these groups pay a premium price and/or accomplish wildlife improvement projects for the increased opportunity. Nonetheless, to provide for the common interests of all hunters, adapting a reasonable hunter success goal and limiting special interests groups would give all hunters a more equal opportunity to hunt and harvest. Adapting the 25 to 33 percent hunter success goal, which includes antlerless deer harvest when available and flexibility to meet the needs of individual units, would maintain high hunter satisfaction, retain sufficient revenue, and provide equability for hunter opportunity.

As much as possible when populations are at or near carrying capacity, hunter regulation restrictions should be made liberal. Whether archery, muzzleloader, or rifle hunter, liberal regulations provide more opportunity for success, are associated with lower rates of wounding and illegal losses, lead to increased harvests, usually merit higher hunter satisfaction, and harvest a broader array of age and sex classes. Regulations must be liberal to obtain maximum sustained yield. Following is a descending scale of common hunter management schemes from highly restrictive to very liberal hunts:

> No hunt
> Limited-entry: trophy bucks only
> Limited-entry: any buck
> Buck-only: short season length
> Buck-only: regular season length
> Buck-only: with post-season antlerless harvest

Buck-only: with antlerless control permit harvest during the buck-only hunt

Buck-only: with antlerless control permit harvest during pre- and/or post-season and during the buck-only hunt

Either-sex: first few days followed by buck-only

Either-sex: season long

Either-sex: extended season

Either-sex: with additional antlerless control permit harvest during the pre- and post-season, and during the regular either-sex hunt

Limit Deer Populations to Available Rangeland Resources

The first rule for long-term successful management of mule deer unquestionably is: Do not over-utilize the forage resources on either summer or winter range by domestic or wild grazers, but especially not by an over-population of mule deer.

Because grazing always results in higher use and decreased productivity of the forages most palatable to the grazer, some vegetative changes will inevitably occur with almost any grazing. However, the forages comprising the majority of the deer diet in any habitat must not be grazed beyond the degree that those forages begin to loose productivity. Deer have the uncommon ability for a wildlife species to be able to destroy their own habitats, and usually deer can destroy habitat more rapidly and with the effects lasting a longer period of time than almost any other grazer. Elk, and to a lesser degree, moose, and possibly pronghorn, can have identical effects on their habitats.

Monitoring range utilization and condition is more difficult than many deer management activities, such as classification counts, harvest determination, or collecting checking station data, but monitoring range utilization and condition is essential to successful and proper mule deer management. Every good mule deer manager understands and monitors rangeland utilization and condition.

Proper good nutrition is essential for maintaining high reproduction in mule deer. Overused winter or summer ranges decrease the nutritional value in diets and directly effect population dynamics. The rules are simple. Slightly suboptimum nutrition during any interval in the course of the year results in slightly suboptimum population dynamics. Suboptimum nutrition on a regular basis results in suboptimum population dynamics. Poor nutrition results in poor population dynamics. Nutrition and the population dynamics for every deer herd are directly correlated.

The long-term decline of mule deer populations in the West is undoubtedly the direct result of decreased quantity and nutritional quality of year-round dietary forages (Workman and Low 1976; Hancock 1981; Clements and Young 1997; Gill 2001; Utah DWR 1951-2008; Utah DWR 1958-2008). The degree of the forage bottleneck and limitation on a year-round period determines the level of herd population dynamics. Only when year-round forages are plentiful and near maximum nutrient quality do deer herds reach maximum herd population dynamics and productivity.

Sadly, once the vegetative productivity of a range has been depleted by overuse, many years, decades, or even longer time periods are required to recover good range condition. Even more alarming, when soil is eroded from overused ranges, potential range production is essentially permanently reduced.

Reduced range productivity is observed directly not only by declining harvest of deer, but also by reduced reproduction and recruitment rates. Whereas fawn-to-doe ratios on many units were consistently above 90 fawns per 100 does in the pre-1960s, rates on almost all units since the 1980s have been consistently under 80 fawns per 100 does. Clearly, production of nutritional forages for mule deer has generally declined statewide and probably throughout the West. Deer populations must be annually evaluated and balanced with the range resources.

Chapter Synopsis

To manage any deer unit, areas of utilization on both summer and winter ranges as well as migration patterns must be understood and documented. Units having potentially distinct subpopulations must be further defined and evaluated. Accurate data must be annually collected within each geographic herd boundary. These data include total hunter harvest with age and sex determinations, reproduction and recruitment classification counts, monitoring of overwinter forage utilization, and periodic range trend data and analyses. Additional data on any deer herd should be collected to address specific problems. Surveys of hunter opinions must be obtained without bias and thoughtfully considered. Annual livestock grazing must be properly managed on both summer and winter ranges. Planned range improvements must be annually implemented. Predator control programs must be flexible, balanced with the deer population, adaptable to the population trends of the current deer population, and managed in concert for all wildlife species. Elk and deer numbers must be evaluated and balanced with the available limiting rangeland. White-tailed deer must be managed to have minimum negative effects on mule deer. Hunter access to public lands must be carefully evaluated. Hunter management regulations must be set as liberal as possible and provide the highest optimal hunter success and satisfaction, but still meet management goals. Finally, mule deer populations must be annually evaluated, maintained, and balanced within the constraints of available forage resources on both summer and winter rangelands.

Epilogue

*I often wonder what man will do with the mountains . . . will he
cut down all the trees to make ships and houses? If so, what will
be the final and far upshot? Will human destructions like those
of Nature—fire and flood and earthquake—work out a higher
good, a finer beauty? Will . . . all this wild beauty be set to poetry
and song? And what then is coming? What is the human part of
the mountain's destiny?*

John Muir

Throughout this volume I have assumed sustainable mule deer populations and hunting harvest will continue perpetually. What if they do
not? In Utah a few units have been closed for one or more years to allow
the population to recover, and then reopened with limited-entry hunting
restrictions. What if populations decline to the point where recovery is
unlikely, such has been the case with sage grouse in many Utah counties
that have been closed to hunting for decades? What if mule deer populations continue to decline to the level where hunting is no longer feasible? Is it possible mule deer could decline to the level of endangerment
of the species? It has been reported by some researchers that within 50
to 100 years, due to declining habitat, disease, fire, urbanization, hybridization with white-tailed deer, and other negative factors, that the mule
deer species is on track for listing under the Endangered Species Act or
even doomed to extinction. If human starvation became severe within

260

the range of mule deer, would the mule deer vanish from nearby ranges, as have other species in some areas such as Haiti and parts of Asia and Africa where constant starvation has forced desperate measures for human survival? These dire possibilities appear very remote for North America, but perhaps over centuries, they are within the long-term range of possibilities.

Similar to John Muir's statement, "I often wonder what man will do with the mountains," I have often wondered what will be the long-term view and status of mule deer and wildlife in the West. Will humans have the wisdom to restrict their populations to remain in balance with the available land and water resources? Will humans have the foresight to permanently preserve adequate agricultural lands to support us? Will humans provide the means to maintain adequate rangelands to support game and non-game wildlife populations and recreation? In the 13,000 years of occupation, the Native Americans had limited effects on changing the landscape, but in just over 150 years on a sliver of geologic time, our very new civilization has made extensive marks on the western environments. "And what then is coming? What is the human part of the mountain's destiny?" How extensive will human actions alter the waters, the deserts, the valleys, and the mountains?

Wildlife officials and federal and state land managers, ranchers, agriculturalists, elected officials, and the public have a voice and a responsibility in determining the future. With the strength of wildlife law enforcement, Division of Wildlife Resources' purchases of many critical habitats, jurisdiction and regulation of federal lands, increasing numbers of private land conservation easements, and the growing sense of citizen concerns for the environment, the future appears tentatively secure. Maintaining habitat quantity and quality is the key to the future for wildlife and humans. With conscientious decisions at all levels of government, and with the contribution of permanently secured undeveloped private agricultural lands and ranches, I hope and believe that mule deer managers will be able to perpetually maintain sustainable populations of mule deer with harvest objectives.

Appendix

Utah Statewide Buck Harvest, Antlerless Harvest, and Hunters Afield, 1925-2008.

Year	Buck Harvest	Antlerless Harvest	Total Harvest	Hunters Afield	%Success TotalHarvest/ HuntersAfield
1925	1,400	0	1,400	5,650	24.8
1926	2,000	0	2,000	7,000	28.6
1927	3,200	0	3,200	9,100	35.2
1928	4,400	0	4,400	11,300	38.9
1929	5,000	0	5,000	12,800	39.1
1930	6,400	0	6,400	15,600	41.0
1931	7,800	0	7,800	19,500	40.0
1932	7,113	0	7,113	16,600	42.8
1933	8,019	0	8,019	17,700	45.3
1934	11,271	825	12,096	22,413	54.0
1935	9,640	2,008	11,648	25,598	45.5
1936	13,800	0	13,800	29,500	46.8
1937	21,000	0	21,000	38,900	54.0
1938	25,572	2,428	28,000	54,500	51.4
1939	28,552	9,448	38,000	70,612	53.8
1940	32,300	11,700	44,000	74,437	59.1
1941	34,460	15,540	50,000	81,461	61.4
1942	36,784	26,825	63,609	98,884	64.3
1943	40,140	15,568	55,708	96,428	57.8
1944	40,743	11,034	51,777	81,067	63.9
1945	38,966	10,924	49,890	88,004	56.7
1946	43,277	10,094	53,371	106,356	50.2
1947	49,557	12,315	61,872	105,921	58.4
1948	55,766	13,129	68,895	114,416	60.2
1949	47,932	12,602	60,534	106,230	57.0
1950	54,384	19,033	73,417	122,087	60.1
1951	67,329	34,308	101,637	121,757	83.5
1952	56,607	33,554	90,161	128,674	70.1
1953	55,214	30,665	85,879	132,990	64.6
1954	67,679	40,394	108,073	143,152	75.5
1955	75,319	36,598	111,917	154,157	72.6
1956	78,504	44,081	122,585	166,217	73.7
1957	61,475	44,124	105,599	173,656	60.8
1958	71,865	45,376	117,241	174,657	67.1

1959	76,481	49,834	126,315	188,646	67.0
1960	78,992	51,953	130,945	200,266	65.4
1961	79,007	53,271	132,278	202,305	65.4
1962	75,464	45,092	130,556	210,779	61.9
1963	67,392	42,007	109,399	199,219	54.9
1964	73,358	42,242	115,600	198,768	58.2
1965	53,686	34,357	88,043	198,296	44.4
1966	60,229	32,711	92,940	176,943	52.5
1967	55,798	34,255	90,053	172,584	52.2
1968	62,713	32,448	95,161	176,645	53.9
1969	52,287	29,634	81,921	179,971	45.5
1970	70,407	32,582	102,989	196,633	52.4
1971	65,394	33,871	99,265	205,257	48.4
1972	71,631	36,787	108,418	220,611	49.1
1973	53,983	32,587	86,570	225,723	38.4
1974	46,282	8,351	54,633	205,032	26.6
1975	43,734	1,667	45,401	200,550	22.6
1976	56,928	95	57,023	187,450	30.4
1977	67,664	751	68,415	208,761	32.8
1978	65,197	3,085	68,282	216,951	31.5
1979	60,876	5,387	66,263	222,127	29.8
1980	65,444	9,796	75,240	222,542	33.8
1981	80,627	10,182	90,809	225,173	40.3
1982	75,094	10,890	85,984	237,836	36.2
1983	82,552	13,164	95,716	245,618	39.0
1984	63,044	4,233	67,277	199,428	33.7
1985	59,082	5,171	64,253	217,114	29.6
1986	60,713	6,371	67,084	202,549	33.1
1987	66,515	7,760	74,275	210,516	35.3
1988	68,503	22,235	90,738	248,685	36.5
1989	57,731	20,642	78,373	235,712	33.2
1990	58,808	16,975	75,783	231,432	32.7
1991	53,342	13,534	66,876	222,981	30.0
1992	56,533	13,132	69,665	228,747	30.5
1993	26,024	4,296	30,320	146,008	20.8
1994	29,227	699	29,926	89,980	33.3
1995	26,412	1,418	27,830	103,071	27.0
1996	34,577	2,582	37,159	109,394	34.0
1997	29,800	3,247	33,047	112,391	29.4
1998	32,213	2,875	35,088	112,389	31.2
1999	31,463	2,970	34,433	99,851	34.5
2000	33,031	4,520	37,551	103,336	36.3
2001	27,512	4,151	31,663	96,524	32.8
2002	24,363	3,145	27,508	102,718	26.8
2003	22,525	2,524	25,049	90,770	27.6
2004	27,929	2,239	30,168	86,505	34.9
2005	21,520	1,951	23,471	92,235	25.4
2006	30,548	1,856	32,404	101,911	31.8
2007	30,211	2,097	32,308	101,617	31.8
2008	22,857	2,145	25,002	91,750	27.3

MANAGEMENT UNITS

1 Box Elder	10 Book Cliffs	19 West Desert	28 Panquitch Lake
2 Cache	11 Nine Mile	20 Southwest Desert	29 Zion
3 Ogden	12 San Rafael	21 Filmore	30 Pine Valley
4 Morgan Rich	13 La Sal	22 Beaver	
5 East Canyon	14 San Juan	23 Monroe	
6 Chalk Creek	15 Henry Mountains	24 Mt. Dutton	
7 Kamas	16 Central Mountains	25 Plateau	
8 North Slope	17 Wasatch Mountains	26 Kaiparowitz	
9 South Slope	18 Oquirrh-Stansbury	27 Paunsaugunt	

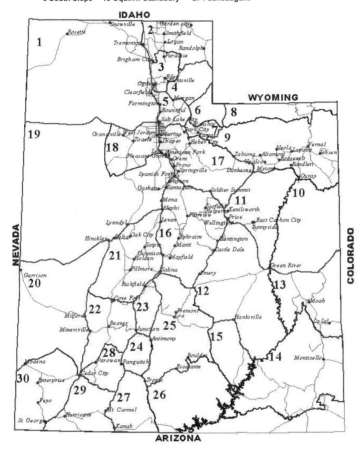

Literature Cited

Ackerman, B. B., F. G. Lindzey and T. P. Hember. 1984. Cougar food habits in southern Utah. J. Wildl. Manage. 48:147–155.

Adams, C. F. 1975. Nutritive value of American foods. USDA Handbook No. 454.

Allen, D. S. and J. B. Delair. 1997. Cataclysm. Bear and Company. Rochester, Vermont.

Anderson, A. E. 1981. Morphological and physiological characteristics. Pgs. 27–97 In: O. C. Wallmo, ed. Mule and black-tailed deer of North America. Univ. of Nebraska Press, Lincoln.

Anderson, B. A. and A. H. Holmgren. Revised, 1996. Mountain plants of northeastern Utah. Utah State Univ. Ext. Serv. Circ. 319. Logan.

Anderson, E. W. and R. J. Scherzinger. 1975. Improving the quality of winter forage for elk by cattle grazing. J. Range Manage. 28:120–125.

Austin, D. D. 1984. Fat depth at the xiphiod process - a rapid index to deer condition. Great Basin Naturalist 44:178–181.

————. 1991. Age specific antler tine counts and carcass weights of hunter-harvested mule deer from Utah checking stations 1932–1988. Utah DWR Salt Lake City.

————. 2000. Managing livestock grazing for mule deer (*Odocoileus hemionus*) on winter range in the Great Basin. Western North American Naturalist 60:198–203.

Austin, D. D., S. D. Bunnell, and P. J. Urness. 1990. Responses of deer hunters to a checking station questionnaire in Utah. Proc. West. Assoc. Game and Fish Comm. 69:208–229.

Austin, D. D. and A. B. Hash. 1988. Minimizing browsing damage by deer: Landscape planning for wildlife. Utah Science 49:66–70.

Austin, D. D. and L. Jordan. 1989. Responses of Utah deer hunters to a checking station questionnaire. Great Basin Naturalist 49:159–166.

Austin, D. D., R. A. Riggs, P. J. Urness, D. L. Turner, and J. F. Kimbal. 1989. Changes in mule deer size in Utah. Great Basin Naturalist 49:31–35.

Austin, D. D. and P. J. Urness. 1976. Weights of hunter-harvested mule deer in Utah. Utah Science 37:11–13.

———. 1983. Over winter forage selection by mule deer on seeded big sage-brush-grass range. J. Wildl. Manage. 47:1204–1207.

———. 1985. Values of four plant communities for mule deer on ranges with limited summer habitat. J. Range Manage. 38:167–171.

———. 1986. Effects of cattle grazing on mule deer diet and area selection. J. Range Manage. 39:18–21.

———. 1987. Consumption of fresh alfalfa hay by mule deer and elk. Great Basin Naturalist 47:100–102.

———. 1989. Evaluating production losses from mule deer depredation in apple orchards. Wildl. Soc. Bull. 17:161–165.

———. 1992. Guidelines for appraising crop losses due to depredating big game. Utah DWR Publ. 92-4. Salt Lake City.

———. 1998. Vegetal change on a northern foothill range in the absence of livestock grazing between 1948 and 1982. Great Basin Naturalist 58:188–191.

Austin, D. D., P. J. Urness, and S. D. Bunnell. 1991. Hunter opinions and questionnaires. Utah Deer Management Workshop, Aug. 1990.

Austin, D. D., P. J. Urness, and D. Duersch. 1998. Alfalfa hay crop loss due to mule deer depredation. J. Range Manage. 51:29–31.

Austin, D. D., P. J. Urness, and L. C. Fierro. 1983. Spring livestock grazing affects crested wheatgrass regrowth and winter use by mule deer. J. Range Manage. 36:589–593.

Austin, D. D., P. J. Urness, and R. A. Riggs. 1986. Vegetal change in the absence of grazing, mountain brush zone, Utah. J. Range Manage. 39:514–517.

Austin, D. D., P. J. Urness, and W. Shields. 1992. Resident Utah deer hunters' preferences of management options. Great Basin Naturalist 52:364–372.

Austin, D. D., P. J. Urness, and M. L. Wolfe. 1977. The influence of predator control on two adjacent wintering deer herds. Great Basin Naturalist 37:101–102.

Bardwell, F. H., E. B. Wilcox, and J. B. Low. 1964. Factors influencing the quality and palatability of venison in Utah. Utah Dept. Fish and Game Publ. 64-6.

Bardwell, F. H., J. B. Low, and E. B. Wilcox. 1968. Venison, field care and cooking. Utah DWR Publ. 69-10. Salt Lake City.

Bartmann, R. M. 1974. Guidelines for estimating deer numbers in connection with claims of damage to growing crops. Colorado Division of Wildlife Resources Publ. 87-5.

Bartmann, R. M., G. G. Whilte, and L. C. Carpenter. 1992. Compensatory mortality in a Colorado mule deer population. Wildl. Mono. 121.

Bartos, D. L. and R. O. Harniss. 1990. Pine Hollow exclosure effect on browsing on an aspen community sprayed with 2-4-D. USDA Res. Note INT-393.

Bayoumi, M. A. and A. D. Smith. 1976. Response of big game winter range vegetation to fertilization. J. Range Manage. 29:44–48.

Beale, D. M. 1992. Fawn mortality among mule deer in southwestern Utah. Utah DWR Misc. Publ. Salt Lake City.

Beetle, A. A. 1970. Recommended plant names. Research Journal 31. Agr. Exp. Sta. Univ. Wyoming. Laramie.

Belsky, A. J. 1986. Does herbivory benefit plants? A review of the evidence. The Amer. Nat. 127:870–892.

Castleton, K. B. 1979. 1984. Petroglyphs and pictographs of Utah. Vol. I & II. Utah Museum of Natural History. Salt Lake City.

Chase, A. 1987. Playing God in Yellowstone: the destruction of America's first national park. Harcourt Braze J. Publ. San Diego, Cal.

Chatfield, C. 1940. Proximate composition of American food materials. USDA Circ. No. 549.

Christensen, E. M. and H. B. Johnson. 1964. Presettlement vegetation and vegetational change in three valleys in central Utah. Brigham Young Univ. Sci. Bull. No. 4 Biol. Series IV.

Clements, C. D. and J. A. Young. 1997. A viewpoint: Rangeland health and mule deer habitat. J. Range Manage. 50:129–138.

Cliff, E. P. 1939. Relationships between elk and mule deer in the blue mountains of Oregon. Trans. N. Amer. Wildl. Conf. 4:560–569.

Collins, W. B. and P. J. Urness. 1983. Feeding behavior and habitat selection of mule deer and elk on northern Utah summer range. J. Wildl. Manage. 47:646–663.

Collins, W. B., P. J. Urness, and D. D. Austin. 1978. Elk diets and activities on different lodgepole pine habitat segments. J. Wildl. Manage. 42:799–810.

Connolly, G. E. 1981. Assessing populations. Pgs. 287–346 In: O. C. Wallmo ed. Mule and black-tailed deer of North America. Univ. of Nebraska Press. Lincoln.

Cook, B. B., L. E. Witham, M. Olmstead, and A. F. Morgan. 1949. The influence of season and other factors on the acceptability and food value of the meat from two subspecies of California deer and antelope. Hilgardia 19:265–284.

Cooke, J. L. 1992. Effects of predator control on desert mule deer numbers. Fish and Wildl. Ref. Serv. Publ. No. 10125-R-1, Final Report.

Costello, D. F. and G. T. Turner. 1941. Vegetation changes following exclusion of livestock from grazed ranges. J. Forestry 39:310–335.

Cottam, W. P. and F. R. Evans. 1945. A comparative study of the vegetation of the grazed and ungrazed canyons of the Wasatch Range, Utah. Ecology 26:171–181.

Cunningham, S. C., C. R. Gustavson, and Warren B. Ballard. 1999. Diet selection of mountain lions in southeastern Arizona. J. Range Manage. 52:202–207.

Daubenmire, R. 1959. A canopy coverage method of vegetational analysis. Northwest Science 33:43–66.

Davidson, W. R. ed. 1981. Diseases and parasites of white-tailed deer. Tall Timbered Research Station Misc. Publ. No. 7. Tallahassee, Florida.

Decker, D. J. and N. A. Connolly. 1989. Motivations for deer hunting. Implications for antlerless deer harvest as a management tool. Wildl. Soc. Bull. 17:455–463.

Dechamp, J. A., P. J. Urness, and D. D. Austin. 1979. Summer diets of mule deer from lodgepole pine habitats. J. Wildl. Manage. 43:154–160.

Doman, E. R. and D. I. Rasmussen. 1944. Supplemental winter feeding of mule deer in northern Utah. J. Wildl. Manage. 8:317–338.

Dolling, J. 2005. Emergency deer feeding in the Northern Region. Utah DWR Final Report. Salt Lake City.

Durrant, S. D. 1952. Mammals of Utah. University of Kansas Publications, Museum of Natural History. Topeka.

Edgerton, P. J. and J. G. Smith. 1971. Seasonal forage use by deer and elk on the Starkey experimental forest and range, Oregon. USDA For. Serv. Res. Pap. PNW-112.

Erickson, J. A., A. E. Anderson, D. E. Medin, and D. C. Bowden. 1970. Estimating the age of mule deer: An evaluation of technique accuracy. J. Wildl. Manage. 34:523–531.

Firestone, R. B., A. West, J. P. Kennett, et al. 2007. Evidence for an extraterrestrial impact 12,900 years ago that contributed to the megafaunal extinctions and the Younger Dryas Cooling. Proc. Natl. Acad. Sci. 104:16016–16021.

Gasaway, W. C., R. D. Boertje, D. V. Grangard, D. G. Kelleyhouse, R. O. Stephenson, and D. G. Larsen. 1992. The role of predation in limiting moose at low densities in Alaska and Yukon and implications for conservation. Wildl. Mono. 120.

Geduldig, H. L. 1981. Summer home range of mule deer fawns. J. Wildl. Manage. 45:726–728.

Geist, V. 1990. Mule deer country. North Word Press, Inc. Minocqua, Wisconsin.

Gill, R. B. 2001. Declining mule deer populations in Colorado: Reasons and responses. Colorado Division of Wildlife Resources Special Report No. 77.

Gruell, G. F. and N. J. Papez. 1963. Movements of mule deer in northeastern Nevada. J. Wildl. Manage. 27:414–422.

Hall, L. K. (ed.). 1984. White-tailed deer-ecology and management. Stackpole Books. Harrisberg, PA.

Hamerstrom, F. N. and F. L. Cambrum. 1950. Weight relationships in the George Reserve deer herd. J. Mamm. 31:5–17.

Hancock, N. V. 1981. Mule deer management in Utah—past and present. Pages 2–27: In F. G. Lindzey, ed. Mule Deer Workshop Proceedings. Ut. Coop. Wildl. Res. Unit. Logan.

Hansen, R. M. and L. D. Reid. 1975. Diet overlap of deer, elk, and cattle in southern Colorado. J. Range Manage. 28:43–47.

Hazam, J. E. and P. R. Krausman. 1988. Measuring water consumption of desert mule deer. J. Wildl. Manage. 52:528–534.

Holmgren, A. H. 1958. Weeds of Utah. Utah State Univ. Agr. Res. Exp. Sta. Spec. Rep. #12.

Hornocker, M. C. 1970. An analysis of mountain lion predation upon mule deer and elk in the Idaho Primitive area. Wildl. Mono. 21.

———. 1992. Learning to live with mountain lions. National Geographic 182:52–65.

Hull, A. C. Jr. and M. K. Hull. 1974. Presettlement vegetation of Cache Valley, Utah and Idaho. J. Range Manage. 27:27–29.

Jennings, J. D. 1978. Prehistory of Utah and the eastern Great Basin. Univ. of Utah Press Anthropology Paper 98. Salt Lake City.

Jensen, C. H., A. D. Smith, and G. W. Scotter. 1972. Guidelines for grazing sheep on rangelands used by big game in winter. J. Range Manage. 25:346–352.

Johnson, K. L. ed. 1989. Rangeland resources of Utah. Cooperative Extension Service. Utah State Univ., Logan.

Jordan, L. A. and J. P. Workman. 1989. Economics and management of fee hunting for deer and elk in Utah. Wildl. Soc. Bull. 17:482–487.

Julander, O. 1955. Deer and cattle relations in Utah. For. Sci. 1:130–139.

Katsma, D. E. and D. H. Rusch. 1980. Effects of simulated deer browsing on branches of apple trees. J. Wildl. Manage. 44:603–612.

Keegan, T. W. and B. F. Wakeling. 2003. Elk and deer competition. Pgs. 139–150 In: deVos, Jr. J. C., M. R. Conover, and N. E. Headrick. Mule Deer Conservation Issues and Management Strategies. Berryman Institute Press, Utah State Univ., Logan.

Keith, J. E., R. S. Krannich, and V. A. Rhea. 1991. Economic analysis of Utah deer hunters' responses to alternative season formats. Institute for Social Science Research on Natural Resources, Utah State Univ., Logan.

Kistner, T. P., C. F. Trainer, and N. A. Hartmann. 1980. A field technique for evaluating physical condition of deer. Wildl. Soc. Bull. 8:11–17.

Krannich, R. S. and D. T. Cundy. 1989. Perceptions of crowding and attitudes about a split deer hunting season among resident and nonresident Utah deer hunters. Institute for Social Science Research on Natural Resources. Utah State Univ., Logan.

Krannich, R. S., J. E. Keith, and V. A. Rhea. 1991. Utah deer hunters' opinions about deer hunting and alternative seasons formats. Institute for Social Science Research on Natural Resources. Utah State Univ., Logan.

Krantz. P. 1992. Fit and trim by spring, you can do it. Better Homes and Gardens. Jan.

Kufeld, R. C., D. C. Bowden and D. L. Shrupp. 1988. Influence of hunting on movements of female mule deer. J. Range Manage. 41:70–72.

———. 1988. Habitat selection and activity patterns of female mule deer in the Front Range, Colorado. J. Range Manage. 41:515–522.

Kufeld, R. C., O. C. Wallmo, and C. Feddema. 1973. Foods of the Rocky Mountain mule deer. USDA For. Serv. Res. Pap. RM-111.

Launchbaugh, K. L. and P. J. Urness. 1992. Mushroom consumption (mycophagy) by North American cervids. Great Basin Naturalist 52:321–327.

Leopold, A. 1931. Game survey of the North Central States. Sporting Arms and Ammunition Manufactures' Institute.

———. 1933. Game management. Univ. Wis. Press. Madison.

Lesperance, A. L., P. T. Tueller, and V. R. Bohman. 1970. Symposium on pasture methods for maximum production in beef cattle: competitive use of the range resource. J. Animal Sci. 30:115–121.

Loft, E. R., J. W. Menke, and J. G. Kie. 1991. Habitat shifts by mule deer: the influence of cattle grazing. J. Wildl. Manage. 55:16–26.

Mackie, R. J. 1981. Interspecific relationships. Pgs 487–507 In: O. C. Wallmo, ed. Mule and black-tailed deer of North America. Univ. of Nebraska Press. Lincoln.

Mackie, R. J., K. L. Hamlin, and D. F. Pac. 1990. Compensation in free-ranging deer populations. Trans. North American Wildl. and Nat. Res. Conf. 55:518–526.

Maguire, H. F. and C. W. Severinghaus. 1954. Wariness as an influence on age composition of white-tailed deer killed by hunters. New York Fish and Game Journal 1:98–109.

McClure, M. F., J. A. Bissonette, M. R. Conover, and D. D. Austin. 1997. Range expansion of white-tailed deer (Odocoileus virginianus) into urban and agricultural areas of Utah. Great Basin Naturalist 57:278–280.

McCullough, D. R. 1979. The George Reserve deer herd. Univ. of Michigan Press. Ann Arbor.

McCullough, D. R., D. S. Pine, D. L. Whitmore, T. W. Mansfield, and R. H. Decker. 1990. Linked sex harvest strategy for big game management with a test case on black-tailed deer. Wildl. Mono. 112.

McKean, W. T., and R. W. Bartmann. 1971. Deer-livestock relations on a pinyon-juniper range in northwestern Colorado. Colorado Division Game, Fish and Parks Proj. W101R. Final Report.

McMahon, C. A. 1964. Comparative food habits of deer and three classes of livestock. J. Wildl. Manage. 29:798–808.

Mendenhall, V. T. 1967. Venison flavors: The fatty free acid content of fat from lean meat tissue. Thesis, Dept of Foods and Nutrition, Utah State Univ., Logan.

Mitchell, J. E. and D. R. Freeman. 1993. Wildlife-livestock-fire interactions on the North Kaibab: A historical review. USDA For. Serv. Gen. Tech. Rep. RM-222.

Neff, P. J. 1968. The pellet-group technique for big game trend, census, and distribution: A review. J. Wildl. Manage. 32:592–614.

Pac, D. F., R. J. Mackie, and H. E. Jorgensen. 1991. Mule deer population organization, behavior and dynamics in a northern Rocky Mountain environment. Montana Dept. of Fish, Wildlife, and Parks Project No. W-120-R-7-18. Final Report.

Papaz, N. J. 1976. The Ruby-butte deer herd. Nevada Dept. Fish and Game Biol. Bull. No. 5.

Plummer, A. P., D. R. Christensen, and S. B. Monsen. 1968. Restoring big-game range in Utah. Utah Dept. Fish and Game Publ. 68-3.

Rawley, E. V. 1985. Early records of wildlife in Utah. Utah DWR Publ. 86-2. Salt Lake City.

Reiner, R. J. and P. J. Urness. 1982. Effects of grazing horses managed as manipulators of big game winter ranges. J. Range Manage. 35:567–571.

Research Committee (D. M. Gaufin, O. Julander, W. L. Robinette, J. G. Smith, and A. D. Smith) 1950a. A review of Utah's big game, livestock, and range relationship problems. Utah Dept. Fish and Game Bull. No. 1.

———— 1950b. Range for big game and livestock in Utah. Utah Dept. Fish and Game Bull. No. 2.

Reynolds, T. A. 1960. The mule deer. Utah Dept. Fish and Game Publ. 60-4.

Rhodes, D. D. and S. H. Sharrow. 1990. Effects of grazing by sheep on the quantity and quality of forage available to big game in Oregon's coastal range. J. Range Manage. 43:235–237.

Riggs, R. A., P. J. Urness, and K. A. Gonzalez. 1990. Effects of domestic goats on deer wintering in Utah oakbrush. J. Range Manage. 43:229–234.

Riordan, L. E. 1970. Differences in range vegetation resulting from grazing by deer, cattle and sheep. Proc. Soc. Amer. For. 57:147–151.

Robertson, J. H. 1971. Changes on sagebrush-grass range in Nevada ungrazed for 30 years. J. Range Manage. 24:397–400.

Robinette, W. L. 1966. Mule deer home range and dispersal in Utah. J. Wildl. Manage. 30:335–349.

Robinette, W. L., J. S. Gashwiler, J. B. Low, and D. A. Jones. 1957. Differential mortality by sex and age among mule deer. J. Wildl. Manage. 21:1–16.

Robinette, W. L., J. S. Gashwiler, and O. W. Morris. 1959. Food habits of the cougar in Utah and Nevada. J. Wildl. Manage. 23:261–273.

Robinette, W. L., N. V. Hancock, and D. A. Jones. 1977. The Oak Creek mule deer herd in Utah. Utah DWR Publ. 77-15. Salt Lake City.

Robinette, W. L., D. A. Jones, and J. S. Gashwiler. 1957. Notes on tooth development and wear for Rocky Mountain mule deer. J. Wildl. Manage. 21:134–153.

Rodgers, K. J., P. F. Folliott, and D. R. Patton. 1978. Home range and movements of five mule deer in a semidesert grass-shrub community. USDA Res. Note RM-355.

Rogers, G. F. 1982. A photograph history of vegetation change in the central Great Basin Desert. Univ. of Utah Press. Salt Lake City.

Severinghaus, C. W. 1949. Tooth development and wear as criteria of age in white-tailed deer. J. Wildl. Manage. 13:195–216.

Skovlin, T. M., R. M. Harris, G. S. Strickler, and G. A. Garrison. 1976. Effects of cattle grazing methods on ponderosa pine-bunchgrass range in the Pacific Northwest. USDA For. Serv. Tech. Bull. 1531.

Smith, A. D. 1948. Livestock and deer grazing affect on Utah vegetation is pointed out. Utah Dept. Fish and Game Bull. 6:1–2. Salt Lake City.

———. 1949. Effects of mule deer and livestock upon a foothill range in northern Utah. J. Wildl. Manage. 13:21–23.

Smith, A. D. and D. D. Doell. 1968. Guides to allocating forage between cattle and big game on big game winter ranges. Utah DWR Publ. 68-11. Salt Lake City.

Smith, G. J. and A. D. Smith. 1959. So you don't like venison. Utah Fish and Game Magazine 15:10–11.

Smith, M. A., J. C. Malechek, and K. C. Fulgham. 1979. Forage selection by mule deer on winter range grazed by sheep in spring. J. Range Manage. 32:40–45.

Stapley, H. D. 1970. Deer illegal kill and wounding loss. Utah DWR Publ. W-65-R-D, A-8. Salt Lake City.

Stoddart, L. A. and A. D. Smith. 1955. Range management. McGraw-Hill Company. New York, New York.

Tebaldi, A. and C. C. Anderson. 1982. Effects of deer use on winter wheat and alfalfa production. Wyoming Fish and Game Dept. Publ. FW-3-R-26. Final Report.

Thomas, J. W. 1970. A comparison of vegetation changes in a mountain brush type after grazing and protection from grazing during 37 years. M.S. Thesis. Brigham Young Univ. Provo, Utah.

Trainer, C. 1975. Direct causes of mortality in mule deer fawns during summer and winter periods on Steens Mountain, Oregon. Proc. West. Assoc. Game and Fish Comm. 54:163–169.

Trout, L. E. and J. L. Thiessen. 1973. Physical condition and range relationships of the Owyhee deer herd. Idaho Fish and Game Misc. Publ.

Urness, P. J. 1980. Supplemental feeding of big game in Utah. Utah DWR Publ. 80-8. Salt Lake City.

———. 1990. Livestock as manipulators of mule deer winter habitat in northern Utah. Pgs. 25-40. In: Can livestock be used as a tool to enhance wildlife habitat? USDA Gen., Tech. Rep. RM-194.

Urness, P. J., D. D. Austin, and L. C. Fierro. 1983. Nutritional value of crested wheatgrass for wintering mule deer. J. Range Manage. 36:225–226.

Utah Division Wildlife Resources. 1951–2008. Utah big game annual reports. Utah DWR Annual Publications. Salt Lake City.

———. 1958–2008. Utah big game range trend studies. Utah DWR Annual Publications. Salt Lake City.

———. 1976. Deer management range limitations. Utah DWR Misc. Memo Publ. Salt Lake City.

———. 1990. Final report of the three point or better evaluation on deer herd unit 28A, North Book Cliffs. Utah DWR Misc. Memo. Salt Lake City.

———. 1997. Third revision of the deer herd unit prioritization system for land acquisition of deer winter range. Utah DWR Misc. Memo. Salt Lake City.

———. 2003. Statewide management plan for mule deer. Utah DWR Salt Lake City.

Utah Wildlife Review, 2002. Spring. Utah DWR Misc. Publ.

Verme, L. J. 1969. Reproductive patterns of white-tailed deer related to nutritional plane. J. Wildl. Manage. 33:881–887.

Wallmo, O. C. ed. 1981. Mule and black-tailed deer of North America. Univ. of Nebraska Press. Lincoln.

Wallmo, O. C. and W. L. Regelin. 1981. Rocky Mountain and Intermountain habitats: Part 1. Food habits and nutrition. Pgs. 386–422 In: O. C. Wallmo, ed. Mule and Black-tailed deer of North America. Univ of Nebraska Press. Lincoln.

Warren, Robert L. 1988. Utah's biggest bucks, second edition. Shields Printing. Yakima, Wash.

Watt, B. K. and A. L. Merrill. 1963. Composition of foods. USDA Handbook 11.

Welsh, S. L., N. D. Atwood, S. Goodrich, and L. C. Higgins. 1993. A Utah flora. Brigham Young Univ. Print Services. Provo, Utah.

Welsh, S. L. and J. G. Moore. 1973. Utah plants. Brigham Young Univ. Press. Provo, Utah.

Whittaker, D. G. and F. G. Lindzey. 1999. Effect of coyote predation on early fawn survival in sympatric deer species. Wildl. Soc. Bull. 27:256–262.

Willms, W. A., A. McLean, R. Tucker, and R. Ritcey. 1980. Deer and cattle diets on summer range in British Columbia. J. Range Manage. 33:55–59.

Wolfe, M. C. 1976. Reliability of mule deer population measurements. Pgs. 93–98 In: G. W. Workman and J. B. Low, eds. Mule Deer Decline in the West, A Symposium. Utah Agr. Exp. Sta., Utah State Univ., Logan.

Wood, T., S. Bickle, W. Evans, J. C. Germany, and V. W. Howard, Jr. 1978. The Fort Stanton mule deer herd. New Mexico State Univ. Agr. Exp. Sta. Bull. 567.

Workman, G. W. and J. B. Low, eds. 1976. Mule Deer Decline in the West, A Symposium. Utah Agr. Exp. Sta., Utah State Univ., Logan.

Yarmoloy, C., M. Bayer, and V. Geist. 1988. Behavior responses and reproduction of mule deer, Odocoileus hemionus, does following experimental harassment with an all-terrain vehicle. Can. Field-Nat. 102:425–429.

The author hunts with his son Jared on the East Canyon Resort.
Maintaining family traditions continues to be one of
hunting's major values.

About the Author

Dennis D. Austin graduated from Utah State University in 1970 and 1972 with BS and MS degrees in range and watershed science. He worked briefly for the Bureau of Land Management and then for the Utah Division of Wildlife Resources for more than 30 years, from 1972 to 2003, as a research scientist and wildlife biologist at Utah State University and on the Cache Wildlife Management unit. He has published over 50 technical reports and over 100 newspaper and magazine articles.

Austin enjoys numerous outdoor activities, including cross-country skiing, biking, hiking, jogging, coaching tennis, stargazing, sleeping under the stars, backpacking Utah's Uinta mountains, western road tripping (especially to Yellowstone and southern Utah National Parks), river fishing, forest grouse and mule deer hunting, gardening, growing fruit trees, compiling and conducting Christmas bird counts and breeding bird surveys, and managing the family's 40-acre Wyoming "Boot Camp" ranch. Dennis Austin and his wife, Ann, currently vice provost for faculty development and diversity at Utah State University, have raised five fine children—two (Mary-Marie and Jared) are devoted to children and family medicine; two (Alicia and Micah) are committed to ecosystem restoration and city management; and one (Daniel) is dedicated to storytelling and philanthropy. Dennis and Ann reside in Hyrum.

Index